Global Insights into Public Service Interpreting

This edited volume sets out to explore interdisciplinarity issues and strategies in public service interpreting (PSI), focusing on theoretical issues, global practices and education and training. Unlike other types of interpreting, PSI touches on the most private spheres of human life, making it all the more imperative for the service to move towards professionalization and for ad hoc training methods to be developed within higher institutions of education. PSI is a fast-developing area which will assume an increasingly important role in the spectrum of the language professions in the future.

An international, dynamic and interdisciplinary exploration of matters related to PSI in various cultural contexts and different language combinations will provide valuable insights for anyone who wishes to have a better understanding when working as communities of practice. For this purpose, the editors have collected contributions focusing on training, ethical issues, professional deontology, the role and responsibilities of interpreters, management and policy, as well as problems and strategies in different countries and regions.

This collection will be a valuable reference for any student or academic working in interpreting, particularly those focusing on PSI anywhere in the world.

Riccardo Moratto is Full Professor of Translation Studies, Chinese Translation and Interpreting at the Graduate Institute of Interpretation and Translation (GIIT), Shanghai International Studies University (SISU) and Honorary Guest Professor at Nanjing Agricultural University. Prof. Moratto is a Chartered Linguist and Fellow Member of CIoL, Visiting Scholar at Shandong University, Honorary Research Fellow at the Center for Translation Studies of Guangdong University of Foreign Studies, and Expert Member of the Translators Association of China (TAC). Prof. Moratto is also an international conference interpreter and a renowned literary translator. He has published extensively in the field of translation and interpreting studies and Chinese literature in translation.

Defeng Li is Professor of Translation Studies and Director of the Centre for Studies of Translation, Interpreting and Cognition (CSTIC) at the University of Macau, China. Previously he taught at the School of Oriental and African Studies of the University of London, where he served as Chair of the Centre for Translation Studies. He also taught at the Department of Translation, the Chinese University of Hong Kong for a decade. He is currently President of WITTA, vice president of the Chinese Corpus-based Translation Studies Association and vice president of the Chinese Cognitive Translation Studies Association.

Routledge Advances in Translation and Interpreting Studies

64 **English and Translation in the European Union**
Unity and Multiplicity in the Wake of Brexit
Alice Leal

65 **The (Un)Translatability of Qur'anic Idiomatic Phrasal Verbs**
A Contrastive Linguistic Study
Ali Yunis Aldahesh

66 **The Qur'an, Translation and the Media**
A Narrative Account
Ahmed S. Elimam and Alysia S. Fletcher

67 **The Translation of Realia and Irrealia in Game Localization**
Culture-Specificity between Realism and Fictionality
Silvia Pettini

68 **Translation and the Global City**
Bridges and Gateways
Edited by Judith Weisz Woodsworth

69 **Gender and Translation: New Perspectives**
New Voices for Transnational Dialogues
Edited by Eleonora Federici and José Santaemilia

70 **Global Insights into Public Service Interpreting**
Theory, Practice and Training
Edited by Riccardo Moratto and Defeng Li

71 **Translation and Interpreting in Australia and New Zealand**
Distance and Diversity
Edited by Judy Wakabayashi and Minako O'Hagan

For more information about this series, please visit www.routledge.com/Routledge-Advances-in-Translation-and-Interpreting-Studies/book-series/RTS

Global Insights into Public Service Interpreting

Theory, Practice and Training

Edited by
Riccardo Moratto and Defeng Li

LONDON AND NEW YORK

First published 2022
by Routledge
2 Park Square, Milton Park, Abingdon, Oxon OX14 4RN

and by Routledge
605 Third Avenue, New York, NY 10158

Routledge is an imprint of the Taylor & Francis Group, an Informa business

British Library Cataloguing-in-Publication Data
A catalogue record for this book is available from the British Library

Library of Congress Cataloging-in-Publication Data
A catalog record has been requested for this book

ISBN: 978-1-03-205318-9 (hbk)
ISBN: 978-1-03-205319-6 (pbk)
ISBN: 978-1-00-319702-7 (ebk)

DOI: 10.4324/9781003197027

Typeset in Times New Roman
by Newgen Publishing UK

Contents

Figures

Tables

Contributors

Amalia Amato is Associate Professor at the Department of Interpreting and Translation (DIT) of Bologna University, Italy, where she teaches interpreting from English into Italian. Her main research interests include interpreter education and training, assessment of interpreting as a process and a product, dialogue interpreting in medical and legal settings, media interpreting, telephone interpreting and interpreting for children and adolescents.

Agnieszka Dominika Biernacka is Associate Professor at the Institute of Applied Linguistics, University of Warsaw, Poland. She is an interpreting researcher/trainer, legal translator and conference interpreter. She is the author or co-author of works on conference and public service interpreting, and legal translation. She is a member of the Polish Association of Hispanists (PSH), Spanish Applied Linguistics Association (AESLA) and European Society for Translation Studies (EST).

Ineke H.M. Crezee is Professor of Translation and Interpreting at Auckland University of Technology, New Zealand. Her 2013 book *to Healthcare for Interpreters and Translators* has now appeared in iterations for Spanish-, Chinese-, Japanese-, Korean- and Arabic-speaking interpreters, while Russian and Turkish adaptations are in progress. Ineke has won numerous awards for her teaching, including two Vice-Chancellor's Teaching Excellence Awards. Ineke was appointed an Officer of the New Zealand Order of Merit (ONZM) for services to interpreter and translator education in 2020. Ineke became New Zealand's first full Professor of Translation and Interpreting in 2020.

Lihua Jiang is currently Professor of Translation and Interpreting, and Assistant Dean of Foreign Studies College at Hunan Normal University, China. She obtained her PhD from Saarland University in Germany and worked as a visiting scholar at Middlebury College of International Studies at Monterey (MIIS), USA. Dr Jiang specializes in interpreting studies and multimodal communication. She has published two monographs: *How Far Can a Community Interpreter Go: Discourse Interpreting Filters* (Verlag

Dr. Kovač, 2011), and *Remote Interpreting Studies with the New Technical Perspective* (Hunan Normal UP, 2020).

Aleksandra Kalata-Zawłocka is Assistant Professor at the Institute of Applied Linguistics, University of Warsaw, Poland, and a founder and former President of the Association of Polish Sign Language Interpreters. She is a researcher, author of academic publications on signed language interpreting and trainer of signed language interpreters. For over a decade she has been actively involved in promoting the development and professionalization of signed language interpreting in Poland.

Nicole W. Lan is a nationally certified (Chinese Accreditation Test for Translators and Interpreters: CATTI) conference interpreter and an interpreter trainer. She has been a simultaneous and consecutive interpreter in medical, legal, financial and educational settings for more than a decade. Before embarking on her PhD studies, she was a research assistant for a project on the roles of medical interpreters in Hong Kong. Her PhD dissertation was on empathic communication in medical interpreting.

Ester S.M. Leung has extensive experience in legal interpreting in the UK, and has been teaching legal translation and interpreting to students at both undergraduate and postgraduate levels. She started conducting impact research in 2010 by researching and teaching ethnic minorities medical interpreting in Hong Kong. She has won multiple grants and awards, such as the "Outstanding Trainer for the Social Enterprise", "Best Knowledge Transfer Project" and Visiting Leadership Program of the US Embassy.

Defeng Li is Professor of Translation Studies and Director of the Centre for Studies of Translation, Interpreting and Cognition (CSTIC) at the University of Macau, China. Previously he taught at the School of Oriental and African Studies of the University of London, where he served as Chair of the Centre for Translation Studies. He also taught at the Department of Translation, the Chinese University of Hong Kong for a decade. He is currently President of the World Interpreter and Translator Training Association (WITTA), vice president of the Chinese Corpus-based Translation Studies Association and vice president of the Chinese Cognitive Translation Studies Association.

Gabriele Mack is Associate Professor at the Department of Interpreting and Translation (DIT) of Bologna University, Italy, where she teaches interpreting between German and Italian. Her main research interests include interpreter education and training, assessment of interpreting as a process and a product, media interpreting, dialogue interpreting in legal settings and interpreting for children and adolescents.

Lara Mantovan is Assistant Professor at Ca' Foscari University of Venice, Italy. She trained as both a linguist and an interpreter. In 2008, she obtained a certification in Italian/Italian Sign Language (LIS) interpreting, and since then, she has been working as a professional interpreter in several settings. In 2015, she earned her PhD with a dissertation exploring the syntax of LIS nominal expressions. Since the end of her PhD, she has been involved as a postdoc in international research projects on sign language linguistics. She has been teaching LIS linguistics and theory of interpreting since 2018.

Christopher D. Mellinger is Associate Professor in the Department of Languages and Culture Studies at The University of North Carolina at Charlotte, USA. Dr Mellinger holds a PhD in Translation Studies from Kent State University, USA. He is the managing editor of the journal *Translation and Interpreting Studies*, co-author with Thomas A. Hanson of *Quantitative Research Methods in Translation and Interpreting Studies* (Routledge) and co-editor with Brian Baer of *Translating Texts: An Introductory Coursebook on Translation and Text Formation*. He has co-edited special issues on community interpreting and technology (*Translation and Interpreting Studies*, 2018) and on translation process research (*Translation & Interpreting*, 2015).

Riccardo Moratto is Full Professor of Translation Studies, Chinese Translation and Interpreting at the Graduate Institute of Interpretation and Translation (GIIT), Shanghai International Studies University (SISU) and Honorary Guest Professor at Nanjing Agricultural University. Prof. Moratto is a Chartered Linguist and Fellow Member of CIoL, Visiting Scholar at Shandong University, Honorary Research Fellow at the Center for Translation Studies of Guangdong University of Foreign Studies, and Expert Member of the Translators Association of China (TAC). Prof. Moratto is also an international conference interpreter and a renowned literary translator. He has published extensively in the field of translation and interpreting studies and Chinese literature in translation.

Eva Ng is an Assistant Professor of the Translation Programme in the School of Chinese, The University of Hong Kong. She previously served in the Judiciary of Hong Kong as a court interpreter, and has researched extensively in courtroom interpreting and forensic linguistics. Her research has appeared in many leading journals. She is the author of the book *Common Law in an Uncommon Courtroom: Judicial Interpreting in Hong Kong*, and Chief Editor of *Interpreting in Legal and Healthcare Settings: Perspectives on Research and Training*.

Lihong Pan is Lecturer in Chinese Interpreting and Business Interpreting. She is the Programme Manager of the MA in Conference Interpreting and Translation Studies and the MA in Business, Public Service Interpreting and Translation Studies at the Centre of Translation Studies (University of Leeds, UK). She is also a veteran conference interpreter.

Aslı Polat Ulaş completed her BA in Translation and Interpreting Studies at Boğaziçi University, Turkey, and received her MA degree in translation and interpreting at Hacettepe University, Turkey. She worked as a public service interpreter at various healthcare institutions in London between 2007 and 2009. She received her PhD in Translation and Interpreting Studies in 2021 at Dokuz Eylül University, Turkey, with a dissertation on the interpreters providing services to Syrian refugees in Turkish public settings. Polat Ulaş currently works as a research assistant at the Translation and Interpreting Department of Adana Alparslan Türkeş Science and Technology University, Turkey.

Laura Volpato is a PhD student in Language Sciences at Ca' Foscari University of Venice, Italy. Her research focuses on communication for deafblind individuals. She has been teaching tactile Italian Sign Language at Ca' Foscari University of Venice from 2018 to 2020. She obtained the certificate of Italian Sign Language interpreter in 2013. Since 2015, she has been working as a professional interpreter, and in 2018, she became a member of ANIOS, the Italian association of sign language interpreters. Before embarking on her PhD programme, she worked as a research assistant for several university projects dealing with deafness and language competence/awareness.

Binhua Wang is Chair/Professor of interpreting and translation studies and Director of the Centre for Translation Studies at the University of Leeds, UK. He is on the editorial board of *Babel*, *Forum: International Journal of Interpretation and Translation* and *Chinese Translators Journal*. His research has focused on various aspects of interpreting and translation studies, in which he has published nearly 50 articles in SSCI/A&HCI journals and CSSCI/Core journals and some chapters in books published by Routledge, Springer, John Benjamins and Palgrave Macmillan. He has authored two monographs in interpreting studies and edited with Jeremy Munday *Advances in Discourse Analysis of Translation and Interpreting* (Routledge, 2020).

Zhiwei Wu is an Assistant Professor at The Hong Kong Polytechnic University. He was an academic visitor at Lancaster University, UK (2014) and a visiting scholar at The Pennsylvania State University, USA (2016–2017). His research interests include interpreting pedagogies, fansubbing and computer-assisted language learning. His publications have appeared in *Interpreting*, *New Voices in Translation Studies*, *Translation & Interpreting* and *Discourse, Context & Media*.

Zhimiao Yang is a PhD student at the Graduate Institute of Interpretation and Translation, Shanghai International Studies University (SISU), China. His research interests include court interpreting studies, psycholinguistics and second-language acquisition.

Cheng Zhan is a Professor at the School of Foreign Languages, Sun Yat-sen University, China, and a research fellow at the Centre for Translation Studies, Guangdong University of Foreign Studies. He obtained his PhD in interpreting studies at Guangdong University of Foreign Studies. An active member of the International Association of Conference Interpreters (AIIC), he focuses on interpreting practice, interpreter training and translation studies in his research efforts. He has published four monographs and ten interpreting textbooks. Currently he is the lead investigator of a research project entitled "The effect of audio description training on cognitive processing competence in interpreting", funded by the Chinese National Humanities and Social Sciences Council.

Junfeng Zhao has a PhD in forensic linguistics, and is Professor and Director of the Centre for Translation Studies, Guangdong University of Foreign Studies (GDUFS), China. Professor Zhao is now the Secretary General of China National Committee for Translation and Interpreting Education, vice president of WITTA, vice director of the Legal Translation Committee of TAC and vice chairman of Translators Association of Guangdong Province, China. From 2014 to 2018 he was the dean of the School of Interpreting and Translation Studies (SITS), GDUFS. He has published extensively in translation and interpreting studies, especially in legal translation and court interpreting.

Acknowledgements

We are truly indebted to all the contributors of this volume, who provided the erudition and wisdom of each chapter. Thank you for answering with patience our editorial queries and responding to our suggestions. Working with you has been a pleasure and, notwithstanding the names on the spine of the book, this volume is really yours.

We would also like to extend our most heartfelt gratitude to Katie Peace, Shubhayan Chakrabarti and all the copyeditors at Routledge. Thank you for your support.

Professor Defeng Li would like to acknowledge the support of The National Social Science Fund of China (project no. 19BYY126).

Introduction

Riccardo Moratto and Defeng Li

Public service interpreting (PSI) "is the type of interpreting that takes place between residents of a community" (Hale, 2011, p. 343). To be more specific, PSI may be perceived as a broad term, or a hypernym; legal, medical and social interpreting are often referred to as its main sub-categories (Pöchhacker, 2004). In the literature, the term "community interpreting" is the most widely used when describing interpreting for public services. "In Canada, interpreters working for public services are also referred to as 'cultural interpreters'" (Mikkelson, 1996, cited in D'Hayer, 2012).[1] In the United Kingdom, the term PSI was introduced in 1994 when the Diploma in Public Service Interpreting (DPSI) was created by the Chartered Institute of Linguists (Hammond, 2007, p. 1, cited in D'Hayer, 2012).[2]

PSI, aimed at providing a public service, such as in healthcare or medical interpreting, legal and police interpreting, as well as interpreting for social services, "is carried out in the context of the public services, where service users do not speak the majority language of the country" (Hale, 2011, p. 343). More specifically, PSI is oftentimes used in courts, hospitals, immigration services, local government, social services, police stations and other sectors of public services presenting a communication need, when services are provided to people who do not speak or are not fluent in the majority language of their host culture or the country they reside in.

Over the years demands for PSI have been on the rise for different reasons. For instance, immigration has increased rapidly in the European Union (EU) over the last few decades and numerous policies have been implemented to facilitate and improve communication between people with different native languages and cultures (Hertog, 2015). As a consequence, interpreting and translation services have also increased exponentially. However, there are numerous issues facing the interpreting profession in the public sector, including lack of financial aids leading to the (mis)use of non-professional interpreters with low-quality standards, unavailability of life-long learning opportunities for interpreters, as well as few training courses for practising interpreters to update their knowledge and skills of language and interpreting, not to mention the lack of a clear-cut career path for many interpreting students or would-be public service interpreters. To address these issues, it

DOI: 10.4324/9781003197027-1

seems imperative not only to provide a precise definition of the profession, to increase the number of languages covered by such professional services, including rare or minority languages, and to educate potential clients, but also to simply raise the awareness of the public on the importance of professional quality standards in the domain of PSI.

Unlike other types of interpreting, "PSI touches on the most private spheres of human life" (Hale, 2007, p. 25). This is the reason why it is absolutely necessary to increase the professional standards of public service interpreters and to develop courses of the highest standards with specific training methods at universities, or more generally, in higher institutions of education. As Corsellis (2008) emphasizes, "[PSI] is a fast-developing area which will assume an increasingly important role in the spectrum of the language professions in the future" (p. viii).

Research in the field of PSI is burgeoning, yet still developing. Nowadays, more than ever, professional interpreters ought to be trained in PSI. In doing so, it is of the utmost importance that research, training methodologies and practical issues proceed hand in hand in an interdisciplinary fashion. As argued by Snell-Hornby (2006),

> in times marked by regional wars or by a sharp economic divide between rich and poor countries, resulting in waves of refugees and asylum-seekers, community interpreting turns into a dire necessity. In some countries, such as Canada, Australia or Sweden, community interpreting services are well developed, but the occupation has nowhere reached the professional status of conference interpreting.
>
> (p. 118)

We believe that an international, dynamic and interdisciplinary exploration of matters related to PSI in various cultural contexts and different language combinations will provide valuable insights for anyone who wishes to have a better understanding of theoretical and pragmatic aspects related to the practice and training of PSI. For this purpose, we have edited this volume of contributions by active PSI researchers focusing on a myriad of issues: training, ethical issues, professional deontology, the role and responsibilities of interpreters, policies, as well as problems and strategies of PSI as practised in different countries and regions.

This volume is divided into three sections, namely theoretical issues, global practices and PSI training. In the first part we will present five studies focusing on theoretical issues of PSI. In Chapter 1 Agnieszka Dominika Biernacka and Aleksandra Kalata-Zawłocka aim to raise awareness on the issue of the universality of ethics by conducting a comparative analysis of two codes of ethics binding upon Polish public service spoken or signed language interpreters. The results show that the two codes have adopted similar approaches to ethical principles such as accuracy, impartiality, confidentiality and professionalism, whereas principles such as respect towards participants of interpreted communication, importance attached to appropriate attire or clients' evaluation of the interpreter's performance have been observed only in the code of ethics for signed language interpreters.

In Chapter 2 Nicole W. Lan and Ester S.M. Leung present two video-recorded interpreter-mediated medical consultations in simulated scenarios involving a doctor played by a medical professional, a patient played by an experienced interpreter and a student-interpreter who interprets for the two parties consecutively. It focuses on the student-interpreter's non-verbal cues in empathic communication. It is found that student-interpreters' empathy can be demonstrated through their management of turn-taking by non-verbal clues, thus emphasizing the importance of empathy for an enhanced interpreting performance. Empathy is perceived as a *conditio sine qua non* of medical interpreter training with a special emphasis on non-verbal devices and it should be emphasized in PSI training courses at all levels.

In Chapter 3 Lihua Jiang aims to investigate the interpreter's latitude for action in a given situation. She presents a set of parameters when an interpreter reproduces a target message and describes them in a Triadic Discourse Interpreting Model (TRIM). This interplay occurs in the form of interpreting filters (IF) through which a source message becomes a target message. The model-derived checklist thus may aid the interpreter to anticipate potential problems and to come up with potential strategies to resort to in order to secure adequate action for a planned assignment.

Chapter 4, co-authored by Junfeng Zhao, Zhimiao Yang and Riccardo Moratto, probes into the way in which court interpreting research can be inspired by Western Rhetoric, by focusing on such core concepts as "persuasion" of Classic Rhetoric, or "identification", "audience" and "multi-value judgment" of New Rhetoric. The analysis centres on the role of court interpreters and the characteristics of court discourse, with the ultimate goal to investigate how court interpreters render legal discourse.

Chapter 5, the final contribution in Part I, investigates children's perceptions and preferences in interpreter-mediated communication with the hope of inspiring and encouraging further research in this area and also *ad hoc* training for interpreters who work with children. Amalia Amato and Gabriele Mack argue that interpreting is still generally considered as a service activity for adults and the perception of interpreting by children is understudied thus far.

The second part features four studies on different discourses and practices of PSI in different countries and regions around the globe. In Chapter 6, based on a corpus of five police interrogations facilitated by trainee interpreters in Guangzhou (China) and their post-task reflections, Cheng Zhan investigates interpreter mediation by means of creation of text ownership and adoption of turn-taking strategies. The results show that the interpreter's role as a mediator is oftentimes so over-performed by trainee interpreters that the interpreter's visibility may end up affecting the natural communication process. Further evidence deriving from post-task reflections shows that trainee interpreters lack accurate understanding of their professional roles which, in turn, may cause ethical problems. The findings may be helpful in PSI training and in closing the gap between PSI training and practice.

In Chapter 7 Agnieszka Dominika Biernacka investigates overlaps in interpreter-mediated institutional talk in the courtroom. The study presents 37 hours of transcribed audio-visual recordings of oral court proceedings in which 12 interpreters working with Polish–English language pairs assisted. Biernacka explores the overlaps from several perspectives, including: (1) the interpreter's participation in the turn-taking system at institutional talk; (2) the interpreter's renditions of institutional talk; and (3) the interpreter's compliance with an ethical principle of accuracy.

In Chapter 8 Aslı Polat Ulaş discusses interpreters providing services between Syrian refugees and Turkish public officials in the units of the Association for Solidarity with Asylum Seekers and Migrants (ASAM), in the legal context and in public healthcare institutions under the EU-funded healthcare project SIHHAT. Polat Ulaş aims to explore interpreters' social, cultural, educational and professional backgrounds, their perspectives on the interpreting activities they are engaged with, as well as their attitudes towards and expectations about PSI. The study adopts Bourdieu's concepts of *habitus*, capital and *illusio* in its analysis. It is concluded that PSI is an unrecognized and thus undervalued service area in Turkey and that most practitioners lack the relevant resources to form a professional identity.

In Chapter 9 Eva N.S. Ng presents a historical review of court interpreting in Hong Kong. from the early colonial days to the present time. Ng argues that in the early colonial times court interpreters enjoyed monopolistic linguistic power in court, but in present-day Hong Kong interpreters often find their performance under the scrutiny of other bilingual court participants and of the digital recording system. This study presents authentic court data, the challenges presented to interpreters in modern-day Hong Kong courts and the limitations of the current system.

The third and final section presents five studies dealing with PSI training and education. In Chapter 10 Christopher D. Mellinger argues for a dialogic pedagogy that is grounded in interpreting studies research to prepare students not only as interpreters but also as informed users of language services.

Chapter 11 discusses some of the challenges of non-language specific interpreter education, especially as they relate to the need to provide students with feedback on their interpreting practice. Ineke H.M. Crezee discusses health interpreting students' feedback on simulated role-play scenarios as well as students' reflections on their own interpreting practice and that of their language peers. The chapter concludes by exploring the potential challenges of moving interpreter training and assessment online as a partial response to the Covid-19 pandemic.

In Chapter 12 Zhiwei Wu argues that research on PSI education seems to be more engaged with curriculum models and programme description, but less with pedagogical designs or procedures. To address this gap, Wu exemplifies a case-based learning design in an Advanced Liaison Interpreting course at a university in Hong Kong. The MA-level course features PSI in educational, healthcare and legal settings. To facilitate students' active inquiry of PSI issues, three metacognitive scaffolds are provided – question prompts, decision matrixes and Toulmin's model of argumentation. Wu argues that the case-based learning design can sensitize students to the complexities inherent in PSI professional practices and thus develop their reflective and critical thinking skills required for professional development.

Chapter 13 presents the first business PSI programme in the UK, established in 2018 at the University of Leeds. After highlighting the particularities of PSI as compared with conference interpreting, Binhua Wang and Lihong Pan propose a framework of PSI competences by integrating representative constructs from relevant research literature, textbooks and professional documents.

Chapter 14, the last chapter of the volume, deals with PSI for deafblind people and social-haptic communication (SHC), a topic that is under-researched in the field of PSI. Laura Volpato and Lara Mantovan argue that PSI for sign language users in Italy is still an under-developed service, mainly because the Italian Government has not yet officially recognised Italian Sign Language (LIS). Following an overview of the currently available training programmes for LIS interpreters in the first part of the chapter, Volpato and Mantovan discuss in detail the training for tactile LIS interpreters, that is, interpreters specialized in working with deafblind signers. They argue that in order to work as a public service interpreter for deafblind individuals, interpreters require several additional skills and they often face more challenges. One of the additional challenges is knowing SHC. The introduction of SHC in the training of (tactile) LIS interpreters thus can dramatically improve PSI for many deafblind people. A proposal for the integration of SHC in public service interpreters' training is described.

We consider it appropriate to close the volume with this chapter on PSI for deafblind people and hope it will serve as a kind reminder to all scholars of PSI studies that there is still much to do to render PSI services truly all-encompassing and fair for all. We certainly hope that an increasing number of students and scholars will conduct studies on less researched aspects on PSI, such as SHC, and become interested in providing interpretation services for deafblind people. PSI has been growing exponentially as a field of research. We hope that this volume may encourage a new generation of scholars to dedicate their full attention to the issues we present in this book, then move beyond to further investigate other theoretical issues and apply their findings in the real world where public service interpreters are increasingly and urgently required. Needless to say, the ultimate goal is to enable all people to enjoy the same access to public services.

Notes

1 Retrieved from www.erudit.org/en/journals/meta/2012-v57-n1-meta0312/1012751ar/
2 Ibid.

References

Chesterman, A. (2006). Questions in the sociology of translation. In J.F. Duarte, A.A. Rosa and T. Seruya (Eds.). *Translation Studies at the Interface of Disciplines* (pp. 9–27). Amsterdam: John Benjamins. https://doi.org/10.1075/btl.68.03che.

Chesterman, A. (2009). The name and nature of translator studies. *Hermes*, 42, 13–22.

Corsellis, A. (2008). *Public Service Interpreting: The First Steps*. London: Palgrave Macmillan.

D'Hayer, D. (2012). Public service interpreting and translation: Moving towards a (virtual) community of practice. *Meta*, 57(1), 235–247.

Hale, S. (2007). *Community Interpreting*. Basingstoke: Palgrave Macmillan.

Hale, S. (2011). Public service interpreting. In K. Malmkjær and K. Windle (eds.). *The Oxford Handbook of Translation Studies*. Oxford: Oxford University Press.

Hammond, J. (Chief Executive). (2007). *The Chartered Institute of Linguists. Preface of DPSI Handbook*. London: IOL Educational Trust.

Hertog, E. (2015). Looking back while going forward: 15 years of legal interpreting in the EU. *Trans*, 19(1), 15–31.

Mikkelson, H. (1996). The professionalization of community interpreting. In M.M. Jérôme-O'Keefe (ed.). *Global Visions: Proceedings of the 37th Annual Conference of the American Translators Association* (pp. 77–89). Alexandria: American Translators Association.

Munyangeyo, T., Webb, G. and Rabadán-Gómez, M. (eds.). (2017). *Challenges and Opportunities in Public Service Interpreting*. Basingstoke: Palgrave Macmillan.

Pöchhacker, F. (2004). *Introducing Interpreting Studies*. London: Routledge.

Snell-Hornby, M. (2006). *The Turns of Translation Studies: New Paradigms or Shifting Viewpoints?* Amsterdam: John Benjamins.

Tomlinson, C.A., et al. (2003). Differentiated instruction in response to student readiness, interest, and learning profile in academically diverse classrooms: A review of the literature. *Journal for the Education of the Gifted, 27*(2/3), 119–145. https://doi.org/10.1177/016235320302700203.

Part I

Theoretical issues

1 One ethics for all?

A comparative study of the Polish codes of ethics for spoken and signed language interpreters

Agnieszka Dominika Biernacka and Aleksandra Kalata-Zawłocka

1.1 Interpreters' ethical conduct and professionalism

Interpreters' ethical conduct and professionalism constitute an important area of research within the discipline of interpreting, be it of spoken or signed languages (cf. Hale 2007; Tryuk 2015; Biernacka 2019; Biernacka & Kalata-Zawłocka 2019; Moratto 2020; Phelan 2020).

What has been particularly drawing the attention of scholars is the guidance with respect to professional practice outlined in codes of ethics, referred to also as codes of conduct or codes/standards of practice, developed by interpreter organisations or institutions employing or educating interpreters. As observed by researchers, these documents may imply differences in their focus, with codes of ethics revolving around the concept of ethical norms, principles, or canons, whereas codes of practice/conduct are centred around interpreters' behaviour (Phelan 2020). As shown by Baixauli-Olmos, these documents differ in their structure and nature of recommendations: "codes of ethics/conduct [are] binding, short and containing rather general principles and standards of practice – informative, longer and containing fairly specific guidelines" (2017, p. 252).

Codes of ethics are referred to as sets of "guidelines for practitioners on how to conduct themselves ethically" (Hale 2007, p. 103), "a principal tool used to guide professional behaviour" (Tate & Turner 2001, p. 53), or documents "intended to hold the interpreter to a high level of ethical behaviour" (Janzen & Korpinski 2005, p. 172). Their primary addressee is the interpreter with his or her "individual awareness and sensitivity" (Baixauli-Olmos 2017, p. 252), "ethical reflection" (Cokely 2000, p. 3), and the ability to confront excessive expectations and/or potential accusations on the part of the recipients of his or her services (Kermit 2020, p. 14). Consequently, decisions made by interpreters can be less arbitrary (Neumann Solow 1981). Furthermore, the codes serve as an educational tool complementing or reinforcing the knowledge acquired in the course of pre-service education and training, and, where

DOI: 10.4324/9781003197027-3

no training has been available, provide interpreters with what is sometimes their only source of guidance and support (Hale 2007).

The role of codes is multi-dimensional; their implications reach far beyond the field of interpreting (Baixauli-Olmos 2017; Phelan 2020). Apart from interpreters, they are helpful to the clients of interpreting services: as a reliable source of information on what standards can be expected of professional interpreters and as protection against interpreters' misconduct and unethical practices (Janzen & Korpinski 2005; Hale 2007; Phelan 2020). Therefore, the codes serve as a sort of a guarantee of interpreters' professionalism and accountability for his or her work-related decisions, thus facilitating the sense of trust between interpreters and their clients (Skaaden 2020).

The existence of codes of ethics is essential for the interpreting profession as a whole. At an internal level, codes work as a binding agent for the collective of practitioners, obliging them to adhere to a common set of rules. This enhances the sense of a professional community, creates mutual understanding, and ensures uniformity of interpreting practices. Individual interpreters feel motivated to follow the rules outlined in the codes knowing that their colleagues are also abiding by them. Moreover, the codes act as regulatory mechanisms, sieving out those who follow the ethical rules from those who do not (Tseng 1992), thus contributing to the better recognition and appreciation of the profession. At an external level, the existence of codes is a signal to the public that their service providers represent a fully fledged profession, and legitimises the profession in the public's eyes, elevating the status of interpreters as trustworthy professionals (Hale 2007). From a broader perspective, researchers (Tseng 1992; Gentile et al. 1996; Valero-Garcés 2014) regard the development of codes of ethics as an inseparable element of the process of professionalisation. Although codes of ethics are facultative by nature, some scholars point out that "they must be obeyed" (Valero-Garcés 2014, p. 5).

1.2 The *Professional Sworn Translator's Code*[1] and *the Code of Ethics of the Association of Polish Sign Language Interpreters*[2]

As regards professional ethics for public service interpreters in Poland, the principles of professional conduct are set forth in the *Professional Sworn Translator's Code*[3] (*Kodeks zawodowy tłumacza przysięgłego*, hereinafter referred to as *PSTC*), prepared and commented by representatives of Polish authorities, practitioners, and academics, and published by the Polish Society of Sworn and Specialized Translators (TEPIS) in 2019.

In spite of both spoken and signed language interpreters being included among the beneficiaries of the *PSTC*, the ethical framework of Polish Sign Language (Polski Język Migowy, PJM) interpreting is established separately by the *Code of Ethics of the Association of Polish Sign Language Interpreters* (*Kodeks etyczny Stowarzyszenia Tłumaczy Polskiego Języka Migowego*, hereinafter referred to as *CEAPSLI*) developed by the Association of Polish Sign Language Interpreters (STPJM).

1.3 Methodological issues

Codes of ethics are powerful tools that shape and regulate the functioning of the interpreting profession they serve, effecting social changes in the realities that surround them. Therefore, they are highly desirable and thus devised by professional associations and institutions in large numbers. The multitude of documents that are currently available results in a diversity of areas they cover (international, national, local) and settings they apply to (medical, legal, administrative, educational, etc.). A study by Bancroft (2005) enumerates 145 different types of ethical documents identified in 25 countries (cited in Phelan 2020, p. 90) which further differ in the scope, structure, principles, or standards they contain as well as in their understanding and the extent of applicability and/or interpretations for all the stakeholders. That multitude raises many questions: (1) "should codes of ethics be broad and cover all possible settings, or is there a need for specific codes for specialised settings?" (Phelan 2020, p. 90); (2) does the concept of ethical conduct imply something else for spoken and signed language interpreting?; and (3) is it possible to draw up a universal code of ethics and what can be done to achieve it?

In order to answer the above questions, this study aims to compare the two codes of ethics binding upon public service interpreters of spoken and signed languages: the *PSTC* and the *CEAPSLI*. Principles and recommendations contained in these documents are analysed in an attempt to find out whether "a uniform code of ethics" (Hale 2007, p. 104) can be proposed for both spoken and signed language interpreters in Poland – not only from the perspective of the need to unify the norms, but also from the point of view of manifesting that irrespective of the interpreter's language pair, ethics is a fundamental aspect of the profession. In particular, the analysis covers the ethical principles of interpreting referred to in these documents, both embedded in the features of spoken and signed languages interpreting modes.

The above-mentioned aspects are a point of reference for a discussion of the principles of ethics from two angles: their occurrence in the two codes explicitly as tenets and entries, and implicitly as notions and concepts, interchangeably.

1.4 Principles of ethics set forth in the *PSTC* and the *CEAPSLI*

In this study, the principles of ethics are organised according to a classification proposed by Hale (2007). In her multifaceted but concise classification, three categories of aspects, as she denominates the principles of ethics, are delineated: (1) "interpreters' responsibility to the authors of the utterances"; (2) "interpreters' responsibility to the profession"; and (3) "interpreters' responsibility to self as a professional" (2007, p. 108).

1.4.1 Interpreters' responsibility to the authors of the utterances

Interpreters' responsibility to the authors of the utterances covers confidentiality, accuracy, and impartiality, (Hale 2007, p. 108).

1.4.1.1 Confidentiality

The tenet of confidentiality is expressly referred to in three[4] paragraphs of the *PSTC*. § 74 provides for the interpreter's right to declare to be bound by a principle of confidentiality. It means that interpreters can, at their discretion, make a declaration in front of their clients that no information will be disclosed to third parties. In § 78 referring to note-taking in interpreting, it is foreseen that for confidentiality purposes, the interpreter is obliged to destroy the notes so that third parties could not restore the data. Furthermore, the concept of *confidentiality* appears implicitly in § 5 where it is referred to as the sworn translator and interpreter's obligation "to keep in secret all facts, circumstances and information obtained in relation with the translation/interpreting done, especially those, the disclosure of which shall threaten security of commercial transactions" (*PSTC* 2019, p. 8). It is then explained that keeping such information secret means that "[t]he translator/interpreter is prohibited to use confidential data to their own benefit" (*PSTC* 2019, p. 8).

The principle of confidentiality listed in the *CEAPSLI* is described as essential for the protection of the interests of all parties to the interpreted event. The principle applies to handling documents, managing data, and all sorts of information regarding these parties. However, the entry also includes two examples of situations in which the obligation to preserve confidentiality may be slightly lessened. First, sharing of information about assignments is allowed among colleague interpreters for the sake of professional consultations. Naturally, extra care must be taken not to disclose information that is confidential or otherwise sensitive (cf. Phelan 2020). Second, is when the disclosure is required by law, during a court trial, or as a response to a life-threatening situation.

As presented, the principle of confidentiality is defined similarly in both codes, although with a different degree of detail. Only the *PSTC* addresses the prohibition to use confidential information to one's benefit. In turn, only the *CEAPSLI* assumes certain exemptions from complying with the obligation to keep in secret all confidential data, while in the case of spoken language interpreters the principle of confidentiality is essential for the profession and perceived as building up trust between the interpreter and the client. Bearing in mind that the *PSTC* addresses both spoken and signed language interpreters, the latter may feel confused about such discrepancy.

1.4.1.2 Accuracy

Accuracy as an entry appears in three[5] paragraphs of the *PSTC*. It is defined in § 17 as rendering the statement "exactly in the form in which it has been conveyed, reproducing the whole content, without omitting, adding or modifying anything" (*PSTC* 2019, p. 11). Moreover, § 75 implicitly provides for a detailed definition of accuracy, which means preserving a grammatical form of an original statement, that is, no grammatical shifts from first- to third-person singular are permitted; in turn third-person singular is reserved for the interpreter and shall be applied in cases where the interpreter needs to address his or her clients by saying "The interpreter asks for an explanation..." (*PSTC* 2019, p. 27).

The concept of *accuracy*, although included in the *CEAPSLI*, is not delineated under a separate tenet, but under the tenets of professionalism and impartiality. The former states that interpreters are obliged to "accurately convey content as well as the spirit of what is being communicated by the use of language that is best understood by the consumer", while the latter postulates "refraining oneself from intentional modifications of the original meaning due to one's own views" (*CEAPSLI* 2009, p. 3). The short guidelines are not accompanied by any additional explanations.

The fact that the two mentions of accuracy appear under two different tenets in the *CEAPSLI* may suggest that the need for precision and faithfulness is thought to be implicitly inherent in the interpreter's professionalism and, as observed by Miguélez (2003), is only achieved as a result of impartiality. However, the lack of a separate entry for accuracy may also imply insufficient focus on this issue.

The comparison of handling the principle of accuracy in both codes shows that the *PSTC* considers accuracy in terms of data- and grammar-oriented transmission of the utterances. In turn, the *CEAPSLI* underlines the importance of the ideas behind what is expressly being "said". Despite this difference, both codes are convergent in terms of the recommendation to convey the original utterances as they are.

1.4.1.3 Impartiality

Impartiality is expressly addressed in two paragraphs of the *PSTC*. First, in § 4, it is prescribed that

> [t]he sworn translator and interpreter shall perform the entrusted tasks with impartiality, without expressing personal opinions or taking the clients' unfounded suggestions into consideration, or representing the views of the client or third parties concerned or involved.
>
> (*PSTC* 2019, p. 7)

Moreover, according to § 4 the concept of impartiality covers a potential conflict of interest, which means that the interpreter is obliged to inform a client of any, be it private or professional, relationship with the other party. Secondly, § 74 provides for the interpreter's right to declare to be bound by a principle of impartiality defined as not being a representative of the judiciary or the parties to the proceedings.

In the *CEAPSLI* impartiality is also outlined under a separate tenet. It states that "the interpreter shall remain impartial towards the content she renders as well as the other participants of the interpreted communication" (*CEAPSLI* 2009, p. 6). It further explains that

> [t]he interpreter, as the only participant of the interpreted event that is proficient in both languages and knowledgeable of the two cultures of interpreting is privileged over the other participants. Successful, high quality communication is possible only when the interpreter maintains impartiality and does not make use of her privilege.

The explanation of impartiality is followed by six practical examples of behaviours with respect to interpreted interaction. Some of the examples of an interpreter's impartial conduct overlap with those mentioned in the *PSTC*, for instance: "refraining oneself from intentional modifications of the original meaning due to one's personal views" or "avoiding expressing one's opinions and judgments on matters connected with the interpreting situation" (*CEAPSLI* 2009, p. 6). Others include such recommendations as: "avoiding drawing attention to oneself for the sake of enabling most natural communication between the interpreting parties", "avoiding emotional involvement in the affairs of the interpreting parties", and "managing communication in a manner ensuring equal realisation by the interpreting parties of their communication goals". One further mention of impartiality can be found among examples of illustrative behaviours listed under the principle of professionalism, where the need to avoid a potential conflict of interest that can affect the quality and efficacy of the interpreting service is highlighted.

It may be assumed that the amount of detail spelled out in the *CEAPSLI*, noticeably higher than in the *PSTC*, reflects the significance of instructing PJM interpreters in this area.

1.4.1.4 Respect for all parties to the communicative event

Respect for all parties to the communicative event is neither explicitly nor implicitly referred to in the *PSTC*. Contrary to that, this principle is discussed in the *CEAPSLI* as a separate tenet that states: "The interpreter shall show respect to both parties to the interpreting" and further elaborates: "Both parties to the interpreting are the key participants of the communication process. The effectiveness of their communication is dependent upon the interpreter's acceptance of their communicative goals and demeanours" (*CEAPSLI* 2009, p. 7). The three exemplary behaviours illustrating compliance with the principle include provision of interpreting to the participants of the communicative event regardless of their nationality, gender, race, colour, disability or sexual orientation, etc.; respect for the selection of a particular interpreter by one of the parties to the interpreting or an individual/

institution employing the interpreter; respect for the client's preference as to the interpreting method. It may be assumed that they were aimed at hindering unfavourable comments about other interpreters and imposing communication methods on their clients (Polish-influenced form of interpreting).[6]

Irrespective of the grounds on which the principle of respect was included in the *CEAPSLI*, it can be claimed that such a recommendation would have the potential to be incorporated in the *PSTC* as a milestone in relations between the parties to the interpreted event.

1.4.2 *Interpreters' responsibility to the profession*

According to Hale, interpreter's responsibility to the profession means "professional conduct issues such as dress, punctuality, and solidarity" (2007, p. 108).

1.4.2.1 Professional solidarity

Professional solidarity is touched upon in five paragraphs of the *PSTC* out of which two (§ 14 and § 15) refer to solidarity as a tenet. In particular, § 14, along with § 13, provides for the sworn translator and interpreter's obligation to help their colleagues in need due to an urgent, unpredictable, or particularly difficult task. According to § 15, professional solidarity is of international dimension and, besides the obligation to assist other practitioners, includes striving to ensure a decent status of the profession. § 12 sets forth an obligation to share knowledge and experience with colleagues and candidates to the profession, while § 8 envisages that the sworn translator and interpreter is obliged to ask his or her colleagues for help.

As regards the *CEAPSLI,* the concept of professional solidarity is expressed under the tenet of "respect for other interpreters", its underlying premise being that "the efficient functioning of the interpreter community is possible only owing to mutual respect and collaboration", and that "mutual relations among interpreters affect the image of their professional group as a whole" (*CEAPSLI* 2009, p. 8). Therefore, ethical conduct of interpreters should include: sharing information about a particular interpreting assignment; providing support, if requested, before, during, and after interpreting; supporting and encouraging colleagues' professional development by assuming the role of a mentor; and reacting to situations of breach of ethical or professional standards. Furthermore, the notion of solidarity is implicitly dealt with as part of the principle of professionalism, under which signed language interpreters are recommended to turn to their colleagues and deaf friends for support in the event of communicative difficulties. In this sense solidarity closely resembles recommendations contained in § 13 and § 14 of the *PSTC.*

It seems then that the principle of solidarity is universal and equally valid for both spoken and signed language interpreters.

1.4.2.2 Punctuality

Punctuality is indicated twice in the *PSTC* as an obligation to be satisfied by practitioners. First, it is covered in § 2 under the heading of "showing particular diligence" (*PSTC* 2019, p. 7), which means that the sworn translator and interpreter should accept only as many assignments as can be performed carefully, diligently, and conscientiously, and in due time. In § 7 it is stated that the interpreter should immediately inform the client if s/he cannot meet the deadline for completing an assignment.

In the *CEAPSLI* punctuality is mentioned only once – under the principle of professionalism – and understood, as in the *PSTC*, as informing about a potential delay in arriving at the assignment or the inability to fulfil it, which should be followed by the interpreter finding himself or herself an appropriate replacement.

Although punctuality is included in the two codes, in the *PSTC* it is regarded as an expression of due diligence, while in the *CEAPSLI* it belongs to the qualities of a professional.

1.4.2.3 Dress code

Dress code is discussed only in the *CEAPSLI* under the tenet of professionalism. It is thus explained that a signed language interpreter shall attach importance to appropriate attire. The occurrence of this recommendation results from certain determinants specific of signed language interpreting; professionals need to pay particular attention to details such as, for example, dark and uniform colours contrasting with the interpreter's hands; avoiding coloured nails, earrings, necklaces, and any such elements, which could be caught up and lead to unexpected interruptions in the act of communication.

1.4.3 Interpreters' responsibility to self as a professional

Interpreters' responsibility to self as a professional includes professional development, role definition, adequate working conditions, and pay rates (Hale 2007, p. 108).

1.4.3.1 Professional development

Professional development is referred to in § 11 of the *PSTC* under the tenet of "improving professional qualifications" (*PSTC* 2019, p. 10). According to this principle, the sworn translator and interpreter is obliged to improve her language competences, translation, and interpreting skills, as well as to develop expertise and acquire knowledge of the provisions governing the national and international legal transactions, as well as the profession itself.

As regards the *CEAPSLI*, the principle of professional development is mentioned twice. First, in a general form, as part of the principle of professionalism, whereby the interpreter is required to update his or her knowledge regarding the evolving language and communication tendencies present in the communities of interpreters and the deaf. The second mention has a form of an entire tenet titled "professional development". The incessant care of the interpreter's qualifications and professional skills embraces both familiarity with up-to-date regulations regarding the interpreting profession as well as linguistic and cultural competences. It may take different forms: pursuing higher education, participating in training courses and workshops, self-learning, or working with mentors. Importantly, professional development is also understood as asking clients for their feedback on the interpreter's performance as well as their reflections and self-evaluations before, during, and after the interpreting assignment.

What the two codes have in common is that they propose similar definitions of professional development. Nonetheless, the *CEAPSLI* makes a reference to assessment of the interpreter's performance by parties to the interpreted event. This contributes to polishing up a picture of the profession, but, unfortunately, is not covered by the *PSTC*.

1.4.3.2 Role definition

Role definition is referred to indirectly in the *PSTC*. First, in the Preamble, it is set forth that the *PSTC* is addressed to professionals (including sworn translators and interpreters, as well as ad hoc court interpreters and signed language interpreters) for the needs of certified translation and interpreting. Thereby, the professional's role is defined as the one consisting in rendering services of both translating and interpreting. Furthermore, in § 2 of the *PSTC* the concept of professional integrity is defined by attributing due diligence, responsibility for implementation of assignments, punctuality, and taking the necessary precautions to the translator and interpreter's conduct.

In the *CEAPSLI* the notion of role is mentioned three times. First, directly, in the Introduction, where the definition of the term "interpreter" is provided alongside "interpretation" and "interpreting party". Here the interpreter is described as "a person that enables mutual communication between the interpreting parties, is equipped with theoretical and practical knowledge of interpreting and belongs to the Association of Polish Sign Language Interpreters" (*CEAPSLI* 2009, p. 1). Next, the notion of the interpreter's role appears in the premise of the tenet of confidentiality that refers to the interpreter as a person of public trust, "whose task is to facilitate linguistic and cultural communication" (*CEAPSLI* 2009, p. 2). Finally, the notion of the interpreter's role appears under the heading of professionalism where it is set forth that the interpreter shall avoid "assuming double or contradictory roles" (*CEAPSLI* 2009, p. 3) It is also strictly connected with the principle of impartiality, according to which it is not the interpreter's role to consult the client's decisions.

Unlike the *PSTC*, which perceives the role of the interpreter as a medium of communication, the definition of role proposed by the *CEAPSLI* is comprehensive and essential for satisfying the principle of impartiality.

1.4.3.3 Accountability for own performance

Accountability for own performance is, as a tenet, touched upon in § 3 of the *PSTC* according to which the sworn translator and interpreter "assumes a personal responsibility for accuracy in translation/interpreting" (*PSTC* 2019, p. 7). Moreover, the interpreter has the right to reject an assignment (§ 6) in the following cases: lack of expertise in a required area; lack of knowledge regarding specialised terminology; lack of time for sufficient preparation; prior commitments making it impossible to assume new ones; unforeseeable circumstances; and unreasonable refusal, on the part of the court, of access to case files.

In the *CEAPSLI*, three of the numerous examples illustrating compliance with the principle of professionalism implicitly relate to the notion of accountability. The first one states that the interpreter respects his or her commitments, ceasing cooperation for serious reasons only. The interpreter's accountability for his or her own performance may be also seen in adjusting to the norms and procedures observed at the place of the interpreting assignment while following the recommendations of the *CEAPSLI* and informing other participants of the interpreted communication of any collision between these two. Eventually, the interpreter's accountability may take the form of earnest preparation before an assignment.

Summing up, interpreters' accountability, although referred to implicitly, consists in that they are capable of making informed commitments. It means that interpreters may decline assignments when they feel that their knowledge and skills are insufficient to ensure a high quality of interpretation or if "some physical, psychological or emotional factors are likely to negatively affect the quality of their services" (*CEAPSLI* 2009, p. 3).

It seems that the main difference between the two codes is that the *PSTC* provides a comprehensive picture of the interpreter who is responsible not only for his or her performance, but also for his or her conduct as a professional: keeping, due filling in, and secure storage of a repertory, in which all assignments are recorded (§ 21); safe keeping of documents and supports so that they cannot be exposed to destruction, distortion, loss, or access by unauthorised third parties (§ 22); as well as protecting the sworn translator and interpreter's seal, which means that it cannot be transmitted to or accessed by third parties (§ 68). In turn, the *CEAPSLI* refers to the interpreter's responsibility in terms of his or her reasonable attitude toward assuming the assignments.

1.4.3.4 Working conditions

Working conditions are addressed in several paragraphs of the *PSTC* and cover a number of possible problems faced by practitioners. First, a disclaimer is made in § 2 that the professional has the right to reject performing the task entrusted to interpreters if "the content of the document, pay rates or working conditions undermine their dignity or integrity" (*PSTC* 2019, p. 7). § 9 concerns the sworn translator and interpreter's obligation to demand adequate pay rates, while the non-competition clause in § 10 prohibits excessively low rates. According to § 70 the sworn interpreter has the right to obtain information concerning the proceedings to which assistance s/he has been appointed, as well as the duration of the proceedings, the clients' expectations, and a possible use of teleconference facilities, all this in order to make sure that s/he is able to meet the requirements of the task entrusted to him or her. According to § 83 concerning working hours, the interpreter has the right to ask for an alternate and for a break when tired. § 71 provides for the sworn interpreter's obligation to suggest the interpreting technique which would best suit a particular communicative event. According to § 78 the interpreter is allowed to take notes in order to support his or her short-term memory. Moreover, the interpreter has the right to ask for access to a document in order to provide sight translation (§ 82). In § 72 it is stated that the interpreter's workplace should ensure good audibility and eye contact with the person whose statements are to be interpreted; this includes teleconferencing. The right of the interpreter to good audibility of the communicative act is repeated in § 74, where it is added that if there are any sound distortions, the interpreter has the right to ask for the statement to be repeated. § 73 provides for the interpreter's obligation to make sure that an interpreter and a foreign language speaking party understand each other, and if not, to inform the client about any difficulties or communication problems. If communication problems result from speech rate and the way of speaking of original speakers, then, according to § 77, the interpreter has the right to ask the speakers to adjust the pace and manner to the interpreter's capabilities. If such distortions of communication result from partial understanding, then the interpreter is required to add the explanations or comments so that clients understand the original statements (§ 79). Also, the interpreter has the right to ask the original speaker to explain specialist terms used (§ 80) or use a dictionary (§ 81).

According to the *CEAPSLI,* working conditions, set forth under the tenet of professionalism, are one of the grounds on which the interpreter may refuse to accept or cease an assignment; that is, when working conditions jeopardise his or her safety and health or are likely to adversely affect the quality of his or her work. What is more, interpreters are obliged to ensure that the external and communicative conditions are appropriate for the provision of interpreting services. Eventually, they are to adjust to the communication needs of their clients and the specificity of the particular interpreted communication. Still under the heading of professionalism, *CEAPSLI* instructs PJM interpreters with regard to remuneration for their work. On the one hand they are advised to accept fair and reasonable payments for interpreting, but on the other, they are encouraged to provide their services free of charge whenever they find it legitimate.

The main difference between the two codes as to working conditions is that the *PSTC* is comprehensive, while the *CEAPSLI* seems to be overly concise. This may evoke justified surprise, as it is signed language interpreters who are typically concerned with appropriate visibility, placement, background etc. What is more, the *CEAPSLI* does not mention lengthy assignments and the need to work with an alternate, even though team interpreting is one of the professional standards which signed language interpreters are obliged to meet (Kalata-Zawłocka 2017).

1.4.3.5 Professionalism

Professionalism is explicitly mentioned in § 1 of the *PSTC*, according to which "a sworn translator and interpreter shall make all endeavours to use their ethical attitude and professionalism to meet the requirements placed before the persons of public trust" (*PSTC* 2019, p. 7). This definition is wide enough to comprise all above-mentioned principles to be satisfied by a professional.

In the case of *CEAPSLI,* the principle of professionalism is discussed extensively under a separate tenet under the same name. It is the longest and most comprehensive of the tenets contained in the code. Its primary focus appears to be professional skills, practical and theoretical knowledge of interpreting. However, it presents 20 examples of behaviours that demonstrate the idea of professionalism reaching far beyond interpreting qualifications. But, as already pointed out, many of the behaviours can be easily linked with other tenets (impartiality, professional development, respect for other interpreters) as well as with implicit notions of role and accountability. As the majority of them have been already discussed in relation to other tenets and notions, interpreters are merely left with recommendations to inform the interpreting parties about any potential (or perceived as such) conflicts of interest, to be ready to present, when necessary, their credentials as well as to refrain themselves from using any consciousness-altering substances before or while interpreting.

On the one hand, the pursuit of detail observed in the *CEAPSLI* reflects the complexity of the concept of professionalism. On the other, the broad repertoire of behaviours that were selected to illustrate professionalism demonstrates that professionalism manifests itself through different principles. Thus, maybe it does not need a separate tenet devoted to it, but could be implicitly interwoven among different parts of the code, as in the case of the *PSTC,* where it is the title of the code that proves that in fact all the provisions included therein concern the attitudes and principles by which a professional translator and interpreter is characterised.

1.5 Conclusion

In spite of different communication channels, both spoken and signed language interpreters are guided by unequivocal ethical principles, which, in both cases, "contribute to making a non-Polish speaking interlocutor understand and be understood" (Biernacka & Kalata-Zawłocka 2019, p. 165).

A significant observation is that the differences in formulating and understanding the ethical principles outlined in the two codes result from different points of departure. Both codes differ in their target readership. In the case of the *PSTC* it is the professional who is capable of taking informed decisions based on recognising both one's rights and obligations. In contrast, at the time when the *CEAPSLI* was developed, the predominant view of interpreting was either as of voluntary work or a part-time job, an occupation rather than a profession. The role of the interpreter was seen as that of a social worker helping those in need rather than a language specialist providing professional communication services (a pattern observed in many countries, cf. Fant 1990). However, there was a strong desire on the part of the community of signed language interpreters and deaf people to change this situation. Thus, the primary motivation behind creating the *CEAPSLI* was to educate interpreters and their clients about the distinction between ethical and unethical behaviours in interpreting. Implementation of the code was a milestone for the communities of signed language interpreters and deaf people as their hitherto awareness of ethical principles was low, if not non-existent (Kalata-Zawłocka 2017). It meant introducing what Cokely calls "the perception of difference" (2000, p. 4). This also explains the huge determination on the part of STPJM to draw particular attention to the notion of professionalism. In order to make it more explicit, it was devised as a separate tenet. By the same token, the tenet of impartiality is being illustrated with numerous examples of recommended behaviours, some of which are characteristic of signed language interpreting, which, both in Poland and elsewhere, grew out of the field of charity, social help, and disability assistance (Fant 1990; Cokely 2005; Kalata-Zawłocka 2017). Thus, introducing a code of ethics brought about an entirely new concept of the PJM interpreter's role that entailed a new understanding of ethical/unethical behaviours requiring clear and precise guidelines.

The intentions of the authors of both codes are also reflected in a grammatical level of the provisions set forth therein. The principles set forth in the *PSTC* pertain either to the interpreter's rights or obligations. The *CEAPSLI* only once resorts to the interpreter's moral obligation of professional secrecy (2009, p. 6), while his or her rights are never explicitly indicated. Instead, the principles guiding the interpreters are introduced as requirements detectable in the use of "shall" in the definitions of particular principles, e.g., "the interpreter shall show respect to the parties of the interpreted event" (2009, p. 7) or in the use of gerunds in the examples illustrating the concepts, e.g., "refraining from giving advice" (2009, p. 6).

In response to the question posed by Phelan (2020) about the need for the codes of ethics to be applicable to all settings or to be restricted to a particular setting, as far as references to interpreting are made in the *PSTC*, particular attention is given to legal interpreting, while other settings are neglected. This results from the fact that the *PSTC* is aimed at sworn translators who, by law, are appointed to render their services for the courts, public prosecutors, the Police, and public administration bodies. In turn, the *CEAPSLI* appears to be more versatile and thus suitable for application in all sorts of settings. Considering that ethical and professional principles need to be unconditionally obeyed by the interpreter, it is suggested that whenever both codes make a reference to the institutional party to the interpreted event, it be referred to as the "institutional client".

What is more, the *PSTC* is weighted towards translation. This may be incomprehensible in that the *PSTC* is supposed to address the needs of all practitioners, be it translators or interpreters, including signed language interpreters. It has been proved that in the case of both codes the degree of generalisation in terms of the settings to which they can be applied is high enough to use them in various public service-related contexts, although the *PSTC* makes explicit references to a legal setting.

The above analysis has led to identification of three levels of similarities between the two documents: (1) similarities of both tenets and notions as demonstrated by the principles of impartiality, solidarity, and self-development (expressed explicitly as tenets and referred to implicitly in other parts of the codes); (2) similarities of tenets, as can be seen from the example of principles of confidentiality; and (3) similarities of notions (covered implicitly, not under a concrete tenet) as in the case of accuracy, punctuality, definition of role, accountability, and working conditions. As regards differences, the list of aspects created by Hale (2007) has been enriched by adding the principles within two categories: respect for all parties to the communicative act as an expression of the interpreter's responsibility to the authors of the utterances (in the *CEAPSLI* only), and professionalism within the category of the interpreter's responsibility to self as a professional (in both codes). The majority of principles of ethics are common for both codes as either tenets or concepts, the only exceptions being the above-mentioned principle of respect for all parties to the communicative act and a dress code, as well as the interpreter's obligation to ask clients for evaluation of his or her performance as contributing to the interpreter's professional development – all three are only included in the *CEAPSLI*.

Summing up, as regards drawing up a universal code of ethics, the study has shown that it is possible due to the basically common principles shared by spoken and signed language interpreters. However, what could help understand these principles, is: (1) organising the content so that the references to the same concept are not dispersed throughout the documents (following Hale's classification of aspects would be recommended); (2) introducing uniform definitions of the same concepts; and (3) adding illustrative examples of interpreters' recommended and stigmatised conducts.

Notes

1 Kodeks zawodowy tłumacza przysięgłego. http://tepis.org.pl/wp-content/uploads/Kodeks-zawodowy-t%C5%82umacza-przysi%C4%99g%C5%82ego-2018.pdf (accessed 4 May 2020).

2 Kodeks Etyczny Stowarzyszenia Tłumaczy Polskiego Języka Migowego. http://nowy.stpjm.org.pl/wp-content/uploads/2016/11/kodeks.pdf (accessed 11 April 2019).

3 According to the traditional Polish taxonomy of public service interpreters, they have been referred to as sworn translators (*tłumacze przysięgli*), which is "an umbrella term for officially appointed professionals who render both translation and interpreting services" (Biernacka 2019: 38).

4 From among these three paragraphs, § 27 of the *PSTC* refers to translation (in particular, it provides for a prohibition of the use of computer-aided translation tools not securing data confidentiality), which remains beyond the interests of this paper.

5 As explained in the case of the notion of *confidentiality*, *accuracy* is also addressed in § 3 and § 63 (both relating to the translator's liability for accurate translation of a source text thus not being subject to this analysis).

6 For more details on sign-supported Polish and transliteration, see Kalata-Zawłocka (2017).

References

Baixauli-Olmos, L. (2017). "Ethics codes as tools for change in public service interpreting: Symbolic, social and cultural dimensions." *JoSTrans*, 28, 250–272.

Bancroft, M. (2005). *The Interpreter's World Tour. An Environmental Scan of Standards of Practice for Interpreters*. Woodland Hills, CA: The California Endowment.

Biernacka, A. D. (2019). *Interpreter Mediated Interactions of the Courtroom. A Naturally Occurring Data Based Study*. Berlin: Peter Lang.

Biernacka, A. D. and Kalata-Zawłocka, A. (2019). "Techniques deployed by sign and spoken language public service interpreters: A comparative study." *Półrocznik Językoznawczy Tertium. Tertium Linguistic Journal*, 4(1), 162–192.

Cokely, D. (2000). "Exploring ethics: A case for revising the code of ethics." *Journal of Interpretation* (RID), 25–60.

Cokely, D. (2005). "Shifting positionality: A critical examination of the turning point in the relationship of interpreters and the deaf community." In: M. Marschark, R. Peterson and E. A. Winston, eds., *Sign Language Interpreting and Interpreter Education*. Oxford: Oxford University Press, pp. 3–28.

Fant, L. (1990). *Silver Threads. A Personal Look at the First Twenty-five Years of the Registry of Interpreters for the Deaf*. Silver Spring, MD: RID Publications.

Gentile, A., Uldis, A. and Vasilakakos, M. (1996). *Liaison Interpreting*. Melbourne: Melbourne University Press.

Hale, S. (2007). *Community Interpreting*. Houndmills, Basingstoke, Hampshire: Palgrave Macmillan.

Janzen, T. and Korpinski, D. (2005). "Ethics and professionalism in interpreting." In: T. Janzen, ed., *Topics in Signed Language Interpreting*. Amsterdam: John Benjamins, pp. 165–199.

Kalata-Zawłocka, A. (2017). *Społeczne i językowe konteksty tłumaczenia języka migowego w Polsce*. Warsaw: Wydawnictwo Wydziału Polonistyki UW.

Kermit, P. (2020). "Introduction." In: M. Phelan, M. Rudvin, H. Skaaden and P. Kermit, eds., *Ethics in Public Service Interpreting*. London: Routledge, pp. 1–23.

Kodeks Etyczny Stowarzyszenia Tłumaczy Polskiego Języka Migowego (*CEAPSLI*). http://nowy.stpjm.org.pl/wp-content/uploads/2016/11/kodeks.pdf (accessed 11 April 2019).

Kodeks zawodowy tłumacza przysięgłego (*PSTC*). http://tepis.org.pl/wp-content/uploads/Kodeks-zawodowy-t%C5%82umacza-przysi%C4%99g%C5%82ego-2018.pdf (accessed 4 May 2020).

Miguélez, C. (2003). "Traducción e interpretación en los servicios públicos de la Unión Europea." In: C. Valero-Garcés, ed., *Traducción e Interpretación en los Servicios Públicos. Contextualización, Actualidad y Futuro*. Granada: Editorial Comares, pp. 35–50.

Moratto, R. (2020). *Taiwan Sign Language Interpreting: Theoretical Aspects and Pragmatic Issues*. New York: Peter Lang. DOI: https://doi.org/10.3726/b17072.

Neumann Solow, S. (1981). *Sign Language Interpreting: A Basic Resource Book*. Silver Spring: National Association of the Deaf.

Phelan, M. (2020). "Codes of ethics." In: M. Phelan, M. Rudvin, H. Skaaden and P. Kermit, eds., *Ethics in Public Service Interpreting*. London: Routledge, pp. 85–146.

Skaaden, H. (2020). "Ethics and profession." In: M. Phelan, M. Rudvin, H. Skaaden and P. Kermit, eds., *Ethics in Public Service Interpreting*. London: Routledge, pp. 147–201.

Tate, G. and Turner, G. H. (2001). "The code and the culture: Sign language interpreting-in search of the new breed's ethics." In: F. J. Harrington and G. H. Turner, eds., *Interpreting Interpreting: Studies and Reflections on Sign Language Interpreting*. Gloucestershire: Douglas McLean, pp. 67–73.

Tryuk, M. (2015). *On Ethics and Interpreters*. Frankfurt am Main: Peter Lang.

Tseng, J. (1992). *Interpreting as an Emerging Profession in Taiwan – A Sociological Model*. Unpublished Master's Thesis, Fu Jen Catholic University, Taiwan.

Valero-Garcés, C. (2014). *Communicating Across Cultures. A Coursebook on Interpreting and Translating in Public Services and Institutions*. Lanham: University Press of America.

2 Empathy as embodied in medical interpreting

A case study of medical interpreter-trainees' turn-taking management

Nicole W. Lan and Ester S.M. Leung

2.1 Background and key definitions

2.1.1 Medical interpreting and patient-centred communication

An increasing number of studies prove that dialogue interpreting is a communication activity that requires an interpreter's active and controlled participation, which in turn affects the construction of meaning and the interactive process of the participants of the communication activity. We use the term "participants" in this research to refer to the doctor, patient, and interpreter because they all "participate" in different ways: sometimes they speak, sometimes listen, and at times they perform a task or an act through speech or non-verbal clues. This is particularly true for healthcare interpreting in which dialogue interpreting is the primary mode (Angelelli, 2003; Wadensjö, 2014). Research on medical interpreters (MIs) in recent years has emphasised the visible and active roles that MIs play in the doctor–interpreter–patient triadic encounter. Education of MIs should, therefore, involve "managing the dynamics of interpersonal interaction, including issues of culture and unequal status, and the interpreter's fraught position 'in-between'" (Pöchhacker, 2009, p. 137). It suggests that MIs are not merely translation machines or conduits who act impartially at all times. Rivadeneyra et al. (2000) pointed out that requests and offers made by patients in monolingual medical interviews numbered almost three times that of bilingual medical interviews, and doctors provided answers or acknowledgements to almost all questions raised by same-language patients, while patients in interpreter-mediated interviews received far fewer answers. Further studies are indeed necessary to examine how the interpreter's presence or non-presence impacts patients' accessibility to and experience of medical services.

DOI: 10.4324/9781003197027-4

2.1.2 Empathy as an embodied simulation and attitude

Empathy is the ability to understand or share others' experiences and emotions. It is an innate biological ability that fulfils human beings' social needs (Hojat, 2007). This section examines the neurological basis of empathy and its connection to non-verbal synchronisation.

Italian neurophysiologist Rizzolatti and his team discovered mirror neurones and the mirror neurone system (MNS) in our premotor and frontal cortex in the 1980s. Mirror neurones fire up on seeing other people performing certain actions and initiate a series of neural activities that evoke the feelings associated with the action. Though imagining or observing alone can stimulate empathy, this is not as powerful as imitation in triggering brain activity in the premotor areas (Carr et al., 2003, p. 5497). Social psychology studies have found that imitation is a key facilitator of empathy; it is also a standard and automatic response to empathy (Iacoboni, 2009). Robinson (2015) suggests that automatic somatic mirroring works on a social regulation level. Specifically, the affective stages of approval and disapproval are not only felt among us but imitated automatically. Gradually, it reinforces the approved behaviours and changes the ones that are disapproved of. Hence, social norms are formed. In the context of a medical interview, for example, a patient whose concern does not receive empathy from the doctor or the interpreter may experience a sense of neglect and disapproval, which turns inward from disappointment and distrust to self-disapproval and gradually suppresses the action of disclosure or narration. This supports the need for empathy in the medical setting. A lack of empathy expression, or its suppression, is conceivably rather inhumane or unnatural. Patients expect empathy from service providers, and a lack of it disappoints them and discourages them from trusting medical professionals and following the advice and treatment they receive from them.

Empathy can be further dissected into emotional, moral, cognitive, and behavioural dimensions (Neumann et al., 2012), or affective, cognitive, and behavioural aspects (Bylund & Makoul, 2005). In medical contexts, two primary dimensions are most commonly discussed: (1) cognitive empathy, which is the ability to understand the patient's perspective and feelings, to confirm this understanding, and to act on the understanding to help the patient; and (2) affective empathy or emotional empathy, which is the ability to emotionally resonate with the patient (Mercer & Reynolds, 2002). In particular, non-verbal behaviours of medical professionals are found to have significant interactional, social, and psychological impacts on patients' satisfaction and health outcomes. For instance, affiliative non-verbal behaviour, such as eye gaze and proximity of the doctor to the patient, is related to higher patient satisfaction (Mast, 2007) and hence to a higher tendency of the patient to follow treatment instructions, thus generating better health outcomes. There are reciprocal influences between non-verbal behaviour, psychopathology, and therapeutic processes, as presented by Philippot et al. (2003), who argue that non-verbal behaviour not only reflects emotional experience but also acts as a diagnostic tool, an index of the pathological process, and a regulator of emotion and interaction, and thus it can create and maintain the therapeutic relationship, which is as instrumental as medication in the patient's recovery.

There has been a surge in demand for medical interpreting services for languages that were previously perceived as marginal in the host countries and had usually been dealt with on an ad hoc basis because there are no established college-level programmes for the languages of these minorities (Angelelli, 2006). Most ethnic minority languages are not taught at local universities. Training of MIs can only be offered as non-degree short courses for candidates who are immigrants or heritage speakers. In Australia, Hale and Ozolins (2014) conducted a short preparatory course to prepare bilinguals who speak languages of limited diffusion for the National Accreditation Authority for Translators and Interpreters (NAATI) test. But the study concludes that short courses conducted with English as the medium of instruction may not be as helpful as desired in building interpreting skills and that the pathway for these groups of bilinguals to become professional interpreters needs to be re-examined.

While identifying the inadequacies of short courses in enhancing skills such as interpreting, which typically takes time and practice, we have to acknowledge the prevalence of such programmes across the world and explore innovative and effective ways of training with more supportive and sustainable professional development for these MIs. Otherwise, we risk pushing groups of ethnic minority bilinguals away from proper training and into unprofessional malpractice. Many low language diffusion (LLD) interpreters know the patient's cultural background and have similar life experiences, such as migration from the home country to a more developed region. But this is a double-edged sword; without proper training, the uncontrolled empathy of these interpreters may jeopardise the MI's performance and communication or may cause the empathiser to burn out.

2.1.3 Empathy in MI education: what needs to be investigated?

The service provider's empathy expressed non-verbally significantly affects the quality of medical service delivered. Halpern (2001, p. 10) suggested that doctors should indeed "become more reflective about their emotional responses and learn to use these responses skilfully, rather than try to detach from them and be influenced by them anyway". An interpreter-mediated medical encounter is no exception. It involves, perhaps, a knottier situation in which the MI is bound by professional identity to strike a balance between being too personally involved and too detached so as to appear unsympathetic. The MI, first of all, needs to identify empathic opportunities from the patient and the doctor, then analyse the emotions and intentions behind them before making decisions on how to express empathy responsibly. Overt expression of empathy may blur the role boundary of the interpreter and bring additional emotional attachment to the interpreter, while an ignored empathy opportunity may leave the patient's needs unattended. All decision-making happens in the blink of an eye, yet comes through in affective, cognitive, and behavioural dimensions. Besides acknowledging or responding to an empathy opportunity, it should be transmitted in a way that the other party can also empathise. This adds to the complexity of MI's communication of empathy. The interplay among empathy, medical interpreting, and non-verbal communication is complicated. Despite the proliferation of research in the field of medicine, psychotherapy, and counselling, the focus is still on two-party communication (i.e., the doctor and patient). In mediated medical interviews there are three parties, with the interpreter as a critical link, and whose tasks are basically about comprehension and imitation. So, by studying video-recorded MI role-play assessments, this study aims to explore the following questions:

1 How do MIs communicate empathy, if any, for and to the patient? In other words, how is empathy constructed in an interpreter-mediated medical encounter? What are the differences in the interpreter's performance under different scenarios impinging on the communication process?
2 How do the other medical interview participants (doctor and patient) and observers (video observers) perceive the empathic performance of the interpreters? Is there any discrepancy? Why?

2.2 Methodology and data collection

The oral examination was conducted in the format of role-playing in a room with a triangular seating arrangement that simulated a doctor's consultation room. A camera had been set up in the room for recording, with consent from all participants. Each role-play event lasted about 12–15 minutes, starting from the MI's entrance through to their exit and the assessors' on-site grading. For each examinee, there were on-site participant ratings by the role-play participant I (i.e., the "doctor"), on-site grading by role-play participant II (i.e., the "patient"), and grading by a non-participant of the role-play (i.e., observers) through watching selected clips of the video recordings. Therefore, three sets of ratings were generated from the oral examination and its recordings in order to answer research question #2, how was empathy perceived by others?, and served as level-determiner for high, mid, and low performance, which partly helped to approach research question #1, how was empathy constructed by the MI?

A brief training of the grading rubrics was conducted with the "doctor" (played by medical professionals) and the "patient" (played by experienced MIs/language consultants) to enhance grader reliability. The construct and conceptualisation of "empathy" as discussed in the literature review of this paper were introduced to the participants from cognitive, affective, and behavioural perspectives. A five-point scale was given to measure each rater's subjective impression of how the interpreter generally behaved empathically in the role-play, with 1 being "shows no or little empathy" and 5 being "shows lots of empathy". The participant raters gave their ratings only on the ones they role-played with, immediately after the role-play was finished. Observer raters were asked to watch the recordings and independently give ratings for each candidate. Because of the length of each candidate's video recording, it would not be feasible to have the observer-raters watch the entire recording. Therefore, a part of each recording was selected and combined to produce a watchable duration (usually of 30 minutes or less). Murphy et al. (2014) made statistical comparisons of various lengths of videos and found that 30-second or 1-minute slices from after the first minute of interaction may sufficiently represent certain non-verbal behaviours, particularly for "gaze, nods, and smiles", regardless of behaviour, so the first 1.5–2 minutes of an interaction is enough to represent behaviour from the whole interaction. Therefore, two segments of 30 seconds have been selected as representative of each MI. The first segment is of the first 1.5–2 minutes of the conversation, during which the interpreter delivers the doctor's message to the patient regarding how the medical condition has deteriorated. The other segment comes from approximately two-thirds into the conversation, when the patient describes their struggles in life and asks the interpreter to keep this information confidential (not telling the doctor). Included in the video clip is how the interpreter listens to the information and how they react to it afterwards. There are two reasons for choosing the two pieces: (1) it provides a glimpse into how the interpreter deals with the doctor's information and the patient's information, respectively, which entails how they process the verbal and non-verbal information (the doctor vs. the patient; the medical discourse vs. the life discourse; the first language vs. the second language); and (2) both segments provide the interpreter with empathy windows or empathy opportunities. To be more specific, the first segment is a delivery of bad news which calls for some level of empathy, whilst the other one is an articulated, verbalised empathisation need by the patient requested of the interpreter, asking the MI to understand them and hence respect their decision not to tell the doctor. Consistent rules have been applied in selecting clips for each interpreter, but not every conversation proceeds at the same speed, and therefore, a few seconds of leeway are given for some instances where the doctor/patient, instead of the interpreter, takes up most of the selected duration. The purpose is to focus on the interpreter and capture as much as possible how the interpreter acts and reacts.

2.2.1 Dialogue transcript

Medical encounters, both inpatient and outpatient ones, are either a first-time consultation or a follow-up visit. Based on the data collected in the preliminary study, revisits in public hospitals account for almost all hospital visits that require interpretation services. Therefore, the dialogue devised for the assessment role-play was also a revisit scenario. According to Tebble (2014), the typical structure of a doctor–patient consultation follows these procedures: (1) symptom description or presentation; (2) disease history-taking; (3) physical examination; and (4) diagnosis and prescription. These components and procedures are subject to change, especially during a follow-up visit in which the focus shifts from giving a diagnosis to tracking the condition development and treatment progress or making necessary adjustment to the treatment plan. Medical conversations consist of two types of voices: the voice of the lifeworld and the voice of medicine. As its name suggests, the voice of medicine refers to information about the medical/technical details typically present in the above-mentioned procedures (1), (3), and (4). Lifeworld, on the other hand, refers to topics of everyday life, which are most commonly seen in procedure (2). The more attention that is given to the lifeworld, the better outcomes and more humane treatment patients will receive (Barry, Stevenson, Britten, Barber, & Bradley, 2001b). Therefore, the script is written with both voices as components and adapts transcriptions from audio recordings of hospital dialogues.

Table 2.1 is the dialogue structure we used in the research. It is set in the Haematology Department. A 47-year-old patient who was diagnosed with stage 1 non-Hodgkin lymphoma (NHL) a few months ago is revisiting the doctor for a check-up.

The dialogue transcript was distributed to the assessors – i.e., the "doctor" and "patient" – 2 weeks before the examination. Explanations were provided for the purpose of the transcript, as well as the construct of the examination, key terminology and components, and possible responses of the interpreters, through phone calls and/or face-to-face meetings based on the participant's availability. The assessors were not required to remember the transcript by

Table 2.1 Structure and turn-analysis of the transcript of the role-play

Turn as scripted	*Role*	*Main idea*
Turns 1–2	Doctor	Breaks the bad news (i.e., deterioration of the condition based on lab results) and gives a prognosis of the disease
	Patient	Confused and struggling to accept the news
Turns 3–5	Doctor	Gives possible reasons and dispenses advice (eat sensibly and rest more)
	Patient	Expresses frustrations (with treatment and medication side-effects)
Turns 6–7	Doctor	Enquires into patient's workload and gives advice
	Patient	Turns to the medical interpreter (MI), expresses concern and doubt about the doctor's ability to understand the patient's dilemma (his/her pressing need to work and support his/her disabled child). Requests that the MI does not share this with the doctor
Turn 8	Doctor	Stresses the importance of rest and a healthy diet. Gives prescriptions

heart or follow it verbatim. In order to facilitate a natural conversation and encourage communication with the assessed, the assessors were encouraged to treat the transcript as an outline so long as the critical terminology and key steps were covered.

2.3 Case analysis and discussion: Turn-taking management and empathy

2.3.1 A primary observation of the interpreters' turn-management and empathic performance

This paper examines in particular, the student interpreters' turn-taking management and empathy using conversation analysis. As a listener as well as a speaker, the interpreter could request a turn, deny a given turn, or backchannel. Although it is arguably difficult to determine whether a specific response function is backchannelling, the research of Adolphs and O'Keeffe (2008) proposed a framework for general categorisation which includes: (1) continuers (CON); (2) convergence (CNV) tokens; (3) engaged response (ER) tokens; and (4) information receipt (IR) tokens, the definitions of which are given below (ibid., p. 84). We integrated these form-and-function-oriented categorisations into our analysis of the interpreter-mediated conversations. Below are our primary observations of the INT's management of turns and empathy:

1 *Continuer (CON)*: small nods, gazing or eye contact, note-taking, torso leaning forward, smiling, "hmm" were noted from the MIs. Among the responses, note-taking by interpreters suggests "I am paying attention, so please continue" because an interpreter can only take notes when he or she is paying close attention and analysing the message heard. Patients and doctors also see it as part of an interpreter's job to jot down notes and take them as an encouragement for continuous speech. Some interpreters take notes while nodding, leaning forward, or maintain regular eye contact, while others do not take notes but gaze at the speaker to show acknowledgement. However, when the speaker conveys messages of high complexity, the interpreter might have to pay undivided attention for better comprehension, processing, and memorisation, and therefore there is no note-taking at this point.
2 *Convergent (CNV) cue* is a type of response more often seen in casual conversations for rapport building and is less expected by professionals in workplace encounters such as medical interpreting interactions. An interpreter is expected to refrain generally from showing approval or disapproval towards the client. Typical verbal CNV messages such as "I agree" or "that is great" that indicate stance or judgement were not observed from our data. However, disapproving emotions, such as annoyance or impatience, could be observed from non-verbal behaviours, albeit subtle.

3 *Engagement (ER)* includes clear and multiple nods, long gazes, compassionate frowning (as opposed to disapproval frowning), placing a hand over one's chest, and a softened tone of voice. This category is a reliable indicator of empathy, as its definition suggests, and indicates the engagement of emotion and understanding, and these kinds of responses were observed from the MIs.
4 *Receipt of information (RI) responses* shown by the interpreters observed include nodding, stopping taking notes, putting down notes, turning away from the original speaker to the next one, and verbal acknowledgement such as "OK". It is an institutional category of responses that often happen at the end of an utterance that show recognition of the receipt of the message and suggests a readiness to deliver interpretation to the other party while maintaining the distance between the different participant roles of the doctor, interpreter, and patient.

Our analysis focused mainly on Turns 3–5 of the dialogue structure (see Table 2.1) in which the interpreter is faced with an unexpected dilemma; that is, upon hearing the patient's request (hereinafter referred to as the Request) to not share their story with the doctor, s/he must decide whether or not to respect the patient's decision. This part was chosen for two reasons and examined from cognitive and affective perspectives. First, it contains no medical terminology or typical note-taking items/memory burdens (e.g., a listing of numbers, names of people or places), which would free the interpreter from technical challenges that may compromise their performance. According to the Effort Model of Gile (2009), the main efforts that the interpreter makes include listening and comprehension before remembering and rendering the utterance in English to the doctor. The focus of this analysis is placed on the empathy responses and communication, and on how the interpreter handles the unexpected, which reflects the MI's view of their role and the function of empathy in medical communication. This part depicts a struggling parent with cancer who has to support a disabled child and cannot afford to rest properly. This was a very real character which most of our "patients" felt the impulse to play enthusiastically. The everyday language used in this part of the conversation also helped participants to assimilate into the situation. As a result, the patient's distress and determination to keep the information from the doctor could be shown non-verbally with greater intensity, compared to other segments in which pure medical information was exchanged. This made for a more productive subject of analysis since multimodality (empathy expressed not just by words) in turn triggers more empathy from the interpreter who might regulate their empathy response to a certain extent.

The following sections compare and summarise the performance of a high (4.1–5.0) Japanese–Cantonese interpreter and Urdu–English interpreters of relatively low performance (1.0–2.9). The purpose is to identify commonalities in turn-taking strategies, especially the use of backchannelling cues that correlates to their empathy performance. The analysis was based on the interpreter's turn-taking strategies employed before, during, and after the

Request. Transcription of the dialogue adopts the Jeffersonian Transcription Notation.[1] In the transcription, "erm" and "urh" are romanisations of the speaker's speech fillers, and "lah" is a pragmatic particle in colloquial Cantonese which indicates the tone of the sentence.

2.3.2 Case analysis of a higher-range performer

The interpreter (INT) was a mid-30s Chinese female with the language combination of Cantonese and Japanese. The doctor (DOC) was a Chinese female medical professional who spoke Cantonese in the role-play. The patient (PAT) was a Japanese male. The INT got 2 out of 5 in participant empathy rating from the DOC, and 4 from the PAT. Her observer rating was 4.4, which was the second highest among all INTs.

2.3.2.1 Before the request

Generally speaking, the INT was softly spoken, agreeable, and attentive to the PAT. She held the palm-size notepad in her left palm at all times which enabled her to navigate her upper torso with flexibility while regularly maintaining eye contact with the PAT to show interest and attention. There was notably a high number of backchannelling cues such as CON, with nods, gazes, raised eyebrows while taking notes, as seen from Figure 2.1. She also acknowledged

Figure 2.1 Before the request: interpreter demonstrates a high number of backchannelling cues while listening and taking notes.

RI with nods or a verbalised "hmm" at the end of the DOC or PAT's turn. Her attention was devoted to the speaker or listener of the turn as evidenced by the direction her torso and head were facing. Her lower torso and slightly tilted head also encouraged the PAT to feel comfortable and speak more. The significant amount of backchannelling cues she delivered formed the basis of her empathic performance which was highly regarded among the raters.

2.3.2.2 During the request

She appeared to be unclear of the PAT's message at first and stopped taking notes. She then gazed at the PAT as he maintained eye contact with her and explained with gestures his family background. She also interrupted the PAT's narration. Interruption is not uncommon in conversations, especially in interpreter-mediated encounters. Interpreters do it for clarification or segmentation of speech. Here she began the interruption with an apology that was followed by a partial recap of the previous message (Line 117). Then she used phrases such as "no problem, OK" to reassure the PAT that the message was received.

115	P	erm (..) °I mean° my job↑ (.) °is° at a construction site (.) >but this < hope you do not(.) tell the doctor (.)	えっと（。。）°あの°私の仕事は↑°あの°工事现场で働いていて＞でこれちょっと＜先生には（。）言わないでほしいんですけど（。）
116	P	I ::: ac- actually understand (.) °I mean° the doctor:: wanted me to stay- stay home:: °meaning° to rest and heal ↓:: I understand it all (.) (.hhh) but::: I mean>this I cannot do< If you ask me why (.) °I mean° I ah have a kid° with a little bit of °disability °meaning° a disable child:: I cannot stop supporting him (.) therefore (.hhh) ::: (..) meaning (.) >I cannot stop working< therefore:: then-	あの：：ま-まぁわかってますけど （。）°あの°先生は私家にいてほしいっまぁ家-家で（。）あの：：疗养病気を直してほしい まぁわかってるんですけど（。）(.hhh) でも：：ちょっと＞それできないんですよ＜なぜかというと（。）°あの° 私には°ちょっと° ハンディキャップこう障害のある子供：：サポートしなきゃいけなくて（。）(.hhh) で：：まぁ（。）＞仕事やめられないんですね＜で：：ま-
117	I	ah- >excuse me< <your family is> (.) er::: has a disabled child (.) [yes(.) small child (.) small child (.)] have a child [at home] (.) no problem okay - then- >let me state it to the doctor< [ah(.)]	あ-＞すみません＜＜あなたの家族が＞（。）er(..)ハンディキャップという[そう（。）子供、子供、家に] 子供があ（。）[ええ] あります(..です)え（。）＞ちょっと先生に说明しましょう[あ-]＜
118	P	but (.) this (..)I feel that the doctor would not be able to understand (.)°so°>hope you do not tell<	でもこれ（。。）先生理解できないと思うんで（。）°あの°＞言わないでほしいんです＜

Figure 2.2 During the request: interpreter displays an embarrassed smile.

However, even though the PAT made it clear not to disclose the information to the DOC (Line 115) she offered to render it (Line 117) and pointed with both hands to the DOC, to which the PAT immediately said no and raised his hand to form a "don't" gesture (Line 118). She then realised the dilemma she had been put in. She responded with an embarrassed smile, gritting her teeth, and quickly glanced away (Figure 2.2). She pulled her head slightly further from the PAT, creating a subtle distance of reluctance. During this turn, there was an observable amount of decrease in backchannelling cues from the INT. But she quickly withdrew herself and indicated to the PAT that she agreed to the request with a nod at the end of the turn.

2.3.2.3 After the request

The INT appeared hesitant in her non-verbal and verbal rendition to the DOC (Lines 119–120). She frequently referred to her notes, holding them up and close to her even though she did not write much in the previous turn. She looked up and away explaining what had happened (Figure 2.3). Her right hand was rubbing her left index finger forcefully, showing a certain level of stress (Figure 2.3). When the DOC replied with an "OK doesn't matter" and expressed her respect for the PAT's request (Line 121), the INT seemed

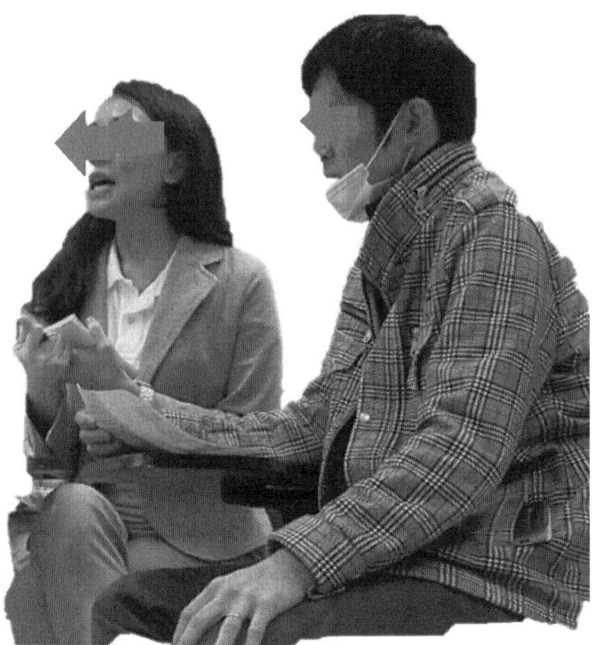

Figure 2.3 After the request: interpreter rubs her hands together as she speaks to doctor.

relieved and immediately rendered it to the PAT (Line 121) even before the DOC finished her turn. She did it swiftly in a whisper-like manner before continuing to take notes of the DOC's second half of the message. This type of overlapped speech had never been observed when the INT was a listener. Nonetheless, it was a self-initiated assuring and caring move for the ease and comfort of the PAT. As a result, her turn-management decision to whisper and quickly come back to the original speaker did not interfere with the progress of communication.

119	I	Because I first (..) already (.) asked (.) him two questions and one was his occupation lah ↑ and the other one was his work how long it took <and then erm he chose to > (.) erm (.) erm not wanting to answer [oh::::]	因为我先 (..) 己经 (.) 问咗 (.) 佢个问题一个就系佢个职业啦↑另外一个就系佢返工(要返几耐嘅) <咁样erm佢就选择系> (.) erm (.) erm 唔想答嘅 咁样嘅 [喔::::]
120	I	Because (.) right (.) he is a bit (..) erm (..)er (1) family (..) <his own problem> so↑ but just now (.) er you- (.) er that is- er (..) doctor you said really wanted (…) he chose (..) erm (..) not to answer	因为 (.) 系啰 (.) 佢就会有啲 (..) erm (..)er (1) 屋企 (..) <自己嘅问题> 咁↑但系头先就系话 (.) er你- (.) er即- erh (..) 医生你话好想佢选择系 (..)erm (..) 唔回答嘅

121	D	°Okay° (..) doesn't matter lah↑ ah : then ↑ (..) if he doesn't want to tell me↑ (.) then::: >this is his<his choice lah (.)ah[それは大丈夫です] then↑ (.) then (.) but he has to pay attention to his own health ah ↑ so those (..)	°OK° (..) 唔紧要啦↑ 下: 咁↑ (..) 如果佢唔想话比我听呢↑ (.) 咁::: >呢个系<佢个选择啦(.)下[それは大丈夫です] 咁呢↑ (.)就(.)但系佢必须要注意佢自己健康喎下↑ 咁嗰啲(..)

Although the PAT rated her empathic performance as 4 out of 5, the DOC gave her a lower score (2 out of 5) because she "was not convinced the INT understood what the PAT said in a couple of turns", as she commented after the assessment. As verified by an examination of the recording and transcription, her unsatisfactory language and interpreting skills did cause a few communication glitches in the other parts of the role-play script, which is discussed in the thematic sections later.

2.3.3 Case analysis of a lower-range performer

In this case, the DOC was a Chinese female medical professional who spoke English in the role-play, and the PAT was a male Urdu-speaking Pakistani. The INT was in her 40s; her language combination was Urdu and English. The INT got 4 out of 5 from the DOC and 3.75 from the PAT, which was above the average empathy score, but her observer rating was only 2.4, which fell on the lower end. The difference was significant because the major interruption of the turn-taking occurred in segment #(2). Even though she performed above average overall empathically, her bilingual observer rating is far from satisfactory. Below is a detailed analysis of what happened.

2.3.3.1 Before the request

As a listener, the INT demonstrated a significant number of backchannelling cues to the speakers, including CONs and RIs but with few ERs. She managed to take notes while maintaining eye contact and nods, providing swift and smooth interpretations after a turn. When faced with extended medical information such as the DOC's explanation of lymphoma, she requested a pause by engaging the DOC with a gaze, tilting her head, slightly raising her right palm and nodding with a polite smile (Figure 2.4).

When providing renditions of the DOC's message to the PAT, she maintained her turn to speak by continuous gesturing that helped illustrate different stages of cancer development (Figure 2.5).

But after her turn to speak, she immediately turned and faced the DOC without any room for the PAT to respond to her utterance (Figure 2.6). She also invited the DOC to speak by facing and extending both of her arms to the DOC (Figure 2.6). She controlled the turn-taking by suppressing the turn of the PAT.

Figure 2.4 Before the request a: interpreter raises her palm with a smile and tilts her head to request a pause from doctor.

Figure 2.5 Before the request b: interpreter speaks to patient with gestures.

2.3.3.2 During the request

The PAT's role, in this case, was emotionally charged. His lines were delivered with several accompanying non-verbal cues such as head tilts, a raised voice, and varied intonation (Line 63). However, the INT seemed to have a hard time empathising with the PAT. She first stopped taking notes, and looked

Figure 2.6 Before the request c: interpreter speaks to doctor and invites doctor to speak with gesture.

up at the PAT with frowned eyebrows. Before requesting a turn, she directly cut off the PAT (Line 63) by stating her role and gestured a "blocking" sign in front of her torso (Figure 2.7). With the use of a falling tone and slowing down the speed, she made her point louder and unquestionable.

	Speaker	*Translation of the transcription*	*Original utterance*
63	P	er。 <I work at a construction site::> but you don't have to tell the doctor (.) (.hhh) because I know (..) the doctor wants me to stay home (..) er:: and rest (hhh.) throughout the treatment::: but it's impossible for me↓	مریض; مین ایک تعمیراتی جگہ پر کام کرتا ہوں لیکن آپکو یہ ڈاکٹر کو بتانے کی ضرورت نہیں ہے کیونکہ یہ چاہتے ہیں میں گھر میں رہوں .علاج کرواؤں،آرام کروں
64	I	but I::: have to tell her↓<about your home> (.) your job related↓	ترجمان;بٹ آئی. (انگریزی میں).لہجے میں تھوڑی ہچکچاہٹ) لیکن مجھے اس کو بتانا ہے آپکے گھر.. آپ کی نوکری سے ریلٹڈ (مریض روکتا ہے)

The PAT persisted and kept explaining his difficulty and tried to convince her not to tell the doctor. However, the INT had already turned to the DOC and, after scribbling down a few words, she was ready to speak to the DOC even though the PAT was still looking, talking, and gesturing to her. The INT did not turn to the PAT but only looked at him while gesturing and whispered

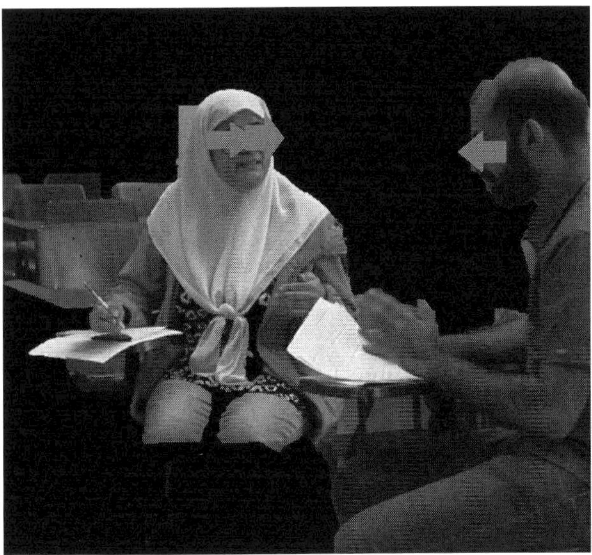

Figure 2.7 During the request: interpreter requests patient to stop talking by gesturing "stop".

"excuse me" three times (Line 66). While the INT tried to suppress PAT's turn by facing away and gesturing "stop", the PAT did not back down. The tug-of-war between INT and PAT here lasted for about 5 seconds until the PAT stopped talking.

	Speaker	*Original utterance*
66	I	excuse me:::excuse me:::excuse me↑

2.3.3.3 *After the request*

After taking a few breaths to clear her thoughts, the INT began to explain what had happened in the third-person pronoun to the DOC (Line 67). She changed her open hand gestures into tightly crossed ones (Figure 2.8), and she avoided eye engagement with the DOC during Lines 67–68. She suppressed the DOC's response by using a few "urh"s because she had more to say (Line 68). She returned to a smile and opened up her hand as she justified her use of "he" to represent the PAT's voice (Figure 2.9).

67	I	(2) urh:::urh::urh urh:he's urh a construction worker (.) he urh:: he needs to feed his children↑ (.) He cannot just stay at home (..) without work
68	I	(1) urh:: urh:urh >sorry I have to use he because he was asking he asked me not to tell you< so: huh==

Figure 2.8 After the request a: interpreter rubs her hands together facing the doctor.

Figure 2.9 After the request b: interpreter smiles with an open gesture.

2.3.4 Coding of themes for discussion

Informal interviews were conducted with the participant and observer raters to elicit data and explore their perceptions. Reoccurring words such as "emotionally engaged", "engaged", "nodding along", and "eye contact" were coded accordingly. With the case analyses above and the patterns which emerged from the video data, the foci of discussion were on the following themes: overlapping speech, turn-requesting, backchannelling, emotional engagement, interpreting competence, and empathic performance.

2.3.5 Overlapping and turn-requesting

Overlapping of speech is inevitable in naturally occurring conversations including interpreter-mediated dialogues. There are three or four types of overlaps, depending on the type of categorisation. For example, Schegloff (2000) includes the verbalised continuers such as "hmm" and anticipatory overlaps such as finishing the original speaker's thoughts. For medical mediated conversations, overlapping becomes even more hectic than in regular dialogues because any two of the participants could be talking over each other. In the role-play in this study, overlapping was observed from a few candidates who struggled with long utterances or complex information that seemed to be beyond their competency. For instance, one of the male Pakistani INTs abruptly interrupted the DOC and the PAT four times when he needed clarification or time to jot down notes. In tri-party communication such as the role-play in the study, overlapping also happened by engaging in a third interlocutor. The Pakistani INT mentioned earlier directly turned away and spoke to the DOC while the PAT was still speaking to her. As a result, the PAT had to stop when he realised the INT was not engaged any more. Such cut-offs were regarded as poor turn-taking management as they were unannounced to the other interlocutors and prevented a smooth taking of turn.

Other interpreter-trainees in this study, who started as listeners, were seen to request a turn to speak in a manner acceptable to the speaker. Common cues preceding such requests were gazing, a stop of note-taking, slowly raising a hand, and more frequent nods, with or without a verbal enunciation of the request such as "excuse me, can I translate this part first?". These nonverbal expressions were often perceived as cues that cushioned the interruption. Turn requests by such cues were observed among the top five empathy scorers which meant interruptions, even when they were not backchannelling, could still be deemed as acceptable and undisruptive when preceded by cues of acknowledgement.

2.3.6 Backchannelling and emotional engagement

Backchannelling was instrumental in indicating emotional engagement when it was in synchronisation with the speaker's message. In the case analyses in the previous sections, a salient distinction between how the two Cantonese–Japanese INTs interacted with the patient was the intensity of backchannelling. While the top scorers provided an array of proxemic and kinesic backchannelling cues such as forward-leaning, constant nods, and eye engagement combined with pronounced verbal acknowledgement, those in the mid-range of the scoreboard maintained a stiffer and composed posture with a limited number of gestures and facial expressions that suggested emotional engagement.

2.3.7 Interpreting competence and empathic performance

The INTs' empathy performance scores did not necessarily align with their interpreting competence in this study. An example of this is the Cantonese–Japanese INT analysed in Section 2.3.2, as indicated in the transcription excerpt Lines 81–87.

Line 85–87 showed that the INT was struggling to understand the PAT's description of "a bitter taste" and hence she asked for repetition. Similar incidents occurred twice in her case and it was clear from her request for repetition and her hesitant renditions to the service users (i.e., the DOC and PAT) that her language proficiency was lacking, but she was nonetheless rated as empathic and her service satisfactory.

However, we must emphasise that this study is not suggesting that the display of empathy is a replacement for interpreting skills. Nevertheless, raising student-interpreters' sensitivity to the use of empathic communicational cues would help to reduce the negative impact of inadequate interpreting. Such awareness would be especially beneficial for early-stage interpreter training when students are still honing their skills to become fully fledged professionals.

2.4 Summary of findings

2.4.1 How is empathy constructed by an MI?

The interpreter's empathetic communication was constructed not only verbally but non-verbally through the provision of various backchannelling cues, primarily through CONs, such as nods, gazes, and torso- and head-facing, and ER,s, which function at an affective level to indicate emotional resonance. On the other hand, when the INT was the speaker, an accurate and affective nonverbal rendition of the patient's message was considered more empathic than an under- or over-representation of the original, which was perceived as either aloof or exaggerated, sometimes even "rude", according to the raters' comments. This study also found that backchannelling cues were perceived to be more effective in conveying empathy compared to other turn-taking strategies. It was found that backchannelling cues were, in essence, a representation and display of the embodied synchronisation of emotions between the speaker and the listener, the act of which could satisfy the patient's need to be engaged and listened to in the interaction, and hence had a higher level of perceived empathy.

2.4.2 How is empathy perceived by the other participants and observers?

Empathy was also perceived by the other participants when the interpreter was able to form an equal and supportive relationship with the patient during the consultation. It was evident from the analyses that proxemics, haptics, vocalics, kinetics, and chronemics all affected the relation-building, and non-verbal cues of trust, warmth, genuineness, and rapport received higher ratings of empathy. These empathic cues include but are not limited to the following: proactively achieving a closer distance with the interlocutor; always maintaining direct torso and facial orientation; an increased and direct gaze and nods; lowering of the torso to achieve a similar effect to touching; more open and animated postures or facial expressions; more pitch variety; fewer silences or latencies; a softened voice and rising tones when seeking confirmation or requesting pauses; adopting speech patterns; and displaying vocal pleasantness. It is worth noting that the documentation of the interpreter's mimicking of the patient's facial expressions, gestures, and speech patterns correlated highly with high empathy perception scores, and the opposite behaviour correlated with low scores, which again confirmed the empirical neuroscience findings that the MNS is responsible for human beings' empathy response and that individuals usually want to be imitated by interactants.

2.5 Conclusion: Implication for curriculum changes for medical interpreting training

The empirical evidence from this study revealed some aspects of empathy communication useful for the training and assessment of MIs in the future and it could be implemented by other regions which also currently lack a developed or standardised accreditation system. This study did not set out to prescribe any empathic behaviours, but rather, through the exploration and identification of the process of empathic behaviours, raise awareness of the significance of empathy for medical interpreting. Even though favourable acts in turn-taking management and relationship management have been identified, it cannot be assumed that copying these acts will guarantee successful empathic communication. Furthermore, it must be understood that empathy could be observed and displayed through an array of non-verbal cues and that individual differences could be distinctive.

As pointed out earlier, empathy is biologically rooted in the MNS and manifested in verbal and non-verbal interpersonal synchrony, but it is also an attitude of positive regard and respect for others that requires warmth and genuineness. As verified by findings from turn-taking management, the genuineness or authenticity of interpreters' empathy requires a basis of accurate understanding, which is not easily achieved through mere verbal messages, nor the non-verbal nuances "between the lines". Some participants in this study demonstrated plenty of continuers as backchannelling cues that were not synchronised with the patient's verbal and emotional messages and they were regarded as having a low level of empathy. Knowing that it was an assessment, test-takers strove to perform well, but only by arriving at a dual understanding of the other's situation through verbal and non-verbal messages can one genuinely empathise with another person. The level of authentic empathy is perceivable to interlocutors and observers via the combination of verbal and non-verbal cues and reflects the MI's attitude and willingness to understand the other interlocutor's message somatically. Interpreters in training must be taught that empathy is not just about understanding how others feel, but also requires the sensitivity and multimodal facility to communicate the empathetic elements to those people. Identified patterns that are perceived as empathic could shed light on how training materials or modules could be developed for mediated communication, which can ultimately enhance healthcare outcomes.

Our findings also verify and support the pressing need to include empathy as part of MI training and assessment. Even though during the intervention, the concepts of patient-centred care and empathy were taught and emphasised, 16 out of 26 interpreters chose to report the patient's personal story to the doctor against the patient's wishes. This was a strong indication of how entrenched the doctor-centred culture was in the consultation room, or, in the interpreter's mind. The in-depth analyses of the data went on to show the complexity of the obstacles to be overcome in MI education. Adult learning or vocational training has its unique features and a change of mindset comes before a behaviour change. Raising awareness is a vital priority instead of a top-down regulation. Second, each culture has its level of acceptance when it comes to new concepts in healthcare, such as "patient-centred care", according to their value systems and customs. Therefore, if the authority is deeply vested with the doctor and patients are assumed to be ignorant of their sickness, participation in the negotiation of their treatment is impossible and it is unlikely that the power dynamics can be easily changed. Third, short-term courses that last a month or two can only have a limited effect on behavioural changes. Continuous practicum or mentorship should also be adopted to change adult behaviours. Raising empathic sensitivity should be one of the objectives of medical interpreting training and an important attribute of MIs as well.

Note

1 Jeffersonian Transcription Notation is described in Jefferson, G. (1984). Transcription notation, in Atkinson, J. and Heritage, J. (eds.), *Structures of Social Interaction*. New York: Cambridge University Press.

References

Adolphs, S., & O'Keeffe, A. (2008). Response tokens in British and Irish discourse: Corpus, context and variational pragmatics. In *Variational Pragmatics: A Focus on Regional Varieties in Pluricentric Languages* Amsterdam: John Benjamins. (pp. 69–98). Accessed on July 27, 2020, from https://dspace.mic.ul.ie/bitstream/handle/10395/1796/.

Angelelli, C. V. (2003). The interpersonal role of the interpreter in cross-cultural communication: A survey of conference, court and medical interpreters in the

US, Canada and Mexico. In *The Critical Link 3 Interpreters in the Community Proceedings of the Third International Conference on Interpreting in Legal Health and Social Service Settings Montréal Canada 2001*. Amsterdam: John Benjamins. (pp. 15–26).

Angelelli, C. V. (2006). Validating professional standards and codes: Challenges and opportunities. Interpreting, 8(2), 175–193. https://doi.org/10.1075/intp.8.2.04ang.

Barry, C. A., Stevenson, F. A., Britten, N., Barber, N., & Bradley, C. P. (2001b). Giving voice to the lifeworld. More humane, more effective medical care? A qualitative study of doctor–patient communication in general practice. *Social Science and Medicine*, *53*(4), 487–505. https://doi.org/10.1016/S0277-9536(00)00351-8.

Bylund, C. L., & Makoul, G. (2005). Examining empathy in medical encounters: An observational study using the empathic communication coding system. *Health Communication*, *18*(2), 123–140. https://doi.org/10.1207/s15327027hc1802_2.

Carr, L., Iacoboni, M., Dubeau, M.-C. M.-C., Mazziotta, J. C., & Lenzi, G. L. (2003). Neural mechanisms of empathy in humans: A relay from neural systems for imitation to limbic areas. *Proceedings of the National Academy of Sciences*, *100*(9), 5497–5502. https://doi.org/10.1073/pnas.0935845100.

Gile, D. (2009). *Basic Concepts and Models for Interpreter and Translator Training*. *Vasa*. Retrieved from http://medcontent.metapress.com/index/A65RM03P4874243N.pdf.

Hale, S., & Ozolins, U. (2014). Monolingual short courses for language-specific accreditation: Can they work? A Sydney experience. *Interpreter and Translator Trainer*, *8*(2). https://doi.org/10.1080/1750399X.2014.929371.

Halpern, J. (2001). From detached concern to empathy: Humanizing medical practice. Accessed on July 27, 2020, from https://repository.library.georgetown.edu/handle/10822/941064.

Hojat, M. (2007). Empathy in patient care: Antecedents, development, measurement, and outcomes. Accessed on July 27, 2020, from www.google.com/books?hl=zh-TW&lr=&id=Kj3NxGwZ9zkC&oi=fnd&pg=PR15&dq=Empathy+in+Patient+Care:+Antecedents,+Development,+Measurement,+and+Outcomes&ots=wlnGBIN7vp&sig=WBAdTNXFAWLvLWdm9Pn50hBD0zU.

Iacoboni, M. (2009). *Mirroring People: The New Science of How we Connect with Others*. Accessed on July 27, 2020, from www.google.com/books?hl=en&lr=&id=FEWWzxLlP8YC&oi=fnd&pg=PP2&dq=Mirroring+People:+The+New+Science+of+How+We+Connect+with+Others&ots=Re3SWpdkTl&sig=WEoYgmCkh7PbXoKAhrvt5lXB7oE.

Mast, M. S. (2007). On the importance of nonverbal communication in the physician–patient interaction. *Patient Education and Counseling*. https://doi.org/10.1016/j.pec.2007.03.005

Mercer, S. W., & Reynolds, W. J. (2002). Empathy and quality of care. *British Journal of General Practice*, *52*(Suppl.), 9–12. https://doi.org/10.1016/j.jpsychores.2014.03.005.

Murphy, N. A., Hall, J. A., Schmid Mast, M., Ruben, M. A., Frauendorfer, D., Blanch-Hartigan, D., … Nguyen, L. (2014). Reliability and validity of nonverbal thin slices in social interactions. *Personality and Social Psychology Bulletin*, *41*(2), 199–213. https://doi.org/10.1177/0146167214559902.

Neumann, M., Scheffer, C., Tauschel, D., Lutz, G., Wirtz, M., & Edelhäuswer, F. (2012). Physician empathy: Definition, outcome-relevance and its measurement in patient care and medical education. *GMS Zeitschrift für Medizinische Ausbildung*, *29*(1), 1–21. https://doi.org/10.3205/zma000781.

Philippot, P., Feldman, R., & Coats, E. (2003). *Nonverbal Behavior in Clinical Settings*. New York: Oxford University Press.

Rivadeneyra, R., Elderkin-Thompson, V., Silver, R. C., & Waitzkin, H. (2000). Patient centeredness in medical encounters requiring an interpreter. *American Journal of Medicine*, *108*(6), 470–474. https://doi.org/10.1016/S0002-9343(99)00445-3.

Robinson, D. (2015). *The Dao of Translation: An East–West Dialogue*. London: Routledge. Accessed on July 27, 2020, from www.google.com/books?hl=en&lr=&id=uk_eCQAAQBAJ&oi=fnd&pg=PP1&dq=dao+of+translation&ots=NHDUFqss_Q&sig=QF0NAJpIe_RgLty4IeWbfTvCsBQ.

Schegloff, E. A. (2000). Overlapping talk and the organization of turn-taking for conversation. *Language in Society*, *29*, 1—63.

Tebble, H. (2014). A genre-based approach to teaching dialogue interpreting: The medical consultation. *The Interpreter and Translator Trainer*, *8*(3), 418–436. https://doi.org/10.1080/1750399X.2014.972651.

Wadensjö, C. (2014). *Interpreting as Interaction*. London: Routledge. Accessed on July 27, 2020, from www.google.com/books?hl=en&lr=&id=vADKAwAAQBAJ&oi=fnd&pg=PP1&dq=Interpreting+as+Interaction&ots=eWYjMzzD2J&sig=QPlJYpSREgmziV3k0yi4iYDux2k.

3 The public service interpreter's latitude for action

A Triadic Discourse Interpreting Model (TRIM)[1]

Lihua Jiang

3.1 Introduction

In contrast to conference interpreting, public service interpreting (PSI) requires the interpreter to interpret "bidirectionally," i.e., "back and forth" into and out of his/her native language in what is often referred to as a "face-to-face" communicative situation. With globalisation and migration processes, PSI has gained increasing importance in the past decade. In fact, most of the interpreting today is considered to be done by PSI (Moody, 2007).

While conference interpreting had established itself firmly by the late 1990s in terms of documented concepts and methods, PSI still today often is used synonymously with non-professional interpreting (Bührig & Meyer, 2004; Sauerwein, 2006) and presents a very heterogeneous picture as far as concepts and methodology are concerned (Hale, 2007). Much of the copious literature centres around problems of its professionalisation and academisation, its development in individual countries, or its problems in particular settings. As an "ad hoc," "non-professional" activity, the different roles of the public service interpreter as compared with those of a conference interpreter have been a matter of controversy to this date (Hale, 2007; Moody, 2007).

While research and academic studies have extensively discussed a wide range of problems associated with the public service interpreter's role conflicts from an ethical, linguistic, and didactic point of view, little interest has been shown to systematise the parameters that influence or determine the interpreter's role in actual interpreter-mediated communicative events. The theoretical and methodological deficits surrounding the concept of PSI are responsible for the conflict of the public service interpreter when presented with the decision for or against faithful ("verbatim" or "conduit") or relatively "free" interpretation (acting as an "advocator" or "cultural mediator") in the actual interpreting situation. In an effort to alleviate the interpreter's predicament, there has been a growing tendency to explore the institutional settings in which PSI takes place, and their influence on the interpreter-mediated communication process (e.g., Hale, 2004; Meyer, 2004; Mikkelson, 2000; Pöllabauer, 2004; Sauerwein, 2006). The visibility issue of the interpreter's role in such settings as court,

DOI: 10.4324/9781003197027-5

medical, or police interpreting has accentuated such traditional opposing views of the interpreter as a "verbatim" reproducer of messages in another language (Goffman, 1981), on the one hand, or as "advocator," "cultural broker," or "conciliator" (Angelelli, 2004a, 2004b; Barald & Gavioli, 2012; Davidson, 2000; Metzger, 1999; Roy, 2000; Rudvin, 2007; Wadensjö, 1998), on the other hand. Socio-linguistic questions and discourse considerations have moved into focus on the threshold of the new millennium, when PSI began to be seen as involving two independent activities, i.e., the translation and the coordination of talk, with the interpreter being considered as an engaged actor in a triad, creating two kinds of talk: relaying a message and mediating the flow of talk (Wadensjö, 1998). Terms like "participation framework," i.e., the interpreter's activity of coordinating utterances arising from assumptions and expectations of the participants in a conversational communication flow, have stressed the interactive component in PSI with distinguishing turn exchanges between the interlocutors and the interpreter, and linguistic forms of turns (such as lengthy lags and overlapping turns).

The public service interpreter's action latitude today, however, is still unresolved, which is reflected and documented, for example, in Miriam Shlesinger's ongoing Tel Aviv project "Grey Goes with the Territory" (Shlesinger, 2008), which vividly illustrates the interpreter's predicament of being caught in a "sandwich position" of serving two masters at the same time. To date, there is no consensus on which communicative parameters determine the individual interpreter's role within those two opposite views of literal "verbatim" renderings ("conduit role") and active "cultural mediation" within a framework of parameters that influence and control the interpretation process in a concrete interpreter-mediated scenario.

3.2 The issues in PSI

The following example shows an interpreted exchange in a Canadian immigration office in the late 1970s with the typical problems associated with PSI as often accentuated in popular descriptions of the phenomenon. The example involves an Italian immigrant who wants to get his legal papers in Canada, relying on his bilingual daughter to interpret the conversation with an English-speaking immigration officer:

> Father to interpreter: Digli che e un imbecile! (Tell him he's an idiot!)
> Interpreter to the immigration officer: My father won't accept your offer.
> Father (angrily, in Italian to daughter): Why didn't you tell him what I told you?
>
> (Harris and Sherwood, 1978: 217)

This example demonstrates two interrelated questions which will be the focus of this study: is the interpreter legitimised to interpret non-verbatim, that is, is it legitimate for the interpreting daughter not to reproduce her father's insulting utterance? Are there criteria that determine whether to render a verbatim message or non-verbatim message in an actual interpreter-mediated communication? Even though we can assume that the daughter by her mediation effort avoided an imminent clash of actual interests which may have led to a possible breakdown of the communication, we so far have no "intersubjectively verifiable criteria" for answering the above questions – not just on an "ad hoc" but on a systematic, more general level. The present study endeavours to shed some light on these questions.

In the search for such parameters, this research will position PSI within the framework of discourse analysis and its essential parameter of (establishing) coherence in communication. Discourse analysis is based on the influential ideas of Sacks, Schegloff, and Jefferson (1974) on turn-taking in conversations with the requirements that

> while understanding of other's turns of talk are displayed to co-participants, they are available as well to professional analysts, who are thereby provided a proof criterion (and a search procedure) for the analysis of what a turn's talk is occupied with. Since it is the parties' understanding of prior turns of talk that it's relevant to their construction of next turns, it is their understandings that are warranted for analysis.
> (p. 728)

Within this framework, discourse analysis provides a valid framework for the complexities in interpreted turns of talk within which the coherence of messages (here indicated by theme-rheme and isotopy considerations) can be investigated: "Turns can be resuming an 'old' or introducing a 'new' topic, contributing to or questioning an idea, changing the topic or tone or commenting to keep the conversation flowing" (ibid., p. 728).

By viewing discourse as an active communicative process of listening and speaking, discourse analysis offers suitable parameters for investigating the interpreter's role, especially because of involving cooperative "speakers/writers who have topics, presuppositions, and who assign information structure and make reference. It is hearers/readers who interpret and who draw inferences" (Brown and Yule, 1983, p. ix). Discourse analysis, therefore, is the theoretical framework for exploring and positioning the interpreter as a cooperative third party in this study. This includes all its implications, i.e., assigning information (structure) and making (isotopic) references and inferences as required, to achieve a shared communicative goal. Within the framework of discourse analysis, "texts" are not considered "as static objects, but as dynamic means of expressing intended meaning" (Brown and Yule, 1983, p. 24). This yields another important parameter in interpreter-mediated discourse, that is, intended or assumed meanings and meaning continuities (coherence and isotopy). The topic and isotopic dimensions of implicit meanings here are thought to produce sense continuity (coherence) in a sequence of utterances. Since hidden meanings are usually left to be discovered by the communicative partners themselves in the coherence-establishing process, in the communications where the communicative partners cannot directly communicate with each other but need an interpreter in the process, the interpreter as a cooperative partner is co-responsible for establishing sense continuity by including assumptions and inferences of his/her own. In the interest of the communication's objectives, it can, therefore, be regarded to fall within the interpreter's responsibility to use the means that he/she thinks are appropriate for assuring continuity of sense (coherence).

Due to its unclear position within the research field of interpreting, PSI has developed a great variety of names with different conceptual components and foci. The lack of consensus on its conceptual features has led to a variety of names which reflects the research deficits on to the general phenomenon and its problems (Hertog & Reunbrouck, 1999, p. 268). Some initial agreements have been reached on its difference from conference interpreting; however, even this distinction has become blurred by its seemingly overlapping features with consecutive interpreting (Kalina, 2002, p. 255).

PSI's synonymous expressions seem to focus on a variety of conceptual issues but lack the verbalisation of a common conceptual core that integrates the various issues into a general concept with distinctive features. There have been several attempts at taxonomies of interpreting, e.g., Harris's taxonomic survey of professional interpreting (1990), Salevsky's survey of the "variable components of interpreting situations" (1993), and Alexieva's "multi-parameter" approach (1997).

All of the pertaining denominations, explicitly or implicitly, include two essential components of PSI: bidirectionality and communicative discourse.

3.2.1 Bidirectionality

This means that the interpretation is rendered "between languages" back and forth from a native language to a foreign language, with a high degree of competence required from the interpreter in at least two languages and cultures. Bidirectionality also means that the messages of the communicative partners are filtered by the interpreter who is then co-responsible for making sense of a message in one language, culture, and context, and reproducing that sense in the target language, culture, and (domain) context. Bidirectionality, therefore, implies the identification and reproduction of (hidden) meaning dimensions in the messages of the communicative partners by the interpreter, and thus, also implies the establishment of coherence by the interpreter in the flow of the original and interpreted messages in a bi-lingual, bi-cultural discourse of varying (domain-specific) actual settings and contexts.

3.2.2 Communicative discourse

The bidirectional discourse situation (in contrast to the monodirectional conference interpreting situation) implies that the communicative partners – including the interpreter – cooperate in terms of having agreed on a shared objective for the communication, which in turn implies that the communicative situation with its partners, topics, and conventions is transparent to all partners. Successful discourse, therefore, presupposes the acceptance of Grice's cooperative principle (1975) by the participants of the discourse, including the interpreter as a third party. The interpreter is, therefore, co-responsible for establishing coherence in the interest of attaining the communicative objective in all types of interpreter-mediated discourse. This applies to everyday as well as specialised (institutional) discourse.

There is an agreement in the literature that the public service interpreter is required to be competent in the relevant domain knowledge which is often equated with terminological knowledge but has recently been extended to cover whole knowledge systems (Will, 2009), and also includes domain-specific norms, e.g., in legal discourse or psychoanalytic procedural knowledge. But the traditional controversy with respect to the degree of action latitude that an interpreter has in an individual scenario is still unresolved within the two extremes of "verbatim," remaining "neutral," "invisible," a "non-person," or actively managing the communication in the way of acting as a cultural mediator, rendering services of "advocacy" or "cultural brokering" or "conciliation" (Merlini & Favaron, 2013, p. 212), as was discussed before. In addition, while there is agreement that linguistic, cultural, and domain-specific knowledge, and the interpreter's communicative competence referred to as "people skills" (Bowen, 2000) or as "discourse management skills" (Pöchhacker, 2004, p. 187), are considered indispensable skills within the discourse analysis framework, it is still unclear which specific knowledge to which degree of specialisation is required for which setting, and how discourse management skills relate to or interrelate with other necessary skills. While it is certainly true that the "Code of Conduct" established in a number of immigrant countries such as the USA, Australia, and Sweden supports the interpreter by specifying the rules of conduct on a collective basis, in an actual situation the individual interpreter is often at a loss as to how active or involved he/she should become.

3.3 A Triadic Discourse Interpreting Model (TRIM): parameters and filters

3.3.1 The parameters

Proceeding from the theoretical framework of discourse analysis, it is suggested that static and dynamic parameters interplay in a triadic discourse communication when an interpreter produces a target message. This interplay is here assumed to take place in the form of a number of interpreting filters (IF) through which a source message (M) passes to become a target message (M'). Interpreting filters reflect the translating and coordinating decisions of the interpreter when formulating a target message in varying degrees of invariance to secure adequacy and coherence of messages from the perspective of the interpreter. This is referred to as the Triadic Discourse Interpreting Model (TRIM).

In its static part, relevant basic parameters as "ingredients" for the analysis of interpreter-mediated communication are identified and described. The communication is triadic in that the message transfer is between three communicative partners A, B, and the interpreter, I, all related to a message, M. In describing relevant parameters in an interpreter-mediated communication, it distinguishes between relatively stable knowledge parameters on a system level and relatively flexible situation-specific parameters, and shows how they interact to influence the interpreted message, M'.

Static parameters describe as knowledge parameters the assumed shared background knowledge in terms of holistic structures which interrelate content and functional elements to reflect the assumed world knowledge in the communicative partners A, B, and the interpreter, I. It is assumed to encompass linguistic, cultural, domain, and general world knowledge as the more or less shared stock of knowledge which is necessary for them to communicate as seen from the interpreter's perspective as well as the shared focus of attention. It also includes characteristic situation-specific knowledge about the actual discourse situation, i.e., type, time, and place characterisations, a shared focus of attention of the communicative partners (from which the topic of the communication emanates), the purpose of the communication, and the interest of the communicative partners in the discourse.

Dynamic parameters in this model show the interplay of these parameters in a tetradic speech act sequence of turns in interpreter-mediated communication. The original Tetradic Model of Speech Acts (Mudersbach, 2004 quoted in Sunwoo, 2008) shows the interaction of communicative partners in a monolingual situation in its four dimensions: communicative partner A's utterance, communicative partner B's reaction, the acknowledgement of B's reaction by A, the acknowledgement of A's acknowledgement by B.

The sequence is interdependent: each turn influences the following turn(s). The reactions and acknowledgements can be positive or negative. If negative, this may be due to unwillingness by one of the partners to cooperate. The communicative partners may not be aware of this "prima facie" but the interpreter needs to realise these underlying meaning dimensions to detect, e.g. "double-bind" strategies of a partner. The tetradic sequence is here shown in its interaction with an interpreter as a "third party." All possible other turns or turn exchanges (e.g., misunderstandings and their clarification or corrections by the interpreter) are explainable within this (recursive) tetradic cycle but will not be shown here in all their details.

Within the tetradic exchange, the dynamic part of the PSI parameters involves understanding and (re)producing an interpreted message. Methodologically, this paper proceeds from a three-phase process analogous to the three-phase translation process in contrast to the two-dimensional cognitive models used in the interpreting literature (Gile, 1995; Albl-Mikasa, 2007), but this research will concentrate exclusively on the (re)production phase.

It is assumed that the source message is influenced by the interpreter's understanding of the message and by his/her decision on which information (of the source message) to transfer and how to transfer it in the interpreting process. The question of "what" is to be interpreted is assumed to be determined by the actual discourse objective and coherence criteria depending on what the interpreter is able to – "locally" (Mudersbach, 2004, p. 260) and on the basis of the previously interpreted actual discourse – qualify as coherent, a-coherent, and non-coherent (ibid., p. 250). Further criteria assumed in the IF are: (1) the general communicative goal and an actual discourse purpose; (2) the coherence of the source message as understood by the interpreter and measured by topic and/or isotopic continuity; (3) potential knowledge differentials which the interpreter needs to balance; and (4) the interest of the partners as perceived by the interpreter in reaching a specified actual discourse purpose.

3.3.2 The interpreting filters

When passing through an interpreter-mediated exchange, an original message (M) is "filtered" by the interpreter into a target message (M'). This process potentially modifies the source message by passing it through a number of interpreting filters which operate on the original message (M) to result in the interpreted message (M'). Discourse IF screen a message (M) according to a number of factors during the process it undergoes from its original state (source message M) to its interpreted message (target message M') by the discourse interpreter. As a result of discourse IF, the interpreted message M' is – when compared to the original M – classifiable as being either invariant ("close" or "verbatim"), partially invariant in two categories: Category I ("restructured") and Category II (asking for clarification), variant ("mediation"), or not existing at all, i.e., zero. During the interpreter's filtering process, a number of filters are assumed to operate on the original message and influence the target message's (M') content and function. They are described here as purpose, coherence (in the sense of topic continuity and isotopic continuity), knowledge, and interest filters, and are activated in that chronological order.

3.3.2.1 The discourse purpose filter

The discourse purpose filter checks whether a message is compatible with the agreed-upon purpose of the actual discourse. It presupposes the cooperation of all discourse partners and their observing of Grice's maxims.

In filtering the original message (M) at this stage, the interpreter is guided by answering the following question: is the source message compatible with achieving the general goal of the communication and the actual purpose of the discourse?

The following example is taken from the author's experience interpreting at an international auto mechanics fair in Frankfurt am Main (Jiang, 2011, p. 120). In the course of a Brazilian purchasing manager's introducing his factory to a Chinese supervisor, the purchasing manager stares at the interpreter and says, "You're a beautiful woman." The male Brazilian client's remark about the female interpreter's looks fall under the discourse purpose filter category. Therefore, utterances similar to those expressed in this example can be left out by the interpreter due to its incompatibility with the general communication goal and discourse purpose.

3.3.2.2 The coherence filter

The coherence filter links an individual message in its topic continuity and its factual, appellative, relationship, and self-indicative isotopy dimensions to previous and subsequent tetradic exchanges. It, thereby, provides for the overall continuity of discourse. It influences the target message in the interpreting process in that it requires judgements relative to whether a message in its many dimensions is in the shared focus of attention ("in focus"), and thus relevant in light of the entire interpreted event.

The questions the interpreter needs to answer here are: are the topic plus the factual, appellative, relationship, and self-indicative dimensions of the source message compatible with the actual purpose of the discourse? Are there signs that indicate whether one of these dimensions is isolated to a particular message (and thus may be neglected and result in zero rendition) or whether it is a continuously (coherently) developed dimension (i.e., linked to/coherent with previous and/or anticipated discourse exchanges) in the sense of an isotopic level which needs to be interpreted?

The coherence filter is a powerful filter from the interpreter's perspective and involves decisions as to the restructuring of a message (summarisation, expanding, reducing) or the deletion of messages (zero renditions).

A coherence filter in the reproduction dimension also checks the local meaning dimensions to be transferred (separate isotopies) against global coherence. Being different from the reception dimension, coherence in the reproduction filter focuses on the transfer of the message in a way to close gaps between different separate isotopies and with a view to top-level isotopy. Thus, interpreters may tone down a message by omitting the relationship and self-indicative meaning dimensions (Schulz von Thun, 1981), structure a message in a way to be fully comprehended by the other primary communicative partner, using additional information to clarify the original message, etc.

In normal communication scenarios, an individual's "ad hoc" understanding of a message in terms of the factual, self-indicative, relationship, and/or appellative dimensions can be understood as establishing factual, relationship, and/or appellative isotopy lines which may reveal hidden meaning layers which are not accessible by the informational theme-rheme category.

3.3.2.3 The topic continuity filter

The topic continuity filter uses topic development in discourse as an indicator of coherence. Explicit or implicit theme progression may establish topic continuity. Explicit theme continuity develops via recurrent or derived topics and implicit theme continuity by establishing thematic progression via textual or world hypothesis with the recipient or analyst.

Shared focus, therefore, is a vital coherence-establishing element in all phases of the interpretation process. This focus is an orienting element during the interpretation process: it helps prevent unethical extensions of the interpreter's job, as in lawyer–plaintiff interactions outside the courtroom (Hale, 1997), and rejects working conditions that are not conducive to coherent discourse. During the interpretation process itself, a shared focus limits distractions, sudden topic changes, or unconscious linguistic mistakes.

The following questions guide the topic continuity filter: is there a change in the original message that must be reproduced in the target message? Is there a shift in theme, shared focus, or perspective in the original message that must be made explicit or that requires clarification?

3.3.2.4 The isotopic continuity filter

The isotopic continuity filter applies Schulz-von-Thun's (1981) assumption that any message contains at least four dimensions: a factual, an appellative, a relationship, and a self-indicative dimension, which are equally applicable to a hearer ("four ears") and a speaker ("four tongues"). It complements the topic continuity filter in not relating to informational units but meaning dimensions which are established by their continuity and which may be hidden to the other communicative partners.

While the factual dimension may seem the least problematic (although it does raise contrastive language and cultural problems), the appellative dimension is of great importance in discourse interpreting because the interchange is often made up by question–answer turns (e.g., in court situations or asylum hearings) which usually imply a strong appellative component. The relationship dimension is equally important because PSI environments frequently involve asymmetric discourse partners (e.g., in doctor–patient relationships or the barrister and defendant in the courtroom) which require careful balancing by the interpreter. And while the self-indicative dimension may seem less crucial, it does provide the interpreter with a judgement as to the credibility of a discourse partner and/or conflict potential arising from the conflicting interests or styles of the discourse partners.

The interpreter, therefore, has to make sure that he/she comprehends the source message in its factual, appellative, relationship, and self-indicative potential, and that he/she filters the target message by deciding: (1) which of the above isotopic dimensions are to be represented in the target message; (2) to which extent; and (3) in which form.

This essay will concentrate on the decisions that fall within the interpreter's action latitude in reproducing a target message, M'. In making these decisions, the interpreter is guided by answering the following question: can the factual, appellative, relationship, and self-indicative dimensions of a message be reproduced in a target message?

The following example shows the realisation of a witness's implied self-indicative isotopic dimension by the interpreter (Sol = Solicitor, Int. = Interpreter, Wit = Witness):

SOL: Did you, sorry Your Worship. Did you say to Ms X that you were gonna go into her home and strangle her?
INT: (Did you say to Mrs X that you were going to go to her house and strangle her?)
WIT: (No, I'm a very educated person to say that.)
INT: No, I'm an educated person, I couldn't say that.

(Hale, 1997, 207)

The above interpreted exchange takes place in the Australian courtroom in which the court interpreter paraphrases the witness's words so as to convey the self-indicative isotopic dimension implied in the message, that is, that he's well educated and has been raised in a proper way, so it would not be his manner to threaten someone in that way. As the interpreter understands the implied self-indicative isotopic line, she makes it explicit in her translated target message by making the cause–effect relationship in M' clearer.

3.3.2.5 The knowledge filter

The knowledge filter proceeds from the concept of knowledge systems and their holistic description (Mudersbach, 1991). Elements of relevant knowledge systems become manifest (are "concretised") in the message exchanges as, for example, linguistic and cultural manifestations or domain knowledge systems.

The question the interpreter needs to ask are: is the message compatible with communicative partner B's language and cultural system and norms and conventions? Does B have sufficient (cultural, domain-specific, norm-related, communicative) knowledge (from the perspective of the interpreter) to understand the message without clarifications or expanding explanations?

The answers to these questions may lead to message restructuring decisions, i.e., to restructured renditions and/or clarification interventions by the interpreter.

Assumed cultural knowledge is of great importance in mediating doctor–patient interactions. Patients from European and African cultures view information receiving as empowerment and believe in obtaining illness-related information as positive. Particularly interesting is the Western physician's concern for Chinese patients' autonomy and self-determination conflicts with Chinese patients' family-centred culture. Without knowing these differences, Western physicians may be troubled by the Chinese family's controlling behaviours and by the patient's indifferent attitude, whereas the Chinese patient and family members may be angered by the healthcare provider's insensitivity in delivering bad news to the patient. The interpreter thus assumes an important role in transferring the information in the culturally appropriate way so as to ensure effective medical communication.

3.3.2.6 The interest filter

The interest filter is of paramount influence on the interpreter's actual filtering of the original message. It provides an answer to the following question: is the source message compatible with the "ad hoc" interest of the individual discourse partner A or B?

If the answer to this question is no, the interpreter will have to balance the diverging partners' interests in order to obtain the discourse purpose.

The following example shows how the interpreter filters the communicative partner's (AW) tone in the situation of conflicting interest between the immigration officer and the asylum-seeker (B1 = immigration officer 1, AW = asylum-seeker, D1 = interpreter 1)

B1: grosse Fluss in ORT 1?
big river in VILLAGE 1?
AW: Mhm.
D1: Okay, and this big river, what is it
AW: The name? I tell you I don't know the name of
D1: called? Ahm.
B1: ((4s)) Als politisch
As a political
AW: the river.
D1: Den Namen weiss ich nicht.
I don't know the name.

(Pöllabauer, 2004, p. 47)

The asylum-seeker expresses impatience ("I tell you…") at the fact that he had already explained that he did not know the name of the river, which could have been perceived as an unwillingness to cooperate or insecurity. The interpreter deletes the self-indicative isotopic meaning dimension. This may have been motivated by trying to secure the purpose of the communication interview, i.e., to get information and evidence from the asylum-seeker in an efficient way. If this unwillingness of the asylum-seeker, however, showed up in other exchanges and would thus form a coherent pattern or isotopy, the interpreter's mediating effort by toning down the original tone of "I don't know the name" may not be an "allowable" moderation of the original message.

3.3.3 Discourse interpreter-filtered message flow and types

The discourse intepreter's filtered M' can now be positioned on a scale from zero to invariant M' with scalar values of partially invariant M' and mediated M' which are determined by the results obtained when passing through the actual discourse purpose, coherence, knowledge, and interest interpreting filters. The assumption of filters makes it possible to specify the conditions under which the filtered M' come about (Table 3.1).

The visualization of the interpreter's filtering process of the original message (M) to the target message (M') is shown in Figure 3.1.

According to Figure 3.1, source messages go through different paths and yield different types of target interpreted messages as follows:

Path 1

Discourse purpose (–): type I (zero M')

Path 2

Discourse purpose (+) → coherence (–) →knowledge differential (+): type II (partially invariant M': Category 1)

Table 3.1 Discourse interpreter's-filtered target message types

Target message types	*Filter presuppositions*[a]	
Type I: zero M'	Discourse purpose	–
e.g. deleting the whole message	Coherence	+
	Compatibility of interest	+
Type II: partially invariant M' (Category 1)	Discourse purpose	+
	Coherence	–
e.g., reducing, expanding, reconstructing, etc	Knowledge differential	+
Type III: partially invariant M' (Category 2)	Discourse purpose	+
	Coherence	–
e.g., asking for clarification	Topic continuity (explicit/implicit)	–
	Isotopy continuity (implicit)	–
Type IV: variant M'	Discourse purpose	+
e.g., mediating techniques like downtoning	Coherence	+
	Topic continuity (explicit/implicit)	+
	Isotopy continuity	+
	Compatibility of interest	–
Type V: invariant M'	Discourse purpose	+
e.g., verbatim or word-for-word translation	Coherence	+
	Compatibility of interest	+

Note:

a + refers to a 'yes' answer for a filter; – refers to a 'no' answer for a filter.

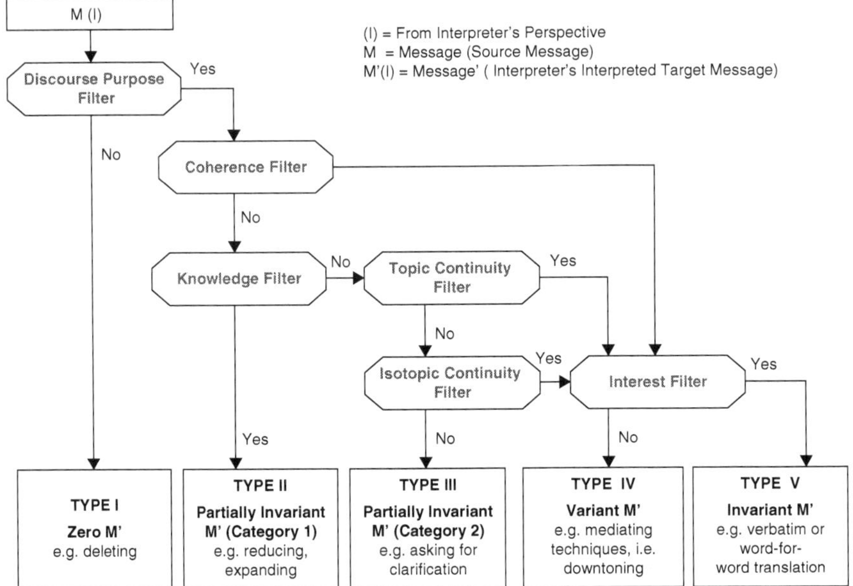

Figure 3.1 Interpreter's filtering process.

Path 3
Discourse purpose (+) → coherence (–) → topic continuity (–) → isotopic continuity (–): type III (partially invariant M': Category 2)

Path 4
Discourse purpose (+) → coherence (–) → topic continuity (–) → isotopic continuity (+) →compatibility of interest (–): type IV (variant M')

Path 5
Discourse purpose (+) → coherence (–) → topic continuity (+) → compatibility of interest (–): type IV (variant M')

Path 6
Discourse purpose (+) → coherence (+) → compatibility of interest (–): type IV (variant M')

Path 7
Discourse purpose (+) → coherence (+) → compatibility of interest (+): type V (invariant M')

3.4 Conclusion

Departing from the problem of whether the interpreter is legitimised to interpret non-verbatim and whether there are criteria that determine rendering a verbatim or a non-verbatim message in an actual interpreted-mediated communication scenario, this chapter has attempted to identify a set of interdependent parameters that influence the interpreter's decisions in an individual actual interpreting situation.

After presenting different communicative factors which are documented in the pertaining literature to influence the interpreter's action latitude and within the framework of discourse analysis, the concept and its static and dynamic parameters of the TRIM were described. The interplay of these parameters was conceptualised as discourse IFs which show how an original message (M) is filtered by the interpreter to become an interpreted message, M'. The resulting typology of interpreted messages (types I–Type V) shows the circumstantial restrictions surrounding the interpreted variations of M' and the interpreter's action latitude to reproduce them in actual interpreting scenarios.

Theoretically, the model can lead to empirical studies on how the M' types apply to different interpreting settings, and questions with regard to the quantity and quality of types related to a number of settings can be investigated. It will also be interesting to look at how the model applies to the comprehension process or to multilingual settings. Moreover, problems like language specificity, misunderstandings, or cultural disparities may be researched by applying the filters to other interpreting settings. Finally, this study stills leaves the question open for empirical researchers to use the identified parameters as indicators for the further investigation of how often certain types of interpreted messages appear in different interpreted communication scenarios and the reasons for that, i.e., more variant interpreted message types are expected to be found in healthcare than in courtroom settings.

In practice, the awareness of certain factors and their interplay at certain stages in interpreter-mediated events will help the interpreter to make on-site decisions. Specifically, for certain settings, that is, the courtroom, hospitals, or police investigations, a checklist as suggested in Table 3.2 could be used, which could be discussed and made an integral part of each interpreter-mediated event, to which all parties have to agree before the actual event.

The checklist proposed in Table 3.2 shows that the interpreter can thus work through the concretisation of the parameters and filters in particular communicative situations and request answers to these questions from the initiator of the interpreter-mediated event. With the answers to these questions, the professional interpreter is able to anticipate potential problems and pre-establish strategies to secure an adequate action for a planned assignment reflecting the interpreter-mediated discourse type and purpose within an overall pre-agreed-upon actual discourse purpose.

In didactics, the parameter constellation and typology proposed can be used in PSI training courses for students to raise their awareness for the knowledge factors, skills, and situational challenges that surround the profession of discourse interpreter. Also, learning assignments can refer to specific situations and make the student aware of how situation-dependent PSI is and

Table 3.2 Interpreter-mediated event checklist

1. What are the prevalent language and culture pair between which the interpretation is to be rendered?
2. What are the place, time, and anticipated duration of the interpreting event?
3. Who is the initiator of the interpreter-mediated event and what is his/her interest?
4. What is the general communication goal of the interpreter-mediated event to which all communicative partners have been committed?
5. What is the actual discourse purpose of the interpreting assignment?
6. What is the type of discourse setting in which the interpreting takes place (e.g., in legal settings, in healthcare settings, or in everyday discourse settings)?
7. Are there certain guidelines, conventions, or norms that the interpreter needs to be aware of?
8. What is the specific topic of the interpreting event?
9. Is there any background material available for preparatory information?
10. What background knowledge (legal, medical, psychotherapeutic) is required by the interpreter other than interpreter-specific know-how (such as interpreting techniques, empathy, code of ethics)?
11. Is there a briefing before the event, and/or a post-event discussion/interchange planned?
12. What are the participants' knowledge profiles (including the communicative partners and the interpreter)?
13. What is the relationship between the communicative partners and the interpreter (between A and B and between A and I and B and I)?
14. Are there divergent interests in all the participants that emanate from the communicative goal and discourse purpose?

how helpful it is in a particular setting to have criteria available that will make reasonable professional interpreting decisions at different stages possible and transparent and justify them.

Note

1 An earlier version of this chapter first appeared in Jiang, L. (2018). *Journal of Foreign Languages and Cultures,* 2, 125–139.

References

Albl-Mikasa, M. (2007). *Notationssprache und Notizentext. Ein kognitiv-linguistisches Modell für das Konsekutivdolmetschen.* Tübingen: Gunter Narr.

Alexieva, B. (1997/2000). A typology of interpreter-mediated events. In: Pöchhacker, F. & M. Shlesinger (eds.). *The Interpreting Studies Reader*. London: Routledge: 218–233.

Angelelli, C.V. (2004a). *Medical Interpreting and Cross-cultural Communication.* Cambridge: Cambridge University Press.

——. (2004b) *Revisiting the Interpreter's Role: A Study of Conference, Court and Medical Interpreters in Canada, Mexico and the United States.* Amsterdam: John Benjamins Publishing.

Barald, C. & L. Gavioli (2012). Introduction: Understanding coordination in interpreter-mediated interaction. In: Wadensjö, C. et al. (eds.). *Coordinating Participation in Dialogue Interpreting*. Amsterdam: John Benjamins Publishing: 1–22.

Braun, S. (2011). Recommendations for the use of video-mediated interpreting in criminal proceedings. In: Braun, S. & J. Taylor (eds.). *Videoconference and Remote Interpreting in Criminal Proceedings*. Guildford: University of Surrey: 265–287.

Brown, G. & G. Yule (1983/2000). *Discourse Analysis*. Beijing: Foreign Language Teaching and Researching.

Bührig, K. & B. Meyer (2004). *Ad hoc-interpreting and the Achievement of Communicative Purposes in Specific Kinds of Doctor–Patient Discourse*. Hamburg: Sonderforschungsbereich Mehrsprachigkeit.

Davidson, B. (2000). The interpreter as institutional gatekeeper: The social-linguistic role interpreters in Spanish–English medial discourse. *Journal of Sociolinguistics*, 4(3): 379–405.

Gile, D. (1995). *Basic Concepts and Models for Interpreter and Translator Training*. Amsterdam: John Benjamins Publishing.

Goffman, E. (1981). *Forms of Talk*. Philadelphia: University of Pennsylvania Press.

Grice, H. P. (1975). Logic and conversation. In: Cole, P. (ed.). *Syntax and Semantics: Speech Acts*. New York: Academic Press: 1–58.

Hale, S. B. (1997). The interpreter on trial. Pragmatics in court interpreting. In: Carr, S. E. et al. (eds.). *The Critical Link: Interpreters in the Community*. Amsterdam: John Benjamins Publishing: 201–211.

—— (2004). *The Discourse of Court Interpreting: Discourse Practices of the Law, the Witness and the Interpreter*. Amsterdam: John Benjamins Publishing.

—— (2007). *Community Interpreting*. Sydney: Palgrave Macmillan.

Harris, B. & B. Sherwood (1978). Translating as an innate skill. In: Gerver, D. & W. H. Sinaiko (eds.). *Language Interpretation and Communication*. New York: Plenum Press: 155–170.

Hertog, E. & D. Reunbrouck (1999). Building bridges between conference interpreters and liaison interpreters. In: M. Erasmus (ed.). *Liaison Interpreting in the Community*. Melbourne: Melbourne University Press: 263–277.

Jiang, L. (2011). *How Far Can a Community Interpreter Go? Discourse Interpreting Filters*. Hamburg: Verlag Dr. Kovač.

Kalina, S. (2002). Interpreters as professionals. *Across Language and Cultures*, 3(2): 169–187.

Merlini, R. & R. Favaron (2013). Community interpreting: Re-conciliation through power management. *The Interpreters' Newsletter*, 13: 205–229.

Metzger, M. (1999). *Sign Language Interpreting: Deconstructing the Myth of Neutrality*. Washington, DC: Gallaudet University Press.

Meyer, B. (2004). *Dolmetschen im medizinischen Aufklärungsgespräch. Eine diskursanalytische Untersuchung zur Arzt–Patienten-Kommunikation im mehrsprachigen Krankenhaus*. Münster: Waxmann.

Mikkelson, H. (2000). *Introduction to Court Interpreting*. Manchester: St. Jerome Publishing.

Moody, B. (2007). Literal vs. liberal: What is a faithful interpretation? *The Sign Language Translator and Interpreter*, 1(2): 179–220.

Mudersbach, K. (1991). Erschließung historischer Texte mit Hilfe linguistischer Methoden. In: *Reihe historisch-sozialwissenschaftliche Forschungen des Zentrums für historische Sozialforschung*. St. Katharinen: Script Mercaturae, 318–362.

—— (2004). Kohärenz und Textverstehen in der Lesersicht. Oder: Wie prüft man die Stimmigkeit von Texten beim Lesen. In: J. House et al. (eds.). *Neue Perspektiven in der Übersetzungs- und Dolmetschwissenschaft.* Bochum: AKS: 249–272.
Pöchhacker, F. (2004). *Introducing Interpreting Studies.* London: Routledge.
Pöllabauer, S. (2004). Interpreting in asylum hearings. Issues of role, responsibility and power. *Interpreting*, 6(2): 143–180.
Roberts, R. P. et al. (eds) (2000). *The Critical Link 2: Interpreters in the Community.* Amsterdam: John Benjamins Publishing.
Roy, C. B. (2000). *Interpreting as a Discourse Process.* Oxford: Oxford University Press.
Rudvin, M. (2007). Professionalism and ethics in community interpreting: The impact of individualist versus collective group identity. *Interpreting,* 9(1): 47–69.
Sacks, H., E. Schegloff & G. Jefferson (1974). A simplest systematics for the organisation of turn-taking in conversation. *Language*, 50(4): 96–735.
Salevsky, H. (1993). The distinctive nature of interpreting studies. *Target*, 5(2): 149–167.
Sauerwein Sami, F. (2006). *Dolmetschen polizeilichen Vernehmungen und grenzpolizeilichen Einreisebefragungen: Eine explorative trans bei lationswissenschaftliche Untersuchung zum Community Interpreting.* Frankfurt: Peter Lang.
Schulz von Thun, F. (1981). *Miteinander reden 1 – Störungen und Klärungen. Allgemeine Psychologie der Kommunikation.* Reinbek bei Hamburg: Rowohlt-Taschenbuch.
Shlesinger, M. (2008). Gray goes with the territory: Certainties and uncertainties in public service interpreting. www.translationconcepts.org/pdf/Miriam_Shlesinger_presentation.pdf (accessed 24 February 2021).
Sunwoo, M. (2008). Operationalizing the translation skopos. In *Proceedings of the Marie Curie Euroconferences MuTra: LSP Translation Scenarios*–Vienna, 30 April–4 May 2007. www.euroconferences.info/proceedings/2007_Proceedings/2007_proceedings.html (accessed 24 February 2021).
Wadensjö, C. (1998). *Interpreting as Interaction*. New York: Longman.
Will, M. (2009). *Dolmetschorientierte Terminologiearbeit. Modell und Methode.* Tübingen: Gunter Narr.

4 Probing into court interpreting studies

Reflections from the perspective of Western rhetoric

Junfeng Zhao, Zhimiao Yang and Riccardo Moratto

4.1 Introduction

The past 20 years have witnessed the shift of court interpreting research to more systematic studies covering a wide range of subject matters. In the past, court interpreting surveys and legal discourse analysis were conducted primarily in common law countries and they covered a variety of topics derived from practical issues (Hale, 2006). These studies mainly focused on the role of interpreters, court interpreting norms, court interpreter training, etc. Since interpreting studies is multidisciplinary at its core, more theories and research methods can be drawn from other disciplines of humanities.

Over the last few decades, China's opening up has been accompanied by an increasing number of trials involving foreign nationals/citizens, foreign companies, and foreign languages, which can be well demonstrated by the routine that at least three foreign-related lawsuits are heard at the Guangzhou Intermediate People's Court on a weekly basis (Zhao & Chen, 2008). However, there is still a lack of qualified court interpreters for trials involving foreign languages. Moreover, compared with court interpreting research in Western countries such as Britain, the United States, and Australia, Chinese court interpreting studies started relatively late and are still lagging far behind. In contrast to Western countries, where rhetoric has been studied mostly in oral materials such as speeches and debates, the application of rhetoric in China is still restricted to written materials such as novels and poems. Compounded by the fact that court interpreting studies is still a budding research field in China, hardly any study on court interpreting from the perspective of rhetoric has been published. The present chapter will approach court interpreting from the perspective of classical and new rhetoric and hopefully will arouse more academic interest in this domain.

Western rhetoric is a discipline covering various research fields. Generally speaking, rhetoric focuses on the communicative activities between speakers and audience. To be more specific, rhetoric studies the techniques of wording and phrasing, such as metaphor, parallelism, personification, and exaggeration. In this chapter, we will focus on the communicative activities between

DOI: 10.4324/9781003197027-6

speakers and audiences in the bilingual courtroom, and conduct a case study on how a court interpreter behaves by means of drawing notions from Western rhetoric, namely, "persuasion", "identification", "audience", and "multi-value judgement", which oftentimes are regarded as the common denominators of court interpreting and rhetoric studies. Persuasion is intended as an attempt to influence a person's beliefs, attitudes, intentions, motivations, or behaviours (Gass & Seiter, 2010, p. 33); identification, also known as consubstantiality, refers to any of the wide variety of means by which a writer or speaker may establish a shared sense of values, attitudes, and interests with an audience (Nordquist, 2020); audience (from the Latin *audire*, meaning "to hear") refers to the listeners or spectators at a speech or performance, or the intended readership for a piece; the concept of multi-value judgement is related to the new rhetoric represented by Perelman (Perelman & Olbrechts-Tyteca, 1971) in which the main principle is the pluralism of value judgements. New rhetoric advocates difference and pluralism, promotes the independent existence and coexistence of different value judgements, and seeks to reach new understanding through conversations (Chen, 2019).

4.2 Classical rhetoric in legal discourse

Originated in ancient Greece (600 BC), classical rhetoric has gone through multiple ups and downs throughout history. Nonetheless, there is still no standard definition of the term "classical rhetoric". The word rhetoric derives from the Greek ῥητορικός (rhētorikós), "oratorical", from ῥήτωρ (rhḗtōr), "public speaker", related to ῥῆμα (rhêma), "that which is said or spoken, word, saying", and ultimately derived from the verb ἐρῶ (erō), "say, speak". Aristotle pointed out in his seminal *Treatise on Rhetoric* that rhetoric is to find out the ways to persuade others in any setting (Aristotle, 1995).

Legal discourse in its essence is institutional. Institutional discourse refers to verbal exchanges between two or more people where at least one speaker is a representative of an institution and where the interaction and the speakers' goals are partially determined by the institution in play (Freed, 2015). For more information on institutional discourse, readers can refer to Drew and Heritage (1992, p. 22). In adversarial trials in many countries under the common law system, speakers in court use various rhetorical devices to make their discourse more convincing, so that the public jury may be influenced by their discourse and make a final verdict that is in their favour. Legal discourse is one of the three types of discourse where rhetoric is most likely to appear, namely political speeches, ceremonial speeches, and litigation speeches (Aristotle, 1995). Aristotle argues that in order to impress the audience, the speaker must pay attention to the content and rhetorical devices of the speech, which clearly demonstrates the relationship between legal discourse and persuasion modes of classical rhetoric.

China does not practise the common law system, and trials in Chinese courts are mainly dominated by judges' questioning and moderating.

Therefore, trials in China are not characterised by adversarial arguments. Trials in China generally consist of court opening, court investigations, court debates, and final statements. Most of the legal discourse in court opening, court investigations, and final statements is prepared before trials in the form of speech scripts. Does this mean that interpreters would receive written texts for sight translation? Yes, but only in the court opening and part of the court investigation. Chinese legal trials are still mainly moderated by the judge, which is quite different from adversarial trials in countries like the United States. Therefore, there will be written texts for speakers in the court opening. Regrettably, though, interpreters do not always have access to the texts before the trial. If they do have access to the written texts, they can do sight translation. The interpreter in the recorded trial in this study did have the texts beforehand and did sight translation for the court opening and part of the court investigation. In other parts of the trials, like court debate and final statement, the discourses are mainly improvised; therefore, interpreters need to do consecutive interpreting.

This does not necessarily mean that rhetorical devices are not applicable to the legal discourse in Chinese trials. For the part that is prepared with scripts beforehand, the legal discourse does follow a certain rigorous and solemn linguistic style, involving a large number of textual rhetorical devices, such as analogy, parallelism, and metonymy. Generally speaking, there are four main parts in Chinese legal trials, namely court opening, court investigation, court debate (similar to cross-examination in American trials), and final statement. In court opening and part of court investigation, there are written texts so that the participants, like the public prosecutor in the recorded trial, only need to read the texts. Ideally, court interpreters have access to the texts, in which case they will do sight translation. In recent years, with the increasing number of court hearings involving foreign nationals in China, the interpretation of improvised legal discourse has been gradually attracting more academic attention.

In his *Treatise on Rhetoric* Aristotle systematically explains the three persuasion modes of classical rhetoric, namely ethos, pathos, and logos, which are commonly used by participants in trials. For centuries, many Western rhetoricians have focused on speech skills and persuasion modes, and they have mainly studied speeches of political figures and court debates (Wen, 2002). In recent years, persuasion modes have been gradually appearing in textual studies of advertising, speech, business negotiation, etc. Although Chinese courts are dominated by the questions uttered by the judges, we still find that the three persuasion modes are widely used in court investigations, court debates, cross-examination of evidence, and final statements.

4.3 New rhetoric in legal discourse

After the revival of rhetoric in the twentieth century (Booth, 1965), many scholars started to explore new strands of rhetoric based on their research fields, hence the name new rhetoric. In the 1960s and 1970s, numerous monographs and articles concerning rhetoric were published, including *The Rhetoric of Fiction* by Booth (1961), *The Philosophy of Rhetoric* by Richards (1965), *Rhetorical Criticism: A Study in Method* by Black (1965), *Classical Rhetoric for the Modern Student* by Corbett (1965), "A generative rhetoric of the paragraph" by Christensen (1965), "The rhetoric of Black power: A moral demand?" by Burgess (1968), *A Rhetoric of Motives* by Burke (1969), *The New Rhetoric: A Treatise on Argumentation* by Perelman and Olbrechts-Tyteca (1969), "The rhetoric of confrontation" by Scott and Smith (1969), *Rhetoric: Discovery and Change* by Young, Becker and Pike (1970), *Language is Sermonic: Richard M. Weaver on the Nature of Rhetoric* edited by Johannesen et al. (1970), *The Rhetoric of the Open Hand and the Rhetoric of the Closed Fist* by Corbett (1969), and *Metaphor and Thought*, edited by Ortony (1979). New rhetoric mainly includes two sub-disciplines: stylistic rhetoric and humanistic rhetoric (Gu, 1990). Stylistic rhetoric is deeply rooted in the texts of classical rhetoricians, and it mainly includes linguistic and literary stylistics. Humanistic rhetoric discusses the role of language symbols in communicative activities, various debating techniques to persuade the audience to accept or believe in certain arguments, and techniques used by writers to evoke readers' responses. It also examines various means for humans to achieve "identification" through symbols, and answers the questions of "what to express" and "how to express" it.

Numerous theories can be drawn from the new rhetoric to study legal discourse, including "audience", "identification", and "multi-value judgement". This chapter will introduce the three most representative principles in new rhetoric and explore the two interdisciplinary research fields of new rhetoric and courtroom interpreting based on one real case of a bilingual court trial in China. We will also probe into the way in which studies on new rhetoric may contribute to improving the quality of interpreting of legal discourse in bilingual court trials.

4.4 A case study

The present study is based on the transcription of a 60-minute unedited recording of a trial in a Chinese court, which is available on China Court Trial Online.[1] In the interest of the privacy of all participants, all personal details were anonymized. All the speakers in the trial are Chinese except the accused, a Nigerian citizen who speaks and understands English. Since the defendant could not understand Chinese, an interpreter was hired by the court to facilitate the proceeding. The whole trial consisted of three parts, namely court investigation, court debate, and final statement of the defendant. In order to find out whether the rhetorical devices in the source discourse were dismissed by the court interpreter, we subcategorized the three persuasion modes into 11 quantifiable parameters specifically for the legal setting. Pathos was subcategorized into confession (CF), empathy (EP), repentance (RP), and promise (PO); ethos

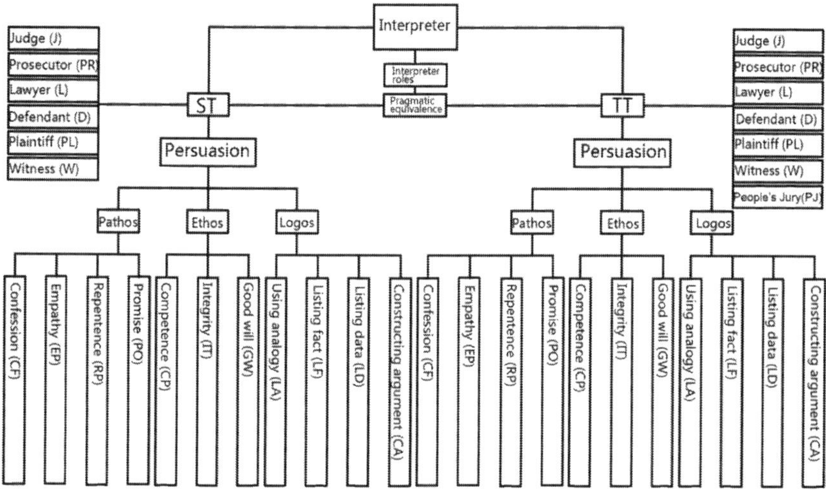

Figure 4.1 The parameters of the three persuasion modes.
Notes: ST, source texts; TT, target texts.

into competence (CP), integrity (IT), and good will (GW);[2] logos into language analogies (LA), listing facts (LF), listing data (LD), and constructing logical arguments (CA). Participants in the trial, mainly including judges (J), lawyers (L), defendants (D), plaintiffs (PL), witnesses (W), and public prosecutors (PR), are also included in Figure 4.1 to discuss the potential effect the interpretation of legal discourse might have on them. We counted the number of these parameters and compared their frequency in the source texts and the target texts to see whether there were any changes in frequency.

4.4.1 Three persuasion modes in legal discourse

The three persuasion modes, namely ethos, pathos, and logos, are at the centre of classical Aristotelian rhetoric and are highly relevant to the legal setting. Therefore, in this section, we will use some excerpts from the transcript to analyse how the three persuasion modes were used in the trial.

4.4.1.1 First persuasion mode: ethos

Aristotle discussed ethos in detail and argued that a speaker's personal characteristics exert a great influence on persuading the audience (Aristotle, 1995). He pointed out that ethos includes three aspects, namely phronesis (competence), arete (integrity), and eunoia (good will). In the legal setting, if a speaker fully demonstrates his phronesis, arete, and eunoia, his legal discourse will be more convincing and more acceptable to the audience (Gallez

& Reynders, 2015). Aristotle also added that ethos has the greatest persuasive effect compared to pathos and logos (Aristotle, 1995).

> 公诉人：本院认为被告人XXX非法持有海洛因77.98克，其行为触犯了中华人民共和国刑法第348条，犯罪事实清楚，证据确实充分，应当以非法持有毒品罪追究其刑事责任。
>
> Prosecutor: The accused held 77.98 g of drug, which violated Article 348 of the *Criminal Law of the People's Republic of China*. The proof has been clearly stated and supported by authentic evidence. Therefore, the accused should be held criminally responsible for the crime of illegal drug possession.

This excerpt is the interpretation of the prosecutor's legal discourse. In order to enhance the credibility of his own discourse, the prosecutor clearly stated his position by combining the defendant's specific crime with relevant legal provisions. The prosecutor demonstrated his competence by citing legal provisions, that is, he made full use of the rhetorical resource of ethos. In other words, the prosecutor "mobilized rhetorical resources to convince the audience" (Gallez & Reynders, 2015, p. 67).

4.4.1.2 Second persuasion mode: pathos

Aristotle conducted a detailed study of human emotions such as fear, happiness, and sadness. He pointed out that in the process of decision-making, human emotions are rational responses to specific scenarios and arguments. Therefore, he proposed the concept of pathos, and pointed out that using pathos puts the audience in the correct emotional state. Under normal circumstances, pathos refers to arousing a certain emotion in the audience, which would make speakers' arguments more convincing, and stimulates the audience to take a certain action. Emotional effects do matter in trials and they can directly influence the final verdict. The rhetorical strategies that can be used to arouse certain emotions in the audience have gained scholarly attention in the field of legal studies. In the legal setting, pathos is mainly employed in court debate and final statements, which can be manifested in several aspects, such as admitting guilt, triggering empathy, stimulating sympathy, expressing repentance, and making promises.

DEFENDANT: Very big, very big, I regret, I'm so much in pain. So I am now very very pain.

This utterance was produced during the final statement after the evidence submission, cross-examination, and court debate. The defendant repeatedly confessed that he was guilty, and obviously regretted his illegal behaviour: his ultimate goal was to try and affect the final verdict by the judge.

Table 4.1 The use of persuasion modes in Chinese trials

Phases	*Speaker(s)*	*Main persuasion mode(s)*
Court introduction	Public prosecutor, judge	Ethos, pathos
Court investigation	Lawyer, public prosecutor, plaintiff, defendant	Logos, pathos
Court debate	Lawyer, public prosecutor	Ethos, pathos, logos
Final statement	Defendant	Pathos

4.4.1.3 Third persuasion mode: logos

Aristotle pointed out that logos is mainly used at the word, argument, or speech level, including reasoning and argumentation. Jiao et al. (2012) summarized and classified Aristotle's "logical argument" into citing examples and logical reasoning. In legal settings, logic construction requires the support of logic, data, facts, analogies, etc.

DEFENDANT: You know, I'm very sorry, if I knew much more about the China law, I wouldn't have that much amount of drugs in my pocket.

In this case, the defendant used a simple backwards reasoning to prove that the reason why he secretly possessed drugs in China was that he did not understand Chinese law and did not know that drug possession violated Chinese law. Using this "logical construction" method is undoubtedly more convincing than directly admitting illegal drug possession. All in all, the use of the three persuasion modes in Western classical rhetoric used in this trial can be summarized in Table 4.1.

The table only shows general conditions. In a specific trial, participants might intentionally or unintentionally resort to these three modes in any part of their legal discourse when necessary. Nonetheless, even though the three persuasion modes of rhetoric are commonly used in legal discourse, in many cases court interpreters fail to recognize the rhetorical devices used in the source discourse and fail to convey the rhetorical effects of such persuasion modes (Gallez & Reynders, 2015).

4.4.2 "Audience", "identification", and "multi-value judgement" in legal discourse

New rhetoric involves a wide range of disciplines and comprises different strands. This study focuses on the concepts of "audience", "identification", and "multi-value judgement", which are relevant to legal interpreting studies because the "audience" in court, such as the judge and the prosecutor, plays a significant part, participants tend to establish the "identification" in their audience, and "multi-value judgement" is required to assess court interpreters' performance. Accordingly, this study aims to illuminate who the "audience" is in the legal setting, and how the "identification" process is established, as well as how these three concepts can influence the quality assessment of court interpreting.

4.4.3 Full consideration of the "audience" in court

New rhetoric shifts the focus from the speakers or writers to their "audience". Writers ought to consider the characteristics of their "audience", such as education level and gender, so that the works they compose can better establish the "identification" in their "audience". Perelman (1971) divided "audience" into three categories, namely the self as audience, a universal audience, and a particular audience. By the self as audience, he meant that sometimes debaters may argue with themselves or question themselves; by universal audience, he meant the ideal audience; by particular audience, he meant the real audience in a particular situation.

Given that legal discourse is institutional in its essence, the main "audience" in Chinese courts comprises judges, lawyers, plaintiffs, defendants, and prosecutors. In mainland China there are no public juries in trials due to the different legal system. In order to protect their own interests to the maximum, before delivering their respective legal discourse, plaintiffs, defendants, and their lawyers carefully investigate the whole case, fully consider the characteristics of their respective "audience", and then prepare the legal discourse that is based on facts and grounded in law, so that their discourse influences their "audience" in their own favour. For example, judges' main "audience" comprises plaintiffs and defendants, so their discourse usually follows a standardized paradigm and includes a large number of legal terms to match this highly professional and solemn setting.

Accordingly, court interpreters need to have a clear understanding of who their "audience" is, which is a prerequisite for good quality. In order to know their "audience" better, interpreters need to fully understand their own role in court first. Court interpreters can facilitate trials, but they are not supposed to interfere with trials in any way. What court interpreters face is not a single "audience", but multiple "audiences", including the plaintiff and the defendant, lawyers, judges, and prosecutors. The Code of Professional Conduct for Public Service Interpreters in the UK establishes that "practitioners shall interpret truly and faithfully what is uttered, without adding, omitting or changing anything; in exceptional circumstances a summary may be given if requested" (NRPSI, 2015, para. 5.4). Therefore, court interpreters must interpret the source legal discourse as faithfully as possible, and exclude their own emotions from their interpretation, so as to safeguard judicial justice.

However, it could happen that some court interpreters unconsciously empathize with either the plaintiff's side or the defendant's side. "Gender, race, and class as relevant dimensions of power disparity are deeply implicated in the standing of the interpreter vis-à-vis other court participants, and the relationship between interpreters and the individuals they assist" (Edwards, 1998; Ahmad, 2007, p. 1051, cited in Aliverti & Seoighe, 2017, p. 149). In some trials, defendants even "cling to [interpreters] as potential saviours, providing not only a linguistic, but also a cultural and legal haven" (Morris, 2010, p. 9). The potentially biased interpretation of legal discourse has gained more attention from Western scholars in recent years (Aliverti & Seoighe, 2017).

It is far from enough to solely rely on court interpreters' efforts to ensure they can play their unbiased role or better identify their "audience" in court trials. Courts and translation and interpreting legislation should also play their part in this endeavour (Zhao & Dong, 2019). Hale (2015) conducted a survey in her court interpreting workshop for judicial staff in 2014. Through her survey, she found that most judicial staff did not have a thorough understanding of the role of court interpreters. They did not have the right expectation of the work of court interpreters and usually were not aware of the value of a brief about trials and relevant materials to the interpreters. This reflects the problem of a lack of norms and regulations in public service interpreting. Hale shared with the attendees the working mode and related requirements of court interpreters in the workshop, after which the attendees confirmed they had not had any similar training before, and such workshops would help them work better with court interpreters.

4.4.4 Establishing the "identification" in the court "audience"

Burke (1969) has to a large extent promoted the development of Western rhetoric in modern times. He proposed the concept of "identification", which has deeply influenced contemporary rhetoric. He believes that the essence of rhetorical activity is "identification", and human beings are always in a mindset of "identification" – consciously or unconsciously – in communicative activities (Burke, 1969; Wen, 2003).

Establishing "identification" is of great importance for both plaintiffs and defendants. This is especially true in the phase of court debates where lawyers for the plaintiff and the defendant refute the evidence submitted by the other side and develop their arguments based on certain logic criteria. In this process, they try to establish the "identification" of the judge with their stand, so that the trial proceeds in a direction that is beneficial to their side. To better establish the "identification" intended by the speakers, court interpreters must first accurately recognize the linguistic style of legal discourse.

According to Joos (1967), there are five styles of spoken language, namely frozen, formal, consultative, casual, and intimate. Given its institutional nature, most court discourse tends to be solemn and formal, such as "下面核实本案的有关证据。首先由公诉人对本案的事实进行举证。建议被告人当庭认罪" (The following is to verify the relevant evidence for this case. First, the prosecutor will submit evidence for the facts of the case. It is recommended that the defendant plead guilty in court). There are also a few that are casual, such as, "I sent money back to my relatives and cloth and I would send to Africa. After selling those cloth in Africa, they would send money back in China. I help them buy again and send back to Africa". Court participants use different language styles and register to target different "audiences" in order to gain their "identification". Therefore, court interpreters should match the style of their interpretation with the original discourse, so as not to affect the intended "identification".

4.4.5 Assessing court interpreting with "multi-value judgement"

The basic principle of new rhetoric represented by Perelman and others is the pluralism of value judgements. New rhetoric advocates difference and pluralism, promotes the independent existence and coexistence of different value judgements, and seeks to reach new understanding through conversations (Perelman & Olbrechts-Tyteca, 1971; Chen, 2019). This "multi-value judgement" can inspire the quality assessment of interpreting in general and court interpreting in particular. Considering the "multi-value judgement" of the new rhetoric, the performance of court interpreters ought to be evaluated from multiple dimensions.

4.5 Problems in the interpretation of rhetorical legal discourse

At present, there is still limited research on the quality assessment of court interpreting in the field of interpreting studies in China. Given the institutional nature of courts, what role do court interpreters play in bilingual courts? What interpreting strategies should court interpreters use? These questions need follow-up research. Based on the observation of our small dataset, we found that there are various rhetorical devices used either consciously or unconsciously by speakers in court. In order to find out whether the court interpreter fully interpreted the rhetorical legal discourse, we counted the number of rhetorical devices in both the source and the target discourse. We found out that court interpreters sometimes fail to interpret the legal discourse involving rhetorical devices for several reasons (Figure 4.2). In this case, speakers in court used CA 58 times, LD 46 times, LF 61, GW 10, CP 24, PO 3, RP 24, EP 8, and CF 13. However, in the interpretation, CA was used 37 times, LD 41 times, LF 44, GW 1, CP 12, PO 1, RP 7, EP 6, and CF 5, which shows an obvious decrease in the use of the aforementioned rhetorical devices. As a result, the intended rhetorical effect of the legal discourse may have been diminished, and the final verdict of the trial may also have been affected. Based on our observation of the data, we outlined the most frequent lack of transfer of rhetorical structures that court interpreters made in our case study when interpreting legal discourse.

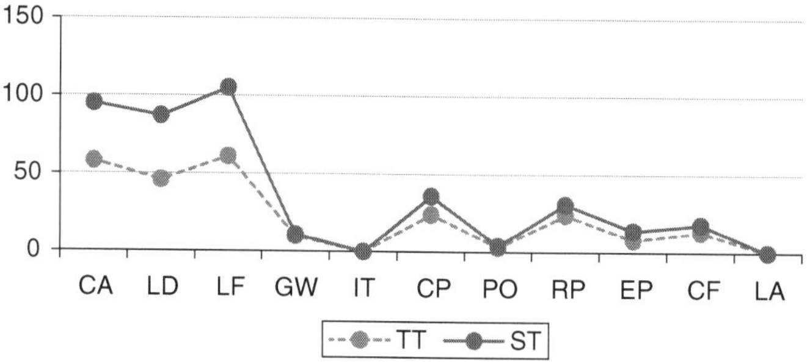

Figure 4.2 The number of rhetorical devices employed in source texts (ST) and target texts (TT).

Notes: CA, constructing logical arguments; LD, listing data; LF, listing facts; GW, good will; IT, integrity; CP, ethos into competence; PO, promise; RP, repentance; EP, empathy; CF, confession; LA, logos into language analogies.

4.5.1 Lack of ethos implied in the source legal discourse

Among the three persuasion modes, ethos may be the most implicit one. It seems that legal discourse with ethos is not that different from that without, but the language impact of the legal discourse is significantly diminished if the part of discourse involving ethos is deleted.

LAWYER: 尊敬的审判长，人民陪审员，我是XX省XX律师事务所的XX律师，本人受XX法律援助处，接受XX的委托，对其涉嫌非法持有毒品一案出庭进行辩护，在接受指派和委托后本人会见了被告，仔细阅读了相关的案件材料，认真研读了相关的法律，现就该案提出以下辩护意见……

(LAWYER: Distinguished presiding judge, jury members, I am XX from XX Law Firm in XX Province. I am entrusted by XX Legal Aid Office to appear in court for the case of illegal drug possession. After receiving the assignment and entrustment, I met with the defendant, carefully read the relevant case materials, and carefully studied the relevant laws. Now I propose the following defence opinions on the case...)

INTERPRETER: The defence opinions presented by the defender……

In this example, the lawyer introduced himself as the defence lawyer for the defendant, and emphasized that he had formally met with the defendant after receiving this task, and also carefully reviewed the relevant laws. Therefore, it is implied in his introduction that he is fully qualified to represent the defendant in this trial. In doing so, he demonstrated his phronesis to the judge and the audience. However, besides the fact that the interpreter deleted a whole chunk of information in the discourse, which is against the norms for interpreting, the interpreter also deleted all the detailed information with rhetorical implications from her interpretation, which consequently did not fully convey the effect that the original ethos was intended to have. In this specific case, though, it is not only a question of deleting rhetorical devices but of omitting a full stretch of the original speech with a consequent serious loss of information.

4.5.2 Influence of improper simplification on pathos

Simplification is an interpreting strategy often used by conference interpreters (Bernardini, Ferraresi & Miličević, 2016). This method can improve the efficiency of communication when there is too much redundant information in conference speakers' discourse. However, this technique is not applicable to court interpreting. Every piece of the detailed information provided in the court by speakers, including each modal particle in the legal discourse may be a key decisive factor leading to the final verdict. Moreover, the use of pathos often involves a lot of repetition in the discourse. If the repeated information is simplified, the emotion-rendering effect of the source legal discourse is bound to be diminished.

DEFENDANT: Very big, very big, I regret, I'm so much in pain. So I am now very very pain.
INTERPRETER: 非常后悔，而且过去几个月我一直承受着痛苦。
(INTERPRETER: I regret it very much, and I have been suffering so much pain over the past months.)

Interpreters in general and public service interpreters such as court interpreters in particular should stick to the principle of impartiality. Due to the solemnity of the legal setting, court interpreters cannot make any changes to the original legal discourse and should be faithful to the original discourse. Mikkelson (2016) listed the professional ethics that court interpreters need to comply with, the very first of which is fidelity. In this excerpt, the defendant expressed his regret multiple times, but only one remained in the interpretation. The court interpreter simplified the source legal discourse because she was not aware of the specific intention of the defendant by saying "pain" twice and the adverb "very" four times. In omitting these expressions, the effect of pathos in the defendant's discourse was weakened.

4.5.3 Incomplete logos

Logic argumentation is common in court trials. The logical reasoning process emphasizes logic links, and every related link cannot be omitted, otherwise the logic would be incomplete or compromised. However, based on the observation on the trial in this study, court discourse involving logos tends to be relatively longer, so that court interpreters will have a relatively larger cognitive load, which in turn will lead interpreters' dismissal of some logic links and incomplete logic in their interpretation.

DEFENDANT: So if she is around, you can ask her you know, I spend most of my time with her, you know, she do visit me always, I do visit her always, every week we do see each other maybe four to five times a week, so I don't have much time on doing drug. The only thing I do is either to send money money to Africa, I will give her the money, she would help me buy things from Taobao Alibaba, everything is on her phone, this is how I buy the goods, is on her phone…

INTERPRETER: 我就花很多时间和她在一起，几乎每个礼拜都会跟她见面四到五次，所以我根本没有时间去做任何违法犯罪的事情。而且，我朋，额，我女朋友也帮助我做一些贸易……

(INTERPRETER: I spent a lot of time with her. I met her four to five times every week. So, I didn't have any time to do anything illegal. Moreover, my friend, emm, my girlfriend also helped me do some trade…)

In this case, the defendant said that he had a girlfriend, and then added that he had known his girlfriend for a long time. Therefore, it can be inferred that he was in a close relationship with her. And then he said that he stayed with his girlfriend every week, so that he didn't have any time to engage in drug dealing. The interpreter indeed interpreted the logic link for the first part of this legal discourse. In the second part of the discourse, the defendant added that he spent the rest of the week sending money back to Africa and also doing online shopping, which confirmed what he mentioned earlier, that he barely went out every week. Since he barely went out every week, it is predictable that he was not engaged in any drug dealing. Unfortunately, the interpreter failed to interpret this part of the logic, which would somehow lead the audience to doubt whether the defendant really had no time to carry out drug dealing.

4.5.4 Unclear understanding of the court interpreter's "audience"

The court interpreter must be unbiased in his or her interpreting, which is especially important in the switching of personal pronouns in the interpretation. In Chinese court trials, interpreters sometimes inadvertently interpret from the perspective of the judge and interpret the discourse of the plaintiff's speech in a third-person stance. This shows their unclear understanding of the "audience", which is likely to affect the final verdict.

DEFENDANT: Evidence I have is I have a girlfriend you know, and this girlfriend, you know, I spend, I met her in 2016, I came to China 2014, I met met her 2014.

INTERPRETER: 他说我是2014年来中国的，2016年6月认识了我的女朋友。

(INTERPRETER: He said that I came to China in 2014 and met my girlfriend in June 2016.)

In this example, the interpreter made a mistake in interpreting the date. Leaving aside this mistake, the interpreter also interpreted using reported speech. Therefore, the interpreter did not remain neutral and shifted the footing in her interpretation (see Goffman, 1979). A shift of person in the interpretation can either empower or disempower defendants. Aliverti and Seoighe (2017) observed some court trials and drew the conclusion that "the intervention of interpreters in court proceedings can have an empowering effect on defendants, but equally, it can be profoundly disempowering. The use of the second person register is another effective way to marginalize and disempower defendants" (p. 146).

4.6 Discussion and conclusion

This study introduced "persuasion modes" from classical rhetoric and "audience", "identification", and "multi-value judgement" from new rhetoric in the analysis of an interpreter's performance in court in a case trial. We found that various rhetorical devices were used in the original legal discourse, which, however, were dismissed by the court interpreter. Moreover, the court interpreter was not fully aware of her role in the trial, and she did not have a clear understanding of her audience either. Consequently, the intended rhetorical effect in the source discourse was diminished. Therefore, we propose the following tips that can be used to help court interpreters better interpret rhetorical legal discourse.

First, court interpreters should stay neutral and stick to the principle of impartiality in their interpretation. One can safely say that court interpreters who do not know their professional boundaries and do not know communication mechanisms may end up acting as gatekeepers and they should be aware of this. Court interpreting is an act of interpreting in the course of judicial proceedings, and the quality of interpreting will have a direct impact on the outcome of judicial proceedings. Especially in criminal trials, the quality of interpreting may even have an impact on the life and freedom of the defendants. Therefore, the most significant standard for the quality of court interpreting is accuracy and completeness (Yu, 2018). As Hale (2015) emphasized when she summarized her experience in holding workshops, court interpreting is a complex and arduous task, which requires all parties involved in court to fully understand the work and fully cooperate with interpreters. This requires the judicial staff to provide case materials, understand the role of court interpreters, understand interpreting difficulties caused by cultural differences, etc. But as court interpreters, they must be faithful to the source discourse while ensuring that the audience can understand their interpretation. Court interpreters should not make any simplification or addition, otherwise the language impact of the legal discourse may be diminished. Moreover, the interpretation would even arouse suspicion about the credibility of the legal discourse.

Second, court interpreters should learn more about rhetorical devices and resources and be more sensitive to them in the source legal discourse. Once the speaker consciously or unconsciously resorts to a certain rhetorical device or a rhetorical resource, court interpreters must promptly identify it and fully render the rhetorical effect in their interpretation. Being more conscious of rhetorical devices in legal discourse can to some extent help court interpreters better deal with more delicate and detailed information in legal discourse. Based on our observation of the transcription of the trial recording, the source legal discourse involving rhetorical devices does not include too many non-equivalent or culture-loaded words or expressions, hence as long as court interpreters are aware of the existence of these rhetorical devices, the quality of their interpretation can be improved.

Third, court interpreters should improve their training in logical thinking. Given that among the three persuasion modes ethos and pathos are relatively more recognizable, and the legal discourse involving ethos and pathos is not usually too long, if court interpreters can recognize the rhetorical devices, it is not that difficult for them to faithfully interpret the source legal discourse. However, based on our observation of the transcription of the trial recording, the logos in legal discourse oftentimes involves legal syllogisms, which tend to lengthen the legal discourse (Jiao, 2015). Moreover, speakers often deliver this type of discourse without any pause, which is aimed at enhancing the impact of their discourse. Consequently, these types of speech can be cognitively challenging for interpreters. In addition, the logic links in the discourse are covert in many cases, hence court interpreters may face more difficulties in interpreting this type of legal jargon. Therefore, court interpreters should add logic training to their daily training routine, which will help them better cope with the legal discourses involving logos in the long run.

This study attempted to probe into interpreting in bilingual Chinese court only at the linguistic level. Paralinguistic information such as phonetics, intonation, rhythm, and stress has not been taken into account. Therefore, in future studies, paralinguistic information can also be included in the data analysis. Moreover, rhetoric is a broad discipline; many other concepts besides "persuasion", "identification", "audience", and "multi-value judgement" can be used to support court interpreting studies. Therefore, it is highly recommended that other rhetoric theories and notions be incorporated into the theoretical basis for court interpreting studies. We hope that this chapter can inspire the training of potential court interpreters in China, and that the team of Chinese court interpreters will grow stronger and become more professional. Meanwhile, we also hope that this study can enrich the scope of court interpreting as an independent discipline.

Notes

1 Link to the trial: http://tingshen.court.gov.cn/live/1198208

2 Competence is a rhetorical device oftentimes used by court staff and especially lawyers to demonstrate their qualification for representing their clients; integrity

is often used by judges and public prosecutors to show judicial justice; good will is used by lawyers especially when they explain legal terms to help their audience understand better, and good will is more frequently used by lawyers in adversarial trials.

References

Ahmad, M. (2007). Interpreting communities: Lawyering across language difference. *UCLA Law Review*, 54, 999–1086.

Aliverti, A. & Seoighe, R. (2017) Lost in translation? Examining the role of court interpreters in cases involving foreign national defendants in England and Wales. *New Criminal Law Review*, 20(1), 130–156.

Aristotle and Buckley, T. (translator). (1995). *Treatise on Rhetoric*. Buffalo, NY: Prometheus.

Bernardini, S., Ferraresi, A. & Miličević, M. (2016). From EPIC to EPTIC — Exploring simplification in interpreting and translation from an intermodal perspective. *Target. International Journal of Translation Studies*, 28(1), 61–86. doi:https://doi.org/10.1075/target.28.1.03ber.

Black, E. (1965). *Rhetorical Criticism: A Study in Method*. Madison, WI: University of Wisconsin Press.

Booth, C. W. (1961). *The Rhetoric of Fiction*. Chicago, IL: University of Chicago Press.

Booth, W. (1965). The revival of rhetoric. *PMLA*, 80(2), 8–12. doi:10.2307/1261264.

Burgess, P. G. (1968). The rhetoric of Black power: A moral demand? *Quarterly Journal of Speech*, 54(2), 122–133. doi:10.1080/00335636809382881.

Burke, K. (1969). *A Rhetoric of Motives*. Berkeley, CA: University of California Press.

Chen, X. W. (2019). The argument of "translation rhetoric". Chinese Translators Journal, 40(3), 44–54. [陈小慰. "翻译修辞学"之辨与辩. 中国翻译, 40(3): 44–54.]

Christensen, F. (1965). A generative rhetoric of the paragraph. *College Composition and Communication*, 16(3), 144–156. doi:10.2307/355728.

Corbett, E. P. J. (1965). Classical Rhetoric for the Modern Student. Oxford University Press.

Corbett, E. P. J. (1969). The rhetoric of the open hand and the rhetoric of the closed fist. *College Composition and Communication*, 20(5), 288–296. doi:10.2307/355032.

Drew, P. & Heritage, J. (1992). Analysing talk at work: An introduction. In Drew, P. & Heritage, J. (eds.). *Talk at Work*. Cambridge: Cambridge University Press, p. 22.

Edwards, R. (1998). A critical examination of the use of interpreters in the qualitative research process. *Journal of Ethnic and Migration Studies*, 24, 197–208.

Freed, A. F. (2015). Institutional discourse. In Tracy, K., Sandel, T. & Ilie, C. (eds.). The International Encyclopedia of Language and Social Interaction. New York, NY: Wiley-Blackwell. https://doi.org/10.1002/9781118611463.wbielsi151.

Gallez, E. & Reynders, A. (2015). Court interpreting and classical rhetoric: Ethos in interpreter-mediated monological discourse. *Interpreting*, 17(1), 64–90. https://doi.org/10.1075/intp.17.1.04gal.

Gass, R. H. & Seiter, J. S. (2010). Persuasion, Social Influence, and Compliance Gaining (4th ed.). Boston: Allyn & Bacon, p. 33.

Goffman, E. (1979). Footing. *Semiotica*, 25(1–2), 1–30.

Gu, Y. G. (1990). Western classical rhetoric and Western new rhetoric. *Foreign Languages Teaching and Research*, 34(2), 13–25. [顾曰国. 西方古典修辞学和西方新修辞学. *外语教学与研究*, 1990(2): 13–25.]

Hale, S. (2006). Themes and methodological issues in court interpreting research. *Linguistica Antverpiensia New Series – Themes in Translation Studies*, (5), 205–228.

Hale, S. (2015). Approaching the bench: Teaching magistrates and judges how to work effectively with interpreters. *Monografías de Traducción e Interpretación*, 7, 163–180.

Jiao, B. (2015). Logic and rhetoric: Two different yet connected elements of legal paradigms. *Legal System and Social Development*, 21(02), 153–166. [焦宝乾.逻辑与修辞:一对法学范式的区分与关联[J].法制与社会发展, 2015,21(02):153–166.]

Jiao, B. et al. (2012). *Introduction to Legal Rhetoric: Discussion from a Judicial Perspective*. Jinan, Shandong: Shandong People's Publishing House. [焦宝乾等. 法律修辞学导论—司法视角的探讨. 山东人民出版社, 2012.]

Johannesen, R. L., Strickland, R. & Eubanks, R. T. (eds.). (1970). *Language is Sermonic: Richard M. Weaver on the Nature of Rhetoric*. Baton Rouge, LA: Louisiana State University Press.

Joos, M. (1967). *The Five Clocks: A Linguistic Excursion into the Five Styles of English Usage* (5th ed.). New York: Harcourt.

Mikkelson, H. (2016). *Introduction to Court Interpreting* (2nd ed.). London: Routledge.

Morris, R. (2010). Images of the court interpreter: Professional identity, role definition and self-image. *Translation and Interpreting Studies*, 5, 20–40.

Nordquit, R. (2020). *What is Identification in Rhetoric?* Retrieved from www.thoughtco.com/identification-rhetoric-term-1691142. Accessed 14 March, 2021.

NRPSI (National Register of Public Service Interpreters). (2015). NRPSI Annual Review of Public Service Interpreting in the UK. Retrieved from www.nrpsi.org.uk/ downloads/AnnualReview2014.pdf. Accessed 20 July, 2021.

Ortony, A. (1979). *Metaphor and Thought*. Cambridge: Cambridge University Press.

Perelman, C. & Olbrechts-Tyteca, L. (1971). *The New Rhetoric: A Treatise on Argumentation*. Notre Dame: University of Notre Dame Press.

Richards, I. A. (1965). *The Philosophy of Rhetoric*. Oxford: Oxford University Press.

Scott, R. L. & Smith, D. K. (1969). The rhetoric of confrontation. *Quarterly Journal of Speech*, 55(1), 1–8. doi:10.1080/00335636909382922.

Wen, K. X. (2002). On the evolution of contemporary English and American rhetoric. *Foreign Language Education*, 23(4), 22–27. [温科学. 论当代英美修辞学的演变. *外语教学*, 2002(7): 22–27.]

Wen, K. X. (2003). The development and innovation of contemporary Western rhetoric theories. *Journal of Fujian Normal University (Philosophy and Social Sciences Edition)*, 21(6), 25–30. [温科学. 当代西方修辞学理论的发展与创新. *福建师范大学学报*（哲学社会科学版）, 2003(6): 25–30.]

Young, R. E., Becker, A. L. & Pike, K. L. (1970). *Rhetoric: Discovery and Change*. San Diego, CA: Harcourt College Pub.

Yu, L. (2018). A primary study on summary interpreting in criminal trials in Chinese mainland. *Asia Pacific Interdisciplinary Translation Studies*, 4(6), 32–47. [余蕾. 中国大陆刑事审判语境下法庭口译中概括口译现象研究. *亚太跨学科翻译研究*, 2018(6): 32–47.]

Zhao, J. F. & Chen, S. (2008). Review and prospect of Chinese and Western court interpretating studies. *Chinese Science & Technology Translators Journal*, 21(3), 20–23. [赵军峰，陈珊.中西法庭口译研究回顾与展望. *中国科技翻译*, 2008（21): 20–23.] https://doi.org/10.16024/j.cnki.issn1002-0489.2008.03.019.

Zhao, J. F. & Dong Y. (2019). The inspiration of the US “Court Interpreter Act” and its amendments to Chinese court interpreting legislation. *Shanghai Journal of Translators*, 34(3), 24–30. [赵军峰，董燕. 美国《法庭口译员法》及其修正案对我国法庭口译立法的启示. *上海翻译*, 2019(3): 24–30.]

5 The best interest of the child in interpreter-mediated interviews

Researching children's point of view[1]

Amalia Amato and Gabriele Mack

5.1 Children's language rights at international level and in Italy

Giving a definition of the terms "fragility" and "vulnerability" is difficult, as convincingly argued by Virág (2015, p. 77ff). Any person, regardless of age, can be frail for a variety of reasons and in many ways, and vulnerability is often a temporary condition induced by transient circumstances. Boys and girls under 18 are considered vulnerable *per se* by national and international legal provisions which recognise their need for special care, especially (but not only) if they are on the move and/or separated from their families.

The fundamental legal provisions concerning children are enshrined in the United Nations (UN) Convention on the Rights of the Child (CRC) (United Nations, 1989), with 196 State Parties[2] and 182 ratifications.[3] Articles 12 and 13 specifically refer to children's language and communication rights. Article 12 guarantees freedom of expression in matters affecting the child and gives due weight to the child's views, and it establishes the obligation to hear the child in any judicial and administrative proceedings affecting her/him. Article 13 grants every child the right to "express his or her views, obtain information, and make ideas or information known, regardless of frontiers". Though it may sound obvious, all these rights can be substantiated only if children can understand them and can communicate their point of view effectively. But linguistic rights are not explicitly granted by international law, although there are initiatives like the Universal Declaration of Linguistic Rights signed in 1996 in Barcelona (UNESCO, 1996a and 1996b).

In Italy, the child's right to be heard when involved in legal proceedings was introduced by decree law no. 154 in 2013, which added article 336-bis to the Civil Code. For unaccompanied children, a major step forward was Act no. 47 of 7 April 2017 ("Provisions on protective measures for unaccompanied foreign minors") stating that no later than 30 days after having been reported to a public authority, unaccompanied children have the right to be heard by qualified staff who collect their story and all the necessary information to grant them protection, with the help of a linguistic mediator if necessary.

DOI: 10.4324/9781003197027-7

5.1.1 Public service interpreting in Italy

In Italy, the shortage of qualified and trained interpreters in the languages of recent migratory flows in legal and other crucial settings – such as health care, education, and psychiatry – raises concerns also in terms of children's rights. So far there is no register or accreditation system for public service interpreters, and according to a comparative research in six European countries, their professional status in Italy is very low and their work is poorly paid, which inevitably affects the quality of their interpreting services negatively (Casadei & Franceschetti, 2009, p. 18). Qualified conference or liaison interpreters rarely accept assignments in public service settings where interpreting is generally performed by linguistic and/or cultural mediators. The first official definition of mediator dates back to 1997, and in the following years local authorities issued multiple and varied job descriptions. Later on, regional and local authorities defined a common job description similar to that of a caseworker who also provides language assistance and interpreting, but it is still ambiguous and comprises so many tasks and roles that it seems impossible they can be all performed by the same person (see Conferenza Regioni e Province Autonome, 2009, pp. 8–9). Moreover, so far there are no common standards for training and qualifications of cultural mediators (Amato & Garwood, 2011).

In legal contexts (see ImPLI, 2012; Falbo, 2013) interpreting is mainly carried out by: (1) in-house police interpreters who work as full-time staff for the Ministry of Interior; (2) former migrants who may or may not be trained as cultural and language mediators and cover languages of lesser diffusion as well as vehicular languages but have no training in interpreting techniques such as consecutive with notes or whispering; and (3) bilinguals acting as *ad hoc* interpreters without any training or experience either in legal matters or in interpreting. Also in health care, interpreting is rarely provided by trained interpreters, and schools have very small budgets to ensure communication with newly arrived foreign pupils.

5.2 Research on interpreting for children

The lack of explicit language rights for children is reflected also in the limited number of interpreting studies in this area. This sharply contrasts with the booming research on interpreting activities performed by children known as language brokering, which raises completely different problems and will not be dealt with in this paper. The following sections give a brief overview of the most salient empirical studies on interpreting for children and present facts and findings that will be referred to when discussing the results of our study.[4]

5.2.1 Interpreting for very young children

A Norwegian research project in public service interpreting for children conducted by researchers from Oslo University College includes a study on very young children's behaviour in interpreter-mediated conversation (Hitching & Nilsen, 2010), to which Nilsen (2013) added some more interviews. Analyses of video-recorded interactions led the authors to conclude that very young children aged 3 or 4 can understand the peculiarity of interpreter-mediated communication and adapt to it, provided they understand and accept the basic rules of turn-taking in consecutive interpreting. Kanstad (2015) confirmed this finding in a study involving a 3-year-old boy who was assisted by an interpreter during his first weeks in a Norwegian kindergarten. The same observation was made by Solem (2014) with *chuchotage* (whispering) and simultaneous interpreting for five children aged between 3 and 7 years.

5.2.2 Interpreting for migrant children and in legal settings

Kanstad's research was part of a multidisciplinary project aimed at both raising awareness and expertise about communication with children via an interpreter and showing how children's rights stated in the UN CRC can be granted (Kanstad & Gran, 2016, p. 21). Interpreting is recognised as an important tool to safeguard children's rights of expression and participation, and to prevent marginalisation (ibid., p. 99). The authors conclude that in increasingly intercultural societies communication via an interpreter should be part of the training of pre-school teachers, and foreign children should have the right to an interpreter, especially in their early days at kindergarten (ibid., p. 95).

The Oslo University College project mentioned above also involved the Norwegian school administration and the Directorates of Immigration and of Integration and Diversity and researched the viewpoints of users, recruiters, and staff working with interpreters as well as interpreters themselves about interacting with minors in public service encounters. One of their conclusions was that interpreting between adults and children does not differ significantly from interpreting between adults, and that interpreters do not need a different toolbox to interpret for children, although it must be extra-large (Hitching & Nilsen, 2010, p. 37). Moreover, interpreters' personal qualities and flexibility seem particularly relevant since some individuals are better at interacting with children than others (Nilsen, 2015). Besides strongly recommending resorting only to trained and experienced interpreters, the Norwegian researchers also suggest that in the public sector interpreter-mediated communication should become a component of professional training in intercultural communication for all staff working with children.

Another research project about interpreting in childcare institutions and care centres for unaccompanied asylum-seeking minors, which was carried out on behalf of the Norwegian Directorate of Children, Youth and Family, collected quantitative and qualitative data (Berg et al., 2018). The use of untrained bilinguals and breach of confidentiality proved to heavily undermine users' trust in interpreting. Telephone interpreting seems rather common in Norway, mainly for logistic and cost reasons (Berg et al., 2018, p. ix), but very little is known about the preferences of young people in this respect. Only Øien, who interviewed 30 asylum seekers aged 15–18, incidentally mentions that some minors seem to prefer the greater distance and impersonality of telephone interpreting when they have to discuss sensitive issues (Øien, 2010, p. 31).

A series of studies based on conversation analysis was carried out in Sweden on a corpus of 26 interviews with Russian children, with the aim "to explore how the participation of unaccompanied asylum-seeking children is interactively constructed in interpreter-mediated asylum hearings" (Keselman, 2009, pp. 34–35). The analyses show "how interpreters can challenge asylum-seeking children's participant statuses" (Keselman, Cederborg, & Linell, 2010, p. 83) and how the development of trust/mistrust can be traced in the interviews (Linell & Keselman, 2010). Another conclusion was that "interpreters are powerful participants who can profoundly influence the fact-finding aspects of asylum investigations" (Keselman et al., 2010, p. 333), and that unprofessional interpreting increases power asymmetry.

Probably the most investigated area of interpreting for minors is the legal one, but once again, although mentioned in a great deal of studies, the specific needs of children rarely become a major focus (e.g., Berg &Tronstad, 2015; Kjelaas & Eide, 2015; Kjelaas, 2016). The voices of children directly involved in interpreter-mediated encounters have been listened to in even fewer cases, but not about their experience with interpreting as such. In their discussion about interviewing practice, Böser and La Rooy (2018) highlight the need to modify protocols like the one by the National Institute of Child Health and Human Development (NICHD) if encounters are interpreter-mediated.[5]

Generally speaking, children tend to learn a new language rather quickly and often act as interpreters themselves for their family or peers, as the vast literature on child language brokering confirms, but the very first "official" contacts with an alien society and a still unknown language are absolutely crucial. Talking about his first weeks in a reception centre near Turin, a 13-year-old Moroccan boy said:

> I didn't understand Italian, there is a mediator but she comes only every now and then. One day I wanted to jump out of the window, which was very high, but I was afraid. That was a prison, not a reception centre. There are windows with bars...
>
> (Rozzi, 2013, p. 63)

Kanstad and Gran rightly voice the need for

> reflections on a more basic level about what view we really have of a child as a person and as an own individual and subject. (...) There may be a danger that the children who share our language are seen as subjects and individuals while those who are more distant due to language and communication difficulties are at risk of being seen as objects.
>
> (Kanstad & Gran, 2016, p. 93)

5.3 Research design and methodology

As the overview on literature in Section 5.2 shows, some aspects concerning interpreting for children have been addressed by research so far, but the perception and preferences of children who need the assistance of interpreters have been largely neglected. We believe that listening to children's opinions about interpreted communication can help improve both existing practice and future interpreter training. For this reason we undertook a study aimed at collecting first-hand information from children about their feelings and preferences during the first interpreter-mediated interview in their life. Participants with no experience of interpreted communication were selected in order to avoid any bias or interference due to previous positive or negative impressions about interpreting. In our study the terms child and children are used as in the CRC to refer to persons under the age of 18.

The study is part of the Co-Minor-In/Quest project series[6] launched in 2012, to our knowledge the first transnational project about interpreting for children in legal settings (see Balogh and Salaets, 2015, pp. 183ff for the results). The Co-Minor-In/Quest II project collected qualitative data about interpreter-mediated interviews involving children via a focus group with professionals and semi-structured interviews (SSIs) with minors to design appropriate tools for joint training and awareness raising among professionals which also incorporate children's feelings and opinions about interpreting.

In this chapter we report about 18 Italian children's perceptions of roles and rapport building during an interpreter-mediated interview as well as some of their preferences, namely seating arrangement and age and gender of the interpreter. In the next sub-section we will describe the study design and highlight some of its limitations.

5.3.1 Study design

One part of Co-Minor-In/Quest II research project involved conducting SSIs with children of three different age groups (6–9; 10–13; and 14–17 years) after their first direct experience of an interpreter-mediated conversation.

Before providing a detailed description of the SSI and discussing the results, it is important to point out the child-centred approach of our study design. Instead of observing children as objects and then writing about them, in this work we consider children the main players and source of information and knowledge, to factor in when adults work with them. In other words, our approach was that of research *with* and *for* children rather than *on* children (Fargas-Malet et al., 2010; Clark et al., 2013; O'Reilly, Ronzoni & Dogra, 2013).

5.3.1.1 Preliminary work

Before starting to organise the interviews, we obtained approval from Bologna University Bioethical Committee and attended a webinar by Terre des Hommes, an international children's rights non-governmental organisation, about how to interview children with full respect of their rights and preferences.[7] The SSI script was prepared by the team of project partners which included six interpreting researchers, a representative of Terre des Hommes, an expert in child rights, a child lawyer, a lawyer, a criminologist, and a development psychologist. The questions addressed reflect the main issues identified during the previous first Co-Minor research project. The SSI script was drafted in English with the wording tailored to the different age groups mainly by the criminologist and the psychologist and then translated into Italian. It included 29 questions grouped into seven thematic chapters covering: (1) personal feelings; (2) understanding of roles and relations between the persons involved; (3) skills of the people involved; (4) space and time arrangements; (5) technical implementation of the interview; (6) trust and rapport; and (7) general feedback. Most questions were open-ended, and during the SSI on only a few occasions small adjustments or additions were made to respond to the children's moves, though with hindsight, it might have been advisable to stick less to the SSI script with the younger children up to the age of 8 (see Einarsdottir, 2007). Two questions were added during the interviews with the teenagers prompted by one of their answers (see Section 5.4.2). For logistic reasons only one pilot interview was conducted with a 6-year-old child (the age group which could potentially be the most difficult to handle), but no adjustments of the script were necessary. We realise that a couple of questions are not completely open, namely the ones asking children to mention what they liked or disliked about the interviewer and the interpreter. Although the wording was meant to help younger children understand these questions, with hindsight the result is a couple of questions that can be perceived as leading.

Children and teenagers were enrolled through the local education authority in Forlì applying the following inclusion criteria: Italian mother tongue, no prior experience with interpreters, and no knowledge of German – the language chosen for the interpreter-mediated interview because it is rarely taught in schools in Italy and it is the mother tongue of one of the researchers. Children with a migration background were excluded considering the probability of previous experience with interpreting and to avoid possible reactivation of negative recollections connected with migration.

5.3.2 The interviews

The interviews were conducted on four afternoons in winter 2017 and involved 18 participants (ten girls and eight boys). Eight children were aged 6–9, four 10–13, and six were teenagers aged 14–17. After watching a short video used as a prompt, each participant took part in two different conversations: during the first one (the interpreter-mediated interview) they talked about the video to an unknown foreigner with the help of an interpreter; during the second conversation (the SSI) they talked with one of the researchers about their experience of communication through an interpreter. The first conversation had no script and unfolded spontaneously according to the participants' answers and reactions since the person acting as interviewer (who had not seen the video) had the goal of obtaining information about the events featured in the video but no other instructions, while the second conversation, in Italian, was based on the SSI script.

A room in our university building was used for the interviews while parents who accompanied children waited in another room, and a third one was used as a waiting room for the interviewer and the interpreter only, when they were idle. Recordings were made with a camcorder and two audio recorders.

In the interpreted interviews different seating arrangements were used for different age groups:[8]

- 6–9 years of age: three chairs in a circle, no table (as there was no furniture of suitable size available)
- 10–13 and 14–17 years of age: five chairs at a rectangular table, with the child/teenager invited to choose where to sit and where to place the interviewer and the interpreter.

The role of interviewer was played in turn by a high school language teacher, a university professor, and a junior lecturer, all German nationals, who had been briefed about the project and how to conduct an interview in a child-friendly way. All interviews were interpreted by the same young male Italian interpreter with German as a B language who had about 4 years of experience as a freelance conference and public service interpreter. He had been instructed to use both consecutive with and without notes and *chuchotage* during the interviews. As suggested by the psychologist and the child rights expert in the research team, the children were put in the position of a witness, but the interviews took place in a neutral environment and were conducted in a very informal style.

Upon arrival, all participants were given the same preliminary information about the interview and namely: (1) that they were going to watch a video; (2) that a person who had not seen it would talk to them to get as much information as possible about what happened in the video; (3) that since that person did not speak Italian, there would be an interpreter who would help them communicate; (4) that they could simply say what they remembered about the video and there were no right or wrong answers; and (5) that they could put an end to the conversation at any time.

After each child had watched on his/her own a 2'30" long video featuring a pickpocketing scene without any violence and with no talk,[9] the interpreter and interviewer came into the room and were introduced by their name and role. During the interpreter-mediated interviews, the researchers were sitting at the back of the room but did not participate or interact in any way. After the interpreted interview and a short pause, the children were asked if they agreed to have another conversation with one of the researchers (the SSI) about the

Table 5.1 Participants' data and length of the 18 interviews

Interviewee's age	*Interviewee's gender*	*Length of the semi-structured interview*
6	M	9′ 05″
6	M	10′ 20″
6	M	10′ 31″
7	M	10′ 51″
7	F	10′ 59″
8	F	9′ 06″
8	F	15′ 14″
9	F	8′ 59″
11	F	14′ 50″
12	M	12′ 23″
12	F	12′ 32″
12	F	13′ 33″
16	M	16′ 04″
16	F	17′ 52″
16	M	18′ 54″
16	M	20′ 53″
17	F	10′ 51″
17	F	16′ 41″

interpreted interview that had just taken place. They were reassured again that there were no right or wrong answers and that they could decide not to answer at all. The second researcher took notes and operated the recorders. Table 5.1 details the 18 interviewees' age and gender and the length of the SSI.

All SSIs were fully transcribed; quotations were translated from Italian for the purpose of this paper. Thematic content analysis was performed coding the answers according to a first set of categories which was cross-checked and adjusted in a second round of analysis.

5.4 Main findings and discussion of semi-structured interviews

In this section we will discuss children's views on four topics: personal feelings, role, age and gender of the interpreter and rapport among participants, and choice of seating arrangement. We are neither trying to generalise these findings nor claiming that they are specific to children only, since there is no adult control group with whom the same study was conducted to compare results. We simply listened to the voice of children and collected their opinions and feelings about their first experience of an interpreter-mediated interaction.

5.4.1 Feelings about the interpreter-mediated interactions

The first question asked to all participants was about how they felt during the interpreter-mediated conversation they had just had. About half of them, especially younger children, admitted they felt nervous before the conversation because of the unknown situation and/or because they could not communicate directly with the interviewer, and indeed, they were faced with a new experience involving persons they had never met before and communication through an interpreter. This feeling is related to trust and rapport, which will be discussed in the next section.

When answering to the question about what children liked in particular during the conversation, two of the younger children said they liked being asked questions about the video, one said he liked being carefully listened to by two adults, and one liked listening to an unknown language. These answers suggest that the initial feeling of anxiety and unease faded away as the interaction unfolded and was over at the end of it. Most of the older children liked the idea of being able to talk to a person they did not know in a foreign language.

The next two questions concerned positive feelings. The first one asked what the children liked most of the interviewer. Most younger children could not answer, but one said: "I understood the interviewer sometimes: when she pronounced my name and said 'OK'". This confirms, from the perception and viewpoint of a child, the importance of social support during interviews, as highlighted in a study which examined the level of support interviewers provided to children:

> Support was identified when interviewers personally addressed the child by his/her name (e.g., "Now Daniel tell me everything that happened from the beginning to the end" or "Tell me more about this person, Sharon") and when neutral reinforcements, unrelated to the content of the child's response, were included.
>
> (Hershkowitz, 2011, p. 113)

Three children between 10 and 13 pointed out that they appreciated the interviewer showing interest for them. One boy said: "She was curious"; one girl stated: "She watched my gestures and looked at me while I was speaking"; another girl said: "She looked really interested", again a form or non-verbal reinforcement. The group aged 14–17 focused on emotional and non-verbal aspects concerning the interviewer: attitude, spontaneity, naturalness, keeping eye contact, patience, willingness to listen were mentioned as the most positive aspects. One boy said: "I didn't understand what she was saying but with her words with her tone of voice with her gaze how she posed more or less I could understand the questions she was going to ask me"; another one stated:

> I liked very much how she expressed herself, even if I didn't understand her language, I liked very much how she acted and how because at the end I could understand something from her tone of voice, from her expression, but the words obviously I couldn't understand them.

This confirms, if need be, the well-known importance of non-verbal and kinetic aspects in communication (Poyatos, 1987), and strongly suggests that interviewers should take them into careful consideration also when working with children who speak another language.

The second question was on what participants liked most about the interpreter. Some of the younger children underlined that the interpreter was there to help them, and one said: "I liked best that he said what I said", which could be interpreted as a reference to dubbing which is widely used in Italy for films and TV programmes. The older children and teenagers mainly appreciated the skills of the interpreter and rated him as very proficient. One of them said: "He tried not to translate literally but to communicate, to make his talk sound Italian and not a translation". Since all teenagers came from a humanities high school, this observation could reflect his personal experience with translations from Latin and ancient Greek in class. In general, being asked questions made children connect this experience to school; in particular, younger children made several references to their teachers and schoolmates during the SSI.

Negative feelings were investigated with a question about whether there had been something that participants disliked during the interview. The only aspect, mentioned by almost all interviewees, was whispered interpreting (*chuchotage*). The reason for this dislike was mainly that it was perceived as overlapping talk and interrupting, and interrupting a person is culturally related to rudeness in Italy. Some also found it confusing since it prevents individuals listening to everything that is being said, and two children aged 10–13 doubted that the interpreter could hear what they were saying since he was translating while they were speaking. These perceptions are in line with the literature on child interviews in legal settings which states that children should not be interrupted in order not to interfere with memory and with the flow of their narrative. This is an aspect which deserves further investigation. Three of the younger children could not answer the question because they said they did not notice that there had been a change of interpreting mode, but the video recordings clearly show them reacting to *chuchotage* by raising their tone of voice and/or by springing up from their chair in an attempt to draw the interviewer's and interpreter's attention to what *they* were saying.

5.4.2 Perception of roles and rapport building

The following section of the SSI concerned the role of the interpreter and the rapport between participants. To understand who interviewees identified as their main conversation partner, they were asked whom they had told the story of the video to. Half of the children up to 13 identified the interpreter as their primary communication partner, and half identified the interviewer. All teenagers said they told the story to the interpreter but two of them specified that the interviewer put the questions and therefore what they said was addressed to the interviewer. Several comments made by children and teenagers show that this choice is also associated with eye contact. One child said: "I looked mainly at the interviewer; the interpreter looked at me *and* at the interviewer".

The question about who had listened most carefully to what the children said received different answers in all age groups, with interesting explanations. One young child said the interpreter listened with more attention because "He was the one who understood me". One older child thought the interpreter listened more carefully because "He had to listen *and* translate", and one teenager said the interpreter listened more carefully since he had to translate, while two others thought the interviewer listened more carefully because she showed attention, gave non-verbal feedback, and tried to follow what was being said even if she did not understand Italian. Again, support and reinforcement by gestures or other non-verbal cues such as nodding and eye contact did not go unnoticed and were mentioned as significant by the older respondents.

Two additional questions asked only to teenagers concerned the interpreter's gender and age. They came up in the interview with the first teenager, who stated that the relatively small age difference with the interpreter had made him feel more at ease, because he felt he would not be judged negatively if he made a "language mistake". Another interviewee said he perceived a younger interpreter as less intimidating while two boys said that in general they would prefer an older interpreter because s/he would be more reliable and reassuring. The interpreter's gender, instead, was not considered significant by any of the teenagers.

5.4.3 Seating arrangements

When preparing the SSI, the group of researchers thought that investigating about the seating arrangement would be relevant for access to non-verbal communication. The above-mentioned comments on this aspect seem to confirm that indeed the possibility to see all participants is perceived as important by children. For the younger ones, three chairs had been arranged in a small triangle with no table (Figure 5.1). When asked where the interpreter was sitting during the interview and where they would like him to sit next time, all children remembered the seating arrangement and said they had liked it and would not change it because it allowed them to watch both the interpreter and the interviewer.

The groups aged 10–17 were offered to choose where to sit and where to place the interviewer and the interpreter at a rectangular table with five chairs, and during the SSI they were asked to explain the reasons for their choice. The four children aged 10–13 chose to sit in front of the interviewer at one of the long sides of the table and placed the interpreter at the short side (Figure 5.1). Two of them specified that they asked the interpreter to sit in that place because: "It is not nice to say it, but the interpreter is a go-between"; "The interpreter is a sort of conduit"; the other two stressed they wanted eye contact with the interviewer and therefore had placed her in front of them,

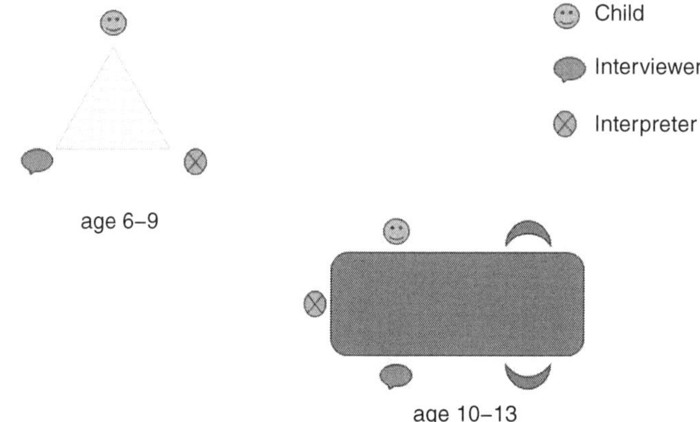

Figure 5.1 Seating arrangement for children aged 6–9 and 10–13.

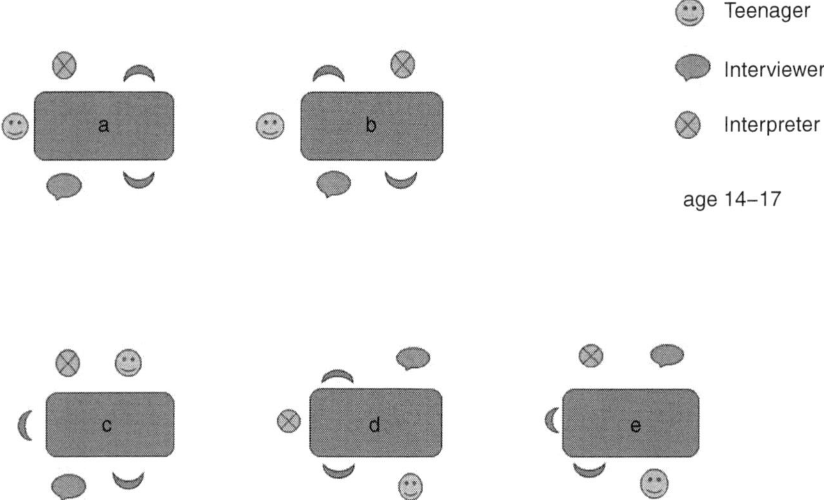

Figure 5.2 Seating arrangements chosen by teenagers (aged 14–17).

and one of them added that she chose that seating arrangement because she wanted to be sure she could hear the interpreter clearly. It could also be that the usual positions of teacher and pupils in a classroom influenced this choice.

The six teenagers instead made five different choices (Figure 5.2) and gave different reasons. Arrangement (a) was chosen by one boy and one girl who decided to sit at the short side of the table and asked the interviewer and the interpreter to sit one in front of the other at the long sides of the table. One of them explained that with this arrangement she could turn her head towards the interviewer or the interpreter when she was talking or listening to one or the other; the second teenager said he wanted to have direct eye contact with both conversation partners. Another boy chose to sit at the short side of the table with the interviewer and the interpreter one in front of the other at the long sides of the table, but the interpreter further away (arrangement b). He explained that for him the primary communication axis was with the interviewer, for whom he showed a strong liking from the very beginning. Arrangement (c) was chosen by another boy who sat at the long side of the table opposite to the interviewer and with the interpreter at his side. He explained that this way he could have eye contact with the interviewer while talking to "his" interpreter. Arrangements (d) and (e) were chosen by two girls who sat at the long side of the table opposite the interviewer, but one of them placed the interpreter at the short side of the table and the other one beside the interviewer, again in order to have direct eye contact with the interviewer.

Most teenagers said they would keep the same arrangement they had chosen if they had a chance to choose again. Trying to find a common denominator in the choices of the teenager group would be an unsuccessful exercise. The information they gave us is that they have individual preferences for seating arrangements and can motivate them and that offering them a choice can make them feel more at ease and possibly more empowered during an interview. This is particularly important when compared to a police psychologist's opinion we collected during a focus group; the police psychologist insisted that the interpreter should be sitting behind the child or teenager because the interviewer should be the sole conversation partner during the interview. Wiener and Rivera (2004) too claim that in psychotherapeutic sessions, whenever possible, the interpreter should sit to the side and a little behind the patient in order not to interfere in the patient–provider relationship.

The children and teenagers in our study wanted to establish eye contact with both the interviewer and the interpreter. Being briefed and placed in a neutral environment, children and teenagers who took part in this research project proved to be well aware of communication axes and components – both verbal and non-verbal – and of who was their main conversation partner (Section 5.4.2), and they attached great attention and importance to non-verbal cues. Their choice and reasons for seating arrangements confirm that seeing both the interpreter and the interviewer made them feel at ease and "in control" of the interaction. This idea is also supported by their negative perception of whispered interpreting: they generally expressed a dislike for it because they felt that not everything that was said could be heard (Section 5.4.1).

5.5 The perspective of children: caveats and conclusions

The aim of this study was to investigate children's feelings, impressions, and preferences after their first experience of communication through an interpreter during an interview. Obviously no general conclusions can be drawn from a small sample like this, nor do we know if our findings apply specifically to children since there was no adult control group. Some aspects, however, converge with what has been reported by other researchers. Results with our age group 6–9 years confirmed for example that young children can communicate successfully via an interpreter (see Kanstad, 2015; Nilsen, 2013; Solem, 2014). Hitching and Nilsen's (2010) conclusion that interpreters' personal qualities and flexibility are particularly relevant was indirectly confirmed by the large number of comments made by all age groups on the interpreter's collaborative attitude and ability to inspire trust. As far as their preferred interpreting mode was concerned, our respondents showed a dislike for *chuchotage*, as observed also by Solem (2014).

Experiencing a new way of communication raised mixed emotions as the interaction unfolded, from (initial) nervousness to (final) satisfaction about the unprecedented opportunity of speaking to a foreigner.

During the interpreted interview, almost all respondents noticed and reacted to verbal and non-verbal signs of attention and interest by the interviewer. Also her careful listening without interruptions was rated positively. Non-verbal communication and kinetic aspects were fully captured also by younger children, which suggests that either letting the child choose the seating arrangement or carefully planning it is probably the best way to allow the child to have eye contact with all participants.

Before drawing conclusions one point should be stressed once again. Although children were placed in the shoes of witnesses, the interviews did not take place in a legal setting or in a police station, and neither a psychologist nor a social worker was present. The interviews were conducted in an institutional context with unknown adults in an unfamiliar environment and the timeframe was rather limited, which must be taken into consideration in order to situate our participant's voices (Spyrou, 2011). Nonetheless this research provides some useful hints about the preferences of our participants which can be summarised as follows:

- being informed (i.e., know what to expect from the interview(er) and who does what and why)
- feeling at ease and not being put under pressure
- being listened to carefully
- not being interrupted
- having eye contact with both interviewer and interpreter
- being allowed to choose the seating arrangement.

Although this list may not be exhaustive and is open to additions, it reflects what the children and teenagers in our study appreciated and hopefully gives hints about what children want and feel when having to communicate through an interpreter. We hope with this study to inspire further research in this area and also, possibly, specialised training for interpreters who work or intend to work with children, in particular (but not only) in legal settings in the best interest of the child, because children can only enjoy their rights if they can understand them and can give their point of view.

Notes

1 This paper was originally published in a longer version on *InTRAlinea* 2021; 23. www.intralinea.org/current/article/the_best_interest_of_the_child_in_interpreter_mediated_interviews
2 www.unicef.org/child-rights-convention/frequently-asked-questions (last accessed 20.02.2021).
3 www.kidsrightsindex.org/Methodology/FAQs.
4 For reasons of space this paper will not touch upon interpreting in paediatric and mental health care settings, nor mention the vast literature on educational interpreting for deaf children. For a general overview, see Seiberlich (2013) and Winston (2015).
5 For a more comprehensive bibliographic overview on previous research in this area, see Van Schoor (2013), complemented by a National Children's Advocacy Center (2016) bibliography and Amato and Mack (2017).
6 See https://site.unibo.it/interpretazione-minori-cominor1/en and https://site.unibo.it/interpretazione-minori-cominor2/en/
7 See Terre des Hommes' Child Safeguarding Policy. www.terredeshommes.org/child-safeguarding-policy/
8 The age groups reflect the Italian school system articulated in 5 years of primary school, 3 years of junior high school, and 5 years of senior high school (in our case in Humanities).
9 The video was produced during a previous EU-funded research project "ImPLI" by Charles University in Prague, Faculty of Philosophy and Art, Institute of Translation Studies. www.youtube.com/watch?v=Yo9yUeEhH7Y&list=PLx15JSWFqoqCm5ycG6CKzxAQHE-YfrgIj&index=2&t=0s.
10 Unless otherwise stated, all links were last accessed on 15.09.2021.

References[10]

Amato, A., & Garwood, C. (2011). "Cultural mediators in Italy: A new breed of linguists." *inTRAlinea*, 13. www.intralinea.org/archive/article/1673.

Amato, A., & Mack, G. (2017). "Interpreters working with children in Italy. Profile, role and expectations". *inTRAlinea*, 19. www.intralinea.org/archive/article/2263.

Balogh, K., & Salaets, H. (eds.) (2015). *Children and Justice: Overcoming Language Barriers. Cooperation in Interpreter-Mediated Questioning of Minors.* Antwerp: Intersentia. www.arts.kuleuven.be/tolkwetenschap/projecten/co_minor_in_quest/children-and-justice.

Berg, B., Caspersen, J., Garvik, M., Paulsen, V., & Svendsen, T. (2018). *Bruk av Tolk i Barnevernsinstitusjoner og Omsorgssentre for Enslige Mindreårige.* Trondheim: NTNU Samfunnsforskning. https://samforsk.brage.unit.no/samforsk-xmlui/handle/11250/2569397.

Berg, B., & Tronstad, K.R. (2015). *Levekår for Barn i Asylsøkerfasen.* Trondheim: NTNU Samfunnsforskning. https://samforsk.no/Publikasjoner/Laevekar_2015_WEB.pdf.

Böser, U., & La Rooy, D. (2018). "Interpreter-mediated investigative interviews with minors: Setting the ground rules." *Translation and Interpreting Studies*, 13(2): 208–229.

Casadei, S., & Franceschetti, M. (2009). *Il Mediatore culturale in sei Paesi europei (Italia, Francia, Germania, Grecia, Regno Unito e Spagna). Ambiti di intervento, percorsi di accesso e competenze. Report di ricerca.* Rome: ISFOL. https://online.unistrasi.it/Avvisi/teormedAll.2.pdf.

Clark, A., Flewitt, R., Hammersley, M., & Robb, M. (eds.) (2013). *Understanding Research with Children and Young People.* London: Sage.

Conferenza delle Regioni e delle Province Autonome. (2009). *Riconoscimento della figura professionale del Mediatore Interculturale.* Document 09/030/CR/C9, Rome, 8 April 2009.

Einarsdottir, J. (2007). "Research with children: Methodological and ethical challenges." *European Early Childhood Education Research Journal*, 15(2): 197–211.

Falbo, C. (2013). *La comunicazione interlinguistica in ambito giuridico. Temi, problemi e prospettive di ricerca.* Trieste: EUT. www.openstarts.units.it/bitstream/10077/9306/1/Falbo_comunicazione_interlinguistica_giur.pdf.

Fargas-Malet, M., McSherry, D., Larkin, E., & Robinson, C. (2010). "Research with children: Methodological issues and innovative techniques." *Journal of Early Childhood Research*, 8(2): 175–192.

Hershkowitz, I. (2011). "Rapport building in investigative interviews of children." In *Children's Testimony. A Handbook of Psychological Research and Forensic Practice*, Lamb, M.E. et al. (eds.). Chichester, UK: Wiley Blackwell, pp. 109–128.

Hitching, T.R., & Nilsen, A.B. (eds.) (2010). *Tolking for Barn – en Statusrapport.* HiO report no. 20. Oslo: Høgskolen i Oslo.

IMPLI (2012). *IMPLI Improving Police and Legal Interpreting 2011–2012. Final Report.* Paris: Institut de Management et de Communication Interculturels. https://site.unibo.it/interpretazione-giuridica-impli/en/contributions.

Kanstad, M. (2015). "Språk, mestring og identitet. Kommunikasjon via tolk i tilvenningsfasen i barnehagen." in *Lek og samspill i et mangfoldsperspektiv.* Kibsgaard, S. & Kanstad, M. (eds.). Bergen: Fagbokforlaget, pp. 117–130.

Kanstad, M., & Gran, J. (2016). *Kommunikasjon med barn via tolk – et flerfaglig samarbeidsprosjekt.* Trondheim: RVTS Midt.

Keselman, O. (2009). "Restricting participation: Unaccompanied children in interpreter-mediated asylum hearings in Sweden." Linköping Studies in Arts and Science, 501.

Keselman, O., Cederborg, A.C., & Linell, P. (2010). "That is not necessary for you to know!: Negotiation of participation status of unaccompanied children in interpreter-mediated asylum hearings." *Interpreting*, 12(1): 83–104.

Keselman, O., Cederborg, A.N., Lamb, M.E., & Dahlström, Ö. (2010). "Asylum-seeking minors in interpreter-mediated interviews: What do they say and what happens to their responses?" *Journal of Child and Family Social Work*, 15(3): 325–334.

Kjelaas, I. (2016). *Barns deltakelse i institusjonelle samtaler. En studie av samtaler mellom enslige asylbarn og miljøarbeidere på omsorgssenter.* Trondheim: NTNU. https://ntnuopen.ntnu.no/ntnu-xmlui/handle/11250/2381994.

Kjelaas, I., & Eide, K. (2015). "Barnets stemme i tolkemedierte samtaler." *Norges Barnevern*, 92(2): 108–122.

Linell, P., & Keselman, O. (2010). "Trustworthiness at stake: Trust and distrust in investigative interviews with Russian adolescent asylum-seekers in Sweden. in *Trust and Conflict: Representation, Culture and Dialogue*. Marková, I. & Gillespie, A. (eds.). London: Routledge, pp. 156–180.

National Children's Advocacy Center (2016). *Interpreters in Forensic Interviews of Children. A Bibliography*. Huntsville, AL: National Children's Advocacy Center. www.nrcac.org/wp-content/uploads/2018/01/interpreters-forensic-interviews-bib.pdf.

Nilsen, A.B. (2013). "Exploring interpreting for young children." *Translation and Interpreting,* 5(2): 14–29. www.trans-int.org/index.php/transint/article/view/224.

Nilsen, A.B. (2015). "Interpreted communication with children in public-sector services." *Translation and Interpreting*, 7(3): 121–131. http://trans-int.org/index.php/transint/issue/view/376.

Øien, C. (2010). *Underveis. En studie av enslige mindreårige asylsøkere*. Oslo: Fafo. www.udi.no/globalassets/global/forskning-fou_i/beskyttelse/underveis-en-studie-av-enslige-mindreaarige-asylsokere.pdf.

O'Reilly, M., Ronzoni, P., & Dogra, N. (2013). *Research with Children. Theory and Practice*. London: Sage.

Poyatos, F. (1987). "Nonverbal communication in simultaneous and consecutive interpretation: A theoretical model and new perspectíves." *TEXTconTEXT*, 2(2–3): 73–108.

Rozzi, E. (2013). *Minori stranieri non accompagnati privi di protezione. Ricerca condotta a Torino nell'ambito del progetto PUCAFREU, Promoting unaccompanied children's access to their fundamental rights in the EU*. For project information in English, see Senovilla Hernandez, D. (2013). *Unaccompanied Children Lacking Protection in Europe. Final Comparative Report/* http://omm.hypotheses.org/files/2018/03/PUCAFREU-comparative-report-EN-1.pdf

Seiberlich, A. (2013). "Annotated bibliography. Interpreting in the educational setting (K-12)". University of Colorado's Distance Opportunities for Interpreter Education Centre.

Solem, L. (2014). *Les enfants utilisateurs d'interprétation. Analyse de la technique d'interprétation et du type de discours utilisés.* Mémoire de recherche en traductologie. Paris: ISIT.

Spyrou, S. (2011). "The limits of children's voice: From authenticity to critical, reflexive representation." *Childhood*, 18(2), 151–165.

UNESCO (1996a). Executive board. *World Conference on Linguistic Rights: Barcelona Declaration*. Document code: 150 EX/37, Paris, 10.10.1996. https://unesdoc.unesco.org/ark:/48223/pf0000104267?posInSet=2&queryId=4b69a590-b69f-4947-8fc9-27a867898624.

UNESCO (1996b). Universal Declaration of Linguistic Rights Follow-up Committee *Universal Declaration of Linguistic Rights.* https://culturalrights.net/descargas/drets_culturals389.pdf.

United Nations. (1989). *The UN Convention on the Rights of the Child. General Assembly Resolution 44/25 of 20 November 1989 (CRC)*. www.unicef-irc.org/portfolios/crc.html.

Van Schoor, D. (2013). *Interpreter-mediated interviews of child witnesses and victims: Status quaestionis.* M.A. thesis, Faculteit Letteren Taal en Communicatie, Antwerp. www.arts.kuleuven.be/english/rg_interpreting_studies/research-projects/co_minor_in_quest/interpreter-mediated-interviews-of-child-witnesses-and-victims-status-quaestionis.

Virág, G. (2015). "Interpreted interviews with highly vulnerable children." In *Children and Justice: Overcoming Language Barriers*, Balogh, B. & Salaets, H. (eds.). Antwerp: Intersentia, pp. 77–93.

Wiener, E.S., & Rivera, M.I. (2004). "Bridging language barriers: How to work with an interpreter." *Clinical Pediatric Emergency Medicine*, 5(2): 93–101.

Winston, E.A. (2015). "Educational interpreting." In *Routledge Encyclopedia of Interpreting Studies*, Pöchhacker, F. (ed.). London: Routledge, pp. 130–135.

Part II

Global practices

6 Mediation of trainee interpreters in police interrogations

Performance and perception of roles

Cheng Zhan

6.1 Introduction

Rabadán-Gómez (2016) defines public service interpreting as consecutive interpreting provided to speakers of languages other than the official language(s) of a country for them to access public services of that country. Among the many domains of public service interpreting, legal interpreting, including various categories such as police interviews and interrogations, lawyer–client conferences, tribunal hearings and court hearings and trials (Hale, 2007), is an area that has generated wide research interest.

In China, traditionally a society with a large population that is predominantly Chinese speaking, it is only in recent years that the need for public service interpreting has increased, mostly in metropolises on the coast. Despite the growing demand for legal interpreting service providers, owing to low-price competitions in the private market and lack of understanding about the complexities of such settings, the linguistic and communicative gap between foreign nationals involved in legal affairs and professionals, such as police officers, judges and lawyers, is often filled by non-professional interpreters, many of whom are trainees at local translation and interpreting (T&I) schools. The extremely charged interactions may present challenges and even ethical problems for them.

Both role performance as a discourse mediator and role perceptions among interpreting practitioners have been studied in various community settings, such as medical consultations and police interviews (Wadensjö, 1998; Angelelli, 2004; Hlavac et al., 2015; Martínez-Gómez, 2015; Drugan, 2017; Gallai, 2017; Zhan and Zeng, 2017). However, the actual performance of trainee interpreters and their self-perceptions of roles have not been sufficiently investigated and corroborated with authentic data, and merit more research input. With the purpose of addressing the risks that may arise from non-professional interpreting in legal settings, this chapter presents and discusses the findings of a study of police interrogations mediated by trainee interpreters, with an analysis of the role performance and role perceptions of them.

DOI: 10.4324/9781003197027-9

This research analyses interpreting done in police interrogations in South China's Guangzhou City. Based on a corpus of five police interrogations facilitated by trainee interpreters in Guangzhou with their post-task reflections, and focusing on discourse management, the research explores how the interpreter performs his/her role, and intends to answer the following questions:

1 How do trainee interpreters manage discourse in police interviews?
2 In what ways does their role performance create issues in the communication?
3 How do the interpreters' roles conform or run counter to their role perception?

6.2 Research background

6.2.1 The interpreter's role in police interrogations

In Hale's (2007) classification of main legal domains, police interrogations involve an antagonistic relationship between the police as questioner and suspect/detainee as answerer. The purpose of this kind of informal or semi-formal dialogue is to gather relevant facts and elicit a confession. As police interrogation is the initial step in the judicial process, the quality of interrogation directly bears upon judicial activities in terms of fairness and efficiency.

The role that interpreters play in such encounters therefore is not only important, but also delicate. The interpreter's role as a visible mediator in different public service domains has already been supported by previous studies. Angelelli's (2004) survey-based revisiting of the role of dialogue interpreters, for example, calls the neutral and invisible role of the interpreter into question, as her analysis shows that the way dialogue interpreters perceive themselves as well as how they perform in the process of interpreting do not conform with their expected role as a conduit. Police interrogations are often charged with emotive and ethical issues. Kredens (2017) therefore argues that having to make ethics-related choices frequently gives rise to a "transgressive shift in the role performed by the interpreter" (p. 74), through which one may gain insight into how this specific group of interpreters perceive their professional practice. Based on her analysis of T&I for the UK police, Drugan (2020) points out that complexity in both the settings and the range of parties and actors involved make collaborations between the interpreter and the police a kind of translaboration in police settings, in which the interpreter plays both the formal role as crime fighter and the informal role as informant. The problem with most of the above proposals, however, is that no authentic data were provided to show how interpreters' role performance conforms to or diverts from professional ethics.

6.2.2 Non-professional interpreters in police interrogations

Another possible problem with interpreted police interrogations is the fact that the professional level of interpreters varies. In contrast to professional interpreters who generally have been certified or trained in a degree programme, non-professional interpreters are seen to be "not possessing the required qualifications or skills to do the job" (Angelelli, 2019, p. 115). Angelelli argues that a major issue for using non-professional interpreters in public service interpreting is lack of guarantee for quality service (ibid., p. 124). Berk-Seligson strongly argues against "the willingness of the police to entrust to non-professional interpreters the task of questioning suspects during investigative police work", and goes so far as to call such behaviour "playing with fire" (Berk-Seligson, 2000, p. 233). Berk-Seligson's argument is corroborated by her analysis of a police interview involving a Spanish speaker assisted by a non-professional interpreter, who, being a constable himself, "in effect became an interrogator" (Berk-Seligson, 2004, p. 141). In a more recent study of public service interpreting done by intercultural mediators, Gil-Bardají (2020) finds that non-professional interpreters show a significant lack of accuracy, with most of the renditions subject to form or content modification, and even free interventions.

Based on review of relevant literature, Wang (2017) points out that non-professional interpreters account for a significant proportion of the private market in China, and summarises the three main differences between professional and non-professional interpreters, namely interpreting competence, experience and observation of professional standards and ethics.

6.2.3 Interpreter's mediation through discourse management

The dialogic structure of public service interpreting means that interpreters cannot work outside the communicative process and are in fact co-constructors of discourse, and their role as a mediator is often performed through discourse management. Based on her investigation of dialogue interpreting with a descriptive discourse analytical approach, Wadensjö (1998) concludes that "in dialogue interpreting, the translating and coordinating aspects are simultaneously present, and the one does not exclude the other" (p. 105). Roy's (2000) qualitative analysis of the dynamics of interactive discourse devotes special attention to turn-taking as an interdependent exchange process with its own unique and complex features. Her analysis has revealed the active role of the interpreter in dialogue interpreting as a cultural mediator. Based on her analysis of the participation framework, Metzger (1999) questions the long-held norm of interpreter neutrality, and argues that interpreters function within the discourse, in the form of triadic interaction. Zhan's (2012) analysis of dialogue interpreting involving government staff interpreters frequently shifting their personal pronouns and footing, and Nakane's (2007, 2011, 2014) comprehensive discussion about interpreters' turn construction, mediation of questioning and responding, and management of silence in police interviews, have offered more evidence from interpreting in different settings. Setting out from Angelelli's (2004) proposal of the continuum of visibility and with data analysis of medical consultations in a hospital in Guangzhou City, Zhan and Zeng (2017) conclude that the Chinese medical interpreters studied perform interpretation with high degrees of visibility by claiming either partial or total text ownership with the aim of exploring conclusion, redirecting turns, expressing solidarity or educating the patient.

Much as discourse management is seen as a strategy of interpreters, researchers are also aware of the risk of affecting the rights of the parties of communication, as one is warned against the possibility of "inaccurate social or psychological evaluations of witnesses" from register and stylistic shifts (Krouglov, 1999, p. 295) or unfaithful rendition caused by misunderstanding of "the goals of the institution and the way they are achieved through discourse strategies" (Hale, 2007, p. 73).

6.3 Research design and process

Data for this research are collected in the city of Guangzhou, which, as one of the major internationalised metropolises as well as the southern gateway to the Chinese Mainland, has a relatively large number of foreign residents and travellers, and therefore demands interpreting services for legal affairs involving non-Chinese speakers.

As many of the police interviews use non-professional interpreters such as interpreting trainees at local T&I schools and institutions, it is not rare to see that interpretation is often performed with much "flexibility". Interpreters in these cases perceive their role performance to be "cultural mediation" or employing "turn-taking strategies".

By analysing typical cases where the interpreter manifests a visible role through discoursal tools including text ownership and turn-taking strategies, and relating them to post-task reflections by the interpreter, the research identifies and describes how trainee interpreters mediate the process of police interrogations, and how their actual role performance may change the communication dynamics and even the direction of the dialogic exchange.

6.3.1 Interpreting for Chinese police

The interpreting tasks studied in this research took place in several locations across Guangzhou, including district police stations, detention house and municipal procuratorate and court. As legal cases involving foreign nationals have seen an increase over recent years (Chen, 2018), municipal as well as community-level police stations in Guangzhou have to come to terms with growing numbers of interviews and interrogations, before the cases go to intermediate or higher People's Courts for trials. As few frontline policemen speak

English, and local police are not equipped with abundant in-house language service resources, communication with foreign suspects or detainees is generally conducted with the help of interpreters sourced from the private market, in most cases interpreting trainees of local higher education institutions, for the payment is not attractive enough to professional interpreters.

6.3.2 *Trainees as non-professional interpreters*

The interpreters studied in this research are students in the first year of their graduate programme in T&I. They have obtained a bachelor's degree in English language, and are studying in a 2-year programme at a local T&I school towards a master's degree. The interrogation was not their first interpreting experience, though most of the interpreting done previously was simulated events in the classroom, which did not offer them an interface with real-world work experience.

For this research, the three non-professional interpreters studied are categorised more accurately as "trainee interpreters", for the boundaries between them and non-professional interpreters are not clear-cut. Wang (2017) categorises non-professional interpreters into three types, with trainees of the interpreting programme being one. For Wang, novice and trainee interpreters can be classified as non-professional interpreters, for they generally lack professional experience and quality, though they have acquired certain interpreting skills and competence. However, being at a stage of professional training towards a degree or certification, this special group of interpreters hardly fit in any of the categories that the terms or modifiers describe, including "naïve", "untrained", "volunteer", "ad hoc", "dual-role" or "bilingual" (Angelelli, 2019, pp. 115–116). The present study will therefore label them as "trainee interpreters" to show that they are in the professional training stage, but are more like non-professional interpreters in terms of competence, quality and management of ethics.

6.3.3 *Data collection*

Himself being an interpreter trainer, the researcher has had access to an archive of interpreting done by students, in the form of audio files with transcription done by students for later review and reflections. Five interpreted police interrogations, which took place between 2016 and 2018, were retrieved for analysis (Table 6.1). These tasks involved three different trainee interpreters, indicated as I1, I2, and I3, who were hired by the police through a local agency on the private market. In all the interrogations, all three parties, including one or two police officers, the interpreter and the suspect/detainee, were present. None of the police officers and suspects/detainees speak the other party's language, so they had to rely on the service of the trainee interpreter throughout the interrogation.

Table 6.1 Interpreted police interrogations studied for this research

No.	*Length (min.)*	*Interpreter*	*Setting*	*Total turns*
1	23	I1	Baiyun District Police Station	219
2	20.5	I2	Anti-Smuggling Bureau of Guangzhou Customs	204
3	10.6	I2	Liwan District Detention House	86
4	16	I3	Anti-Smuggling Bureau of Guangzhou Customs	172
5	21.2	I3	Guangzhou People's Procuratorate	188

6.4 Analysis and discussion

The following session will focus on case analysis of how the interpreter mediates the dialogic interactions by managing turns in the process and totally or partially owning a text (Angelelli, 2004). With the participation of the interpreter, the features of turn-taking in triadic exchanges are somewhat different from a dyad. Whether turn-taking can be conducted smoothly and whether the primary participants can achieve successful communication to realise their respective purpose and expectations largely depend on whether the interpreter can adopt effective and reasonable discourse strategies such as transferring, offering, creating, interrupting, stopping and accepting turns to deal with potential confusion, stagnation, silence or overlapping among primary participants, which might lead to conversational misunderstanding and difficulty.

Apart from managing turns, the interpreters are observed also to create utterance with both original messages from the two parties of communication and messages owned by the interpreter him/herself, and utterance with only interpreter-owned messages, which Angelelli (2004) describes as situations where the interpreter claims partial and total ownership.

A detailed case analysis of text ownership and turn-taking by the interpreter, and of the ways in which such discourse strategies show the interpreter's multiple mediation roles, is presented and discussed below.

6.4.1 Inducing information

It can be inferred from Angelelli's (2004) analysis of medical consultations that when an interpreter creates his/her own text in order to obtain an answer from the patient, triggered by a question, the interpreter is exploring an answer. However, the interpreter is found to often create his/her own line(s) to get more information from the suspect other than what the police officer is asking for. Such effort of the interpreter to reach complete information, by being the owner or co-owner of an utterance so as to meet the expectation of the police, is classified as inducing information.

Example 1 (no. 3 – Liwan District Detention House, turns 56–84) (see Appendix 6.1)

POLICE OFFICER: 叫他把从尼日利亚走私毒品到中国这个事情的经过，从头，按照时间顺序讲清楚。(56)
(Tell him to tell us the whole thing about smuggling drugs from Nigeria to China clearly, from the beginning, in chronological order.)
INTERPRETER: Now tell us the process of how did you smuggle drugs from Nigeria into China from the beginning to the end, especially the time, the place and people connected to this case. (57)
SUSPECT: At the beginning, somebody called me there was something he wanted me to bring to Guangzhou, China. (58)
INTERPRETER: What is the name of the person? (59)
SUSPECT: Emma Oniayebuchi. (60)
INTERPRETER: Can you spell it? (61)
SUSPECT: E-M-M-A, O-N-I-A-Y-E-B-U-C-H-I. (62)
INTERPRETER: When did she call you? (63)
SUSPECT: The time is 25th September. (64)
INTERPRETER: This year? (65)
SUSPECT: 25th September, 2017. (66)
((interpreter writes down the information))
POLICE OFFICER: 他有没有吸过毒？(67)
(Has he ever taken drugs?)
INTERPRETER: Did you smoke drugs? (68)
SUSPECT: I smoke marijuana. (69)
INTERPRETER: 吸大麻。(70)
(He smokes marijuana.)
POLICE OFFICER: 吸了多久？ 他一直吸还是？(71)
(For how long? Does he always smoke or …?)
INTERPRETER: How long have you been smoking marijuana? (72)
SUSPECT: I started to smoke two months ago. (73)
INTERPRETER: 两个月之前开始吸的。(74)
(Started two months ago.)
POLICE OFFICER: 就吸过一次呢还是？(75)
(Did he smoke only once or …?)
INTERPRETER: Just once or more than once? (76)
SUSPECT: I took it once when things were difficult. And I took it to get peace in my heart. (77)
INTERPRETER: 只吸过一次。(78)
(Only once.)
POLICE OFFICER: 你还有没有什么话要补充？(79)
(Do you have anything else to add?)
INTERPRETER: Do you have anything else to say? (80)

SUSPECT: Yeah. I have something to say. I wanna go home. I am innocent. I respect the Chinese law and I am … (81)

INTERPRETER: [Do you have any information **concerning the case**? (82)

SUSPECT: You ask me whether I have something to say. I do. I want to complain, I … INTERPRETER (83): [Any information **related to the case**. Tell the police. (84)

The above interrogation took place in Liwan District Detention House. A Nigerian man was suspected of smuggling drugs into China, and was detained for questioning. It can be seen that the police officer is not an experienced interpreter user, as he keeps speaking to the interpreter and using third-person pronouns (他, he) to refer to the suspect, and only at the end of this encounter (79) turns to the suspect for further information. The illocutionary style of the police officer seems to have turned this dialogue into a two-part one, between the police officer and the interpreter, and between the interpreter and the suspect. The triadic relationships are for most of the time broken. This may have led the interpreter into taking more initiatives to create his own utterances to keep the communication flowing more naturally. When the police officer initiates a turn by demanding that the suspect tell him the whole process of drug smuggling into China (56), the interpreter extends the simple instruction and goes into greater details by giving more specific directions about the time, place and people (57). This clearly is an effort to induce information. The effect of such a partially owned text is twofold. On the one hand, the suspect is made to answer the question in a way that the interpreter feels is elaborative and effective, as it can be seen in the following turns that the suspect did follow the pattern set by the interpreter. On the other hand, the communication may have become more efficient, as the police officer's general question is explained for the suspect and he is guided in answering the question in a more "effective" way.

From turns 58 to 66, the interpreter engages in a dialogue with the suspect. She addresses the suspect directly, interpreting none of the suspect's answer back to the police officer. Without being prompted by an original line from either party, the interpreter keeps asking follow-up questions by creating totally owned texts to induce further information about the person and time. It is clear that the interpreter voluntarily asks the suspect for information the police officer seeks. The interpreter's visibility here is shown by her creation of text, supported by her intention to help the interlocutors induce information. The interpreter's role therefore is shifted from a co-constructor of discourse to an interrogator who owns her text. This ends when the police officer initiates a new question about whether the suspect has taken drugs himself (67). Here the interpreter's rendition is somewhat problematic, as she interprets "吸毒" into "smoke drugs" (68). This may have been a problem of the Chinese expression "吸毒". The verb "吸" literally means "inhale or smoke". But in the collocation of "吸毒", the denotation of the verb is not limited to the single method of "smoke". As the interpreter renders "吸毒" into "smoke drugs" (68), the suspect answers that he smokes marijuana (69). This can be a piece of misleading information, for the suspect may have taken other types of drugs, but marijuana is the one that he has actually "smoked".

Towards the end of the interrogation, the police officer asks if the suspect has anything else to say. The suspect then starts his plea for help, insisting on his innocence. However, his two turns (81 and 83) are interrupted twice by the interpreter, who demands only information pertaining to the case. When the suspect becomes agitated and starts to complain (83), he is cut short again, with the interpreter insisting on information "related to the case". It is interesting how the interpreter feels that the suspect's utterances are not relevant, but as the suspect becomes so upset that he gives up at the end, his legal right is in fact infringed upon. For the interpreter, contrary to what she seeks to achieve, she fails to induce more information from the suspect.

6.4.2 Expressing solidarity

Hale (2007) argues that the already antagonistic relations between the police officer and the suspect/detainee may become more complex with the interpreter's presence. The interpreter needs to redress the imbalance of power, but very often falls into the role of an advocate or a legal representative for the police. In the interpreted interrogations studied, the interpreter is sometimes found to take sides with the police officer and express solidarity by taking initiatives to perform interrogation.

Example 2 (no. 5 – Guangzhou People's Procuratorate, turns 12–36)

POLICE OFFICER: 她来中国几次了？(12)
(How many times has she been in China?)
INTERPRETER: How many times have you ever been to China? (13)
SUSPECT: I do not know the road signs. And I just … (14)
INTERPRETER: [I just ask you the number. Answer what I ask you. How many times have you been to China? (15)
SUSPECT: Three. (16)
INTERPRETER: 三次了。(17)
(Three.)
POLICE OFFICER: 给她说一下那个逮捕证延期的事情。(18)
(Tell her about the renewal of the arrest warrant.)
INTERPRETER: Last time, we gave you an arrest warrant and it meets its deadline. But the case is still under investigation. We should show you another arrest warrant. This is our new arrest warrant. You should still stay here another month. Sign your name and date. (19)

SUSPECT: What? Oh, no. Oh, my god. Oh, no. ((suspect breaks into tears and shakes her head)) (20)
INTERPRETER: 啊，她哭了。她说，我的天呐。(21)
(Oh, she cries. She said, "My god.")
POLICE OFFICER: 你告诉她，触犯法律就是要受到惩罚的。(22)
(You tell her, one shall be punished for violating the law.)
INTERPRETER: As you violated our Chinese law, you must receive punishment. (23)
SUSPECT: I have my children; I have to look after them. Please, please let me go home. Please … ((suspect continues weeping)) (24)
INTERPRETER: Sorry. We will investigate as soon as possible, and please cooperate with us. We will give you light punishment if you tell us the truth. (25)
SUSPECT: OK. Please help me. (26)
POLICE OFFICER: 她带了多少现金过来？(27)
(How much cash did she bring here?)
INTERPRETER: How much money did you take this time? (28)
SUSPECT: I did not take much money. My brother will … (29)
INTERPRETER: [How much cash did you take? Give me the number.
POLICE OFFICER: 多少啊？你就问她具体数字，你别听她讲那么多。这么解释来解释去的，这提审一天都结束不了了。(30)
(Just how much? You just ask her the exact number. Don't listen to her long talks. If she goes on explaining this and that, the interrogation will not finish in a day.)
INTERPRETER: I want to know the cash. The number, please. (31)
SUSPECT 1000 dollars and … I cannot remember. (32)
INTERPRETER: A general number. (33)
SUSPECT: About 1750 dollars. (34)
INTERPRETER: 她说大约1750美元，不过这不是所有用于做生意的钱。(35)
(She said about 1750 dollars, but it's not all for her business.)
POLICE OFFICER: 不是做生意的钱，那是干什么的？(36)
(Not all for business? Then what's it for?)

In this example, an Australian woman is detained for smuggling. The purpose of this interrogation is to inform the suspect of the arrest warrant expiry and renewal, and to gather information for the case. The interpreter's role starts to shift to an interrogator not long after the interrogation starts, when the police officer asks the detainee about her previous visits to China (12), as he interrupts the detainee's turn (14) quickly and starts his own text "I just ask you the number. Answer what I ask you. How many times have you been to China?" It should be noted that the first-person pronoun "I" is used. This is not ethically unproblematic, as the police officer probably has no intention for, or even no idea about, such a coercive instruction. If the "I" used here is the speaker's "I" (Harris, 1990), then one may ask who the speaker really is.

Clearly the interpreter claims total text ownership, and assumes the role of an interrogator, without the police officer demanding him to do so.

At turn 18, the police officer asks the interpreter to tell the suspect about the renewal of the arrest warrant. The instruction is straightforward and very simple. There is no explanation about the whole thing. This indicates that the police officer trusts the interpreter to understand the situation and convey the message fully and accurately. The interpreter's text ownership expressed in turn 19 reveals his awareness of his power and knowledge. He becomes a visible constructor of discourse. The use of first-person plural pronoun "we" makes him an active participant in the interrogation. He then changes his footing at turn 21 to that of a commentator or third-party reporter, when he tells the police officer that the suspect is crying. This again is a violation of the guidelines of legal interpreting.

When the police officer warns the detainee of punishment for violation of the law (22), the Chinese sentence interestingly does not have a subject. While it is perfectly acceptable for a sentence in Chinese to have no subject, the interpreter has to make a choice for a grammatically and pragmatically suitable subject in his translation. Instead of rendering the sentence into a more general one carrying a generic subject (one, for example), he chooses to use the second-person pronoun "you" in his rendition, which in effect changes the modality of the original utterance. The interpreter again sounds as if he is interrogating the detainee. The ethical confusion grows when he starts to put the detainee at ease and express solidarity by assuring her that if she cooperates with the police, which the pronoun "us" denotes, her punishment will be lightened.

Later, the police officer inquires about the sum of cash (27), and the interpreter redirects the flow of communication by interrupting the turn of the suspect and creating a text with total ownership. When the police officer becomes impatient and urges the interpreter not to listen to the explanation of the suspect, the purpose of seeking confession becomes so obvious that the interpreter immediately initiates a couple of turns with the suspect and presses her for a number. However, after the suspect gives her response, the interpreter creates a partially owned text and brings in a piece of information that the money is not all used for her business, which the suspect never says (35). This clearly redirects the interrogation to a new topic, as the police officer follows up by raising the question "Then what's it for" (36). The interpreter's mediation in this case proves to be a conspicuous factor in the information exchange and power relations of the interrogation.

6.4.3 Building rapport

Hale (2007, p. 73) points out that in confrontational situations of legal interpreting, the "inherent animosity between the participants" often gives rise to greater complexities in the role performance of the interpreter, who is entangled in the expectation of the police to be an assistant and the suspect's mistrust in him/her as a police offsider. In police interrogations, as a bilingual person who mediates across languages and cultures, the interpreter easily becomes someone to cling to for help or someone to threaten for information disclosure, and thus may resort to discoursal means to build rapport and redress the imbalance of power.

Example 3 (no. 1 – Baiyun District Police Station, turns 52–66)

POLICE OFFICER: 让他讲讲他和阿拉伍森之后的那天下午做了什么？(52)
(Tell him to say something about what he and Alawsen did later that afternoon.)
INTERPRETER: What did Alawsen and you do that afternoon? (53)
SUSPECT: We sent the package and then went to play football. Then … ((suspects knocks his head on the table)) (54)
POLICE OFFICER: 你给他说让他冷静。((stands up)) (55)
(Tell him to calm down.)
INTERPRETER: Please be quiet. ((suspects keeps hitting himself in the chair)) If you truthfully tell us what you know, we will give you justice. We will help you, if you cooperate with us. (56)
SUSPECT: Help me? Can you call my wife? (57)
INTERPRETER: ° Do not hurt yourself.。 (58)
POLICE OFFICER: 那你还要这么多钱干嘛？(59)
(What did you need this much money for?)
INTERPRETER: Why did you still need that money? (60)
SUSPECT: I just want my children to live better. (61)
INTERPRETER: 他只是想让孩子们过得更好一点。(62)
(He just wants his children to live a better life.)
SUSPECT: I miss my children. I miss them very much. I really have no idea about the drugs in my luggage. When can I go back home? I really miss my children. (63)
INTERPRETER: Don't worry. I'll ask the police officer. (64)
INTERPRETER: 他说他很想念他的孩子们。他真的不知道他行李里有毒品。他问他什么时候能回家。他很想念他的孩子们。(65)
(He said he missed his children. He really didn't know there were drugs in his luggage. He asked when he could go home. He really missed his children.)
POLICE OFFICER: 那要看他交代的情况了。(66)
(Then it depends on how he tells us about the whole thing.)
INTERPRETER: If you tell the truth, you can go back home. (67)

The above interrogation took place in Baiyun District Police Station. In the luggage of an Australian man in his 50s, the airport police found drugs. The man was held in detention and interrogated. The interrogation becomes emotively charged when the suspect starts to knock himself in the chair. In the post-task reflections of the interpreter, she admits that when she saw the violent behaviour of the suspect, she was a bit "shocked and scared". This may explain why the interpreter sounds quite friendly to the suspect and shows sympathy. When the police officer demands that the suspect calm down (55), the interpreter does not strictly render that into an instruction, but utters a much softer request "please be quiet". Such a rendition changes the modality of the discourse and could serve to ease the suspect out of confrontation. As the suspect continues to hit himself, the interpreter creates a totally owned text, saying "If you truthfully tell us what you know, we will give you justice. We will help you, if you cooperate with us". This effort to build a rapport is confirmed by post-task reflections of the trainee interpreter, who claims that she utters the sentence by herself to "control the situation", and that "the suspect became calm after hearing the word 'help'". The interpreter was actually spoken highly of by the police officer for her "quick-wittedness in the face of emergency". This happens twice later in the interrogation (58 and 64), when the interpreter sympathises with the suspect and comforts him with self-initiated turns. When asked about her text creation, the interpreter said that she was fully aware of such a role shift from an interpreter to an advocate, and explained that "as a human being, it was hard not to feel sympathetic for the man". However, even the intention to build rapport may not justify the interpreter's final line in this excerpt, "If you tell the truth, you can go back home". When the interpreter becomes too visible, one may ask whether this truly is desirable in terms of the aims of the participants. As Hale (2007) argues, the interpreter's allegiance should not lie with either the police or the detainee, but rather with the communication process. Interpreters in such settings should resist pressure, or rather in this case, temptation, to take sides.

6.5 Summary and conclusion

Analysis of the five interpreted police interrogations shows that trainee interpreters frequently break away from the norms and ethics of impartiality and fidelity, and take initiatives to mediate the discourse process through the creation of totally owned or partially owned texts and start, interrupt or ignore a turn in dialogic exchanges, with the purposes of inducing information, expressing solidarity or building rapport. The trainee interpreters' role is that of mediation with significant visibility. However, it is also found that the trainee interpreters studied perform their roles with so much flexibility and even transgression that instead of facilitating the communication process, their mediation more often than not changes the discourse modality and meaning, thus creating misunderstandings of the interpersonal intentions of the participating parties, or ethical problems, in extreme cases.

These findings, when juxtaposed with the trainee interpreters' post-task reflections, reveal a gap between their role performance and perception. As students in a graduate programme of T&I, the trainee interpreters of these police interrogations kept a learning journal, and wrote reports on their interpreting tasks. A major part of their reflections is on how they feel about their interpreting performance in the framework of interpreter roles and ethics. Critical reviews of their performance show that the three trainee interpreters are quite satisfied with their performance, although I1 commented that she was perhaps being a bit sympathetic to the suspect, particularly after seeing his violent behaviour and hearing him talk about his children. However, she also reported that her mediation was "spoken highly of" by the police officer onsite.

All three trainee interpreters were aware of the codes of conduct, but they also seemed to assume that they were to accomplish the communicative goals of helping the police gather information and seek confession from the suspect/detainee. Based on such assumption, they described their roles as "a problem solver", "a linguistic controller" (I1), "a service provider", "a co-constructor of conversation" (I2) and "a mediator", "an assistant" (I3). Despite the fact that these descriptions from trainee interpreters may point to slight visibility based on an established conception of professional ethics and norms that they were exposed to in their training process, their actual role performance transgressed such role perceptions.

Given the data size and homogeneity in the training background of the interpreters, the findings of this research cannot reveal the topic in its universality. However, with these specific cases of police interrogations, the research at least reveals a gap between the actual performance of trainee interpreters and their perception of roles. Trainee interpreters not only actively participate in interactions, but also have the power, through discoursal means such as text ownership and turn-taking, to bring changes to the dynamics of dialogic exchanges. Some ethical issues can be detected from there, and merit further analysis with empirical data, so as to qualify the risks involved. It would also be useful to compare non-professional interpreters' performance with that of professionals, to identify the gap in understating and observation of professional norms and ethics that arises from stages of training and different levels of professionalism. At this point, an understanding can be reached that professional training for interpreters and client education need to play a part in shaping non-professional interpreters' perception of their role and helping them deal with challenging interactive tasks where the norms of impartiality and fidelity should still have an important place.

Appendix 6.1

The transcription convention in this paper is drawn from Wadensjö (1998):

[line brackets indicate that people are speaking simultaneously
, continuing intonation (usually with a rising or sustained tone)
. terminating intonation (usually with a falling tone)

?	questioning intonation (usually with a rising tone)
...	open-ended intonation (fading out, ambiguous intonation terminal)
(())	non-verbal feature
Boldface	words spoken with emphasis
° °	part of an utterance framed by these is spoken relatively quietly

References

Angelelli, C. V. (2004). *Medical interpreting and cross-cultural communication*. Cambridge: Cambridge University Press.

Angelelli, C. V. (2019). "Non-professional interpreting and translation (NPIT)." In Angelon, E., Ehrensberger-Dow, M. & Massey, G. (eds.), *The Bloomsbury companion to language industry studies*. New York: Bloomsbury. 115–137.

Berk-Seligson, S. (2000). "Interpreting for the police: issues in pre-trial phases of the judicial process." *Forensic Linguistics*, 7(2), 212–237.

Berk-Seligson, S. (2004). "The Miranda warnings and linguistic coercion: the role of footing in the interrogation of a limited English-speaking murder suspect." In Janet Cotterill (ed.), *Language in the legal process*. New York: Palgrave Macmillan. 127–143.

Chen, Y. (2018). "Big data analysis on foreign civil and commercial cases." *Legal System and Sociery*, 01, 213–214. [陈绎帆. 涉外民商事案件的大数据分析. *法治与社会*, 2018 (01)上:213–214.]

Drugan, J. (2017). "Ethics and social responsibility in practice: interpreters and translators engaging with and beyond the professions." *The Translator*, 23(2), 126–142.

Drugan, J. (2020). "Complex collaborations: Interpreting and translating for the UK police." *Target*, 32(2), 307–326.

Gallai, F. (2017). "Pragmatic competence and interpreter-mediated police investigative interviews." *The Translator*, 23(2), 177–196.

Gil-Bardají, A. (2020). "Ethics, accuracy, and interpreting in social settings: assessing a non-professional interpreter profile." *Translation and Interpreting Studies*, 15(1), 132–152.

Hale, S. (2007). *Community interpreting*. London: Palgrave Macmillan.

Harris, B. (1990). "Norms in interpretation." *Target*, 2(1), 115–119.

Hlavac, J., Xu, Z. & Yong, D. X. (2015). "Intercultural pragmatics at work: (self-)perceptions of intercultural behavior of Chinese and English speakers and interpreters in healthcare interactions." *Intercultural Pragmatics*, 12(1), 91–118.

Kredens, K. (2017). "Conflict or convergence? Interpreters' and police officers' perceptions of the role of the public service interpreter." *Language and Law/ Linguagem e Direito*, 3(2), 65–77.

Krouglov, A. (1999). "Police interpreting: politeness and sociocultural context." *The Translator*, 5(2), 285–302.

Martínez-Gómez, A. (2015). "Bibliometrics as a tool to map uncharted territory: a study on non-professional interpreting." *Perspectives*, 23(2), 205–222.

Metzger, M. (1999). *Sign language interpreting. Deconstructing the myth of neutrality*. Washington, DC: Gallaudet University Press.

Nakane, I. (2007). "Problems in communicating the suspect's rights in interpreted police interviews." *Applied Linguistics*, 28(1), 87–112.

Nakane, I. (2011). "The role of silence in interpreted police interviews." *Journal of Pragmatics*, 43(9), 2317–2330.

Nakane, I. (2014). *Interpreter-mediated police interviews: A discourse-pragmatic approach*. London: Palgrave Macmillan.

Rabadán-Gómez, M. (2016). "Introduction." In Munyangeyo, T., Webb, G., & Rabadán-Gómez, M, *Challenges and opportunities in public service interpreting*. London: Palgrave Macmillan. 1–7.

Roy, C. (2000). *Interpreting as a discourse process*. New York: Oxford University Press.

Wadensjö, C. (1998). *Interpreting as interaction*. London: Longman.

Wang, Y. (2017). "Non-professional interpreting: retrospect and prospect." *Translation Horizons*, 1, 17–27. [王炎强. 非职业口译：回顾与前瞻. *翻译界*, 2017(1): 17–27.]

Zhan, C. (2012). "Mediation through personal pronoun shifts in dialogue interpreting of political meetings." *Interpreting*, 14(2), 192–216.

Zhan, C. & Zeng, L. (2017). "Chinese medical interpreters' visibility through text ownership: An empirical study on interpreted dialogues at a hospital in Guangzhou." *Interpreting*, 19(1), 98–118.

7 Overlaps in interpreter-mediated institutional talk in the courtroom

Agnieszka Dominika Biernacka

7.1 Introduction

Overlaps occur as varieties of a transition space (Sacks et al., 1974; Jefferson, 1986), that is, the instances between particular turns of particular speakers. In other words, in taking turns the speakers break the rules of waiting until the current speaker completes their utterance. More specifically, longer overlaps in which speakers produce at least some fragments of their utterances at the same time in the conversation are interruptions that can be problematic for interlocutors (Liddicoat, 2011, p. 113). Nonetheless, in casual conversations, not all overlaps interrupt a conversation or violate the rules of interaction; instead, they may be a manifestation of the parties' interest in the subject of the talk (Díaz-Campos et al., 2017, p. 290). Apart from being spontaneous indications of the interlocutor's need to speak, overlapping can occur for reasons such as asking for help, breaking up, completing, correcting, seeking clarification, or disagreeing (Wardhaugh, 1985). Therefore, as Truong (2013) puts it, there can be cooperative and competitive overlaps. In cooperative overlapping both the overlapper and the overlappee *cooperate* to make the act of communication develop smoothly in terms of obtaining the information required by both parties. In competitive overlapping the overlapper *competes* with the overlappee; this *competition* takes place because the interlocutor wants to show disagreement or correct what the other party has said.

7.2 Overlapping as an ethical problem of bilingual courtroom interactions

As regards mechanisms in interpreter-mediated talks, overlaps are – along with conflicts of interest, lack of competence, contradictory requirements and expectations of clients, bad working conditions, as well as cultural and personal issues – one of the reasons for interpreters' moral dilemmas (Hale, 2007, p. 116). Roy (1990) finds out that it is impossible to interpret consecutively overlapping utterances produced by several main speakers. She further indicates that interpreters try to solve the problem of potential misunderstanding of those instances where overlapping appears. She specifies

DOI: 10.4324/9781003197027-10

that some interpreters interrupt one speaker to let the other speak while others ignore all overlapping utterances. Yet other interpreters ignore overlapping utterances by interpreting one of them, and then interpreting the other as precisely as the interpreter's memory permits. Others ignore the utterance produced as the second one, interpret the first, and then ask for repetition of the second utterance (Roy, 1990, p. 85). According to Hale (2007, p. 75), such choices are evident and used on a regular basis by interpreters who have to cope with overlapping utterances produced by witnesses and lawyers representing the parties to the proceedings who struggle to obtain and maintain control over the speakers and the content of their talks. This means that the principles arising out of the codes of ethics cannot provide a ready solution to the problematic instances of the act of communication; hence, interpreters must frequently and intuitively decide how to proceed in a particular communicative event (ibid., p. 116). Consequently, in the case of court interpreters, who are obliged to comply with the principle of accuracy, such decisions mean that they either obey or disobey their respective codes of ethics.

In Poland, interpreters are obliged – not only ethically, but also legally – to satisfy a set of rules and principles governing their profession. As regards legal documents, the *Act on the Profession of Sworn Translator* of 25 November 2004[1] sets forth fundamental principles binding upon sworn translators and interpreters who are in general the only ones allowed to render their services before the court. In particular, an oath taken pursuant to the Act by newly appointed sworn translators and interpreters specifies principles such as due diligence, honesty, and professional ethics, to mention just those strictly connected with a broadly understood accuracy. In turn, the principles of professional ethics are included in *The Sworn Translator's Professional Code.*[2] *The Code* defines *accuracy* as the sworn translator's obligation to "translate statements made by foreigners exactly in the form in which they were expressed in writing or orally, rendering the whole content, without omitting, adding or modifying anything", and to respect the style of the original utterance.

Taking both legal and ethical aspects of court interpreting into consideration, it can be speculated that if accurate rendition of the original utterances is a fundamental issue, then judges presiding over particular trials should enable interpreters to comply with this principle. Indeed, studies of the inquisitorial procedure of the Polish monolingual courtroom confirm the question–answer sequence of the talk, the rigid order of turn-taking, and the dialogical form of the talk (Bednarek, 2014, p. 139). These findings can give the impression that no interruptions of the order of speaking by individual parties to the court proceedings occur. At the same time, however, studies in the field of the Polish–English and Polish–Spanish bilingual courtroom show a multidirectionality of interactions (Biernacka, 2019, p. 287). This means that all parties in the act of communication, be it the main speakers or interpreters, interact with one another. This in turn might prove that judges rather do not use their power to impose a specific order according to which the arguing parties would speak. Therefore, it can be speculated that it is inevitable that interpreters are exposed to the need to render such instances as overlapping.

7.3 Research questions

In light of the findings concerning the inherent peculiarities of mono- and bilingual institutional talk, the aim of the analysis is to discuss these overlaps from the perspective of: (1) the interpreter's participation in the turn-taking system at institutional talk; (2) the interpreter's renditions of institutional talk; and (3) the interpreter complying with an ethical principle of accuracy. Therefore, this study intends to answer the following questions:

1 In what way do court interpreters participate in the turn-taking system as far as overlapping is concerned, and in particular, are they only overlappers or only overlappees, or both?
2 How do court interpreters cope with overlaps produced between the main speakers?
3 Do the reasons for overlapping differ depending on which party in the act of communication deploys an overlap?

7.4 Method

In order to find answers to the above questions, this small-scale qualitative study is designed to analyse ten bilingual, Polish–English, episodes of interaction, in which overlapping appears.

The study is limited only to these ten episodes as emblematic of all the overlaps identified within bilateral real-world communicative events, which form part of naturally occurring data obtained during a search query (2013–2014) at the Civil and Economic Divisions of the Regional Court in Warsaw, Poland. The entire Polish–English material comprises a total of 37 hours of oral court proceedings, in which 12 interpreters rendered their services. Taking the bureaucratic obstacles to obtaining such sensible data into account, it is worth emphasizing that the episodes of interaction extracted from the collected material constitute a valuable dataset, thus, despite different aspects having already been analysed (Biernacka, 2019, 2020), should be subject to further research.

The material obtained during the search query was in the form of electronic minutes comprising both the audio-visual recordings and the minutes taken by court clerks during particular court hearings. It is worth calling attention to these electronic minutes as an obligatory procedure introduced in Poland by the Act of 29 April 2010 amending the act – Code of Civil Procedure (Journal of Laws No. 108, item 684). Since the Act came into force on 1 July 2010, the Polish courts have been obliged to take the electronic minutes of all hearings in civil cases. Consequently, the author of this study could only access these electronic minutes, which means that it was impossible to record the proceedings independently.

Table 7.1 Transcription symbols

Symbol	*Meaning*
Judge:	Current speaker
a:::	Long vowel (the longer the sound, the higher the number of colons)
…	Open-ended intonation
.	Falling intonation
,	Slightly rising intonation
?	Rising intonation
court	Words spoken with emphasis
°court°	Words spoken quietly
>the court<	Words spoken faster than the surrounding talk
<the court>	Words spoken slower than the surrounding talk
h	Breathiness
=	No discernible interval between the units of talk
[	Overlaps
(.)	Micro-pause (very short silence)
(0.5)	Half-second pause
(2.0)	Two-second pause
(xxx)	Inaudible words due to technical problems, *chuchotage*, or silence
((looks up)) ((knocking))	Non-verbal element of the talk or information added by the author

As no transcripts of the hearings were available, the author had to prepare them by herself. Technically speaking, the author transcribed the hearings based on both the recordings and the minutes manually, by playing, stopping, rewinding, and winding the recordings. This was because access to the material was on the computers available in the courts' libraries and the author could not use any external programs or transcription applications.

The conventions used for the transcription of the acts of communication subject to this empirical study are a compilation of symbols originally proposed for monolingual talks (Sacks et al., 1974; Jefferson, 1983, 1986, 2004) and then applied for the purposes of the research in the field of interpreting studies (cf. Wadensjö, 1998; Jacobsen, 2004; Biernacka, 2019) (Table 7.1).

The preliminary processing of the transcripts consisted of making all personal data anonymous so that any identification of the interlocutors and circumstances they refer to was impossible. To this aim, the author not only deleted or changed personal information, but also isolated very short episodes of interaction.

Each episode of interaction, or act of communication, forms an integrated whole, in which the parties to the proceedings focus on a particular issue. The episodes of interaction are given in Tables 7.2–7.10, in which original Polish/English talk is on the left side, while the author's verbatim translation into English is in italics on the right side. The verbatim translations are only to help non-Polish-speaking readers to understand the episodes, and not to

Table 7.2 Interpreter-excluded overlapping produced by the petitioner's lawyer

Speaker	*Original Polish/English talk*	*Author's verbatim translation into English*
Petitioner's lawyer	proszę pana (0.2) mówiąc o zdradach rzekomych pana X (.) powiedział pan (.) że o jednej dowiedział się od Y (.) o jednej od Z. =	*Sir, when you speak about the alleged infidelity of X, you said that you learned about one from Y, and about another one from Z.*
Respondent's lawyer	= nie – (0.2) o jednej się dowiedział od partne:ra (.) [tak powiedział.	*No, he learned about one from the partner, he said so.*
Petitioner's lawyer	[czy od partnera (.) przepraszam (.) a o innej że (.) trzeciej jakby (0.2) że widział inną (0.3) co mam >przez to rozumieć<? =	*Or from the partner, I'm sorry, and about another one, that, the third one, that he saw another one. How should I understand this?*
Interpreter	= when you said about Z cheating (0.2) you said that one you learnt from your partner (.) one from X and one you witnessed?	
Witness	yhm.	
Interpreter	what do you mean by that?	
Witness	e::::: (.) the one I witnessed?	
Interpreter	((nodding)) o tej (.) którą widziałem (0.2) tak. =	*About the one I saw, yes.*
Witness	= yes.	
Interpreter	tak.	*Yes.*

instruct the interpreters to provide such renditions from Polish into English as the only correct ones. For this reason, any mistakes in the interpreter's or other interlocutors' talks are copied in the author's verbatim translation. For the same reason the lexical issues are subject to the study only if they are significant for analysis of the overlaps.

7.5 Analysis of episodes of overlapping interaction

The analysis covers ten episodes of interaction where overlaps appear. The author has classified these episodes as either interpreter-excluded or interpreter-included. Interpreter-excluded overlaps are those in which the interpreter is neither an overlapper nor an overlappee. Interpreter-included overlaps are those in which the interpreter is either an overlapper or an overlappee.

7.5.1 Interpreter-excluded overlaps

In the episode of interaction presented in Table 7.2, the petitioner's lawyer becomes an overlapper.

The respondent's lawyer expresses his disagreement with what the petitioner's lawyer says. The transition space between the first turn in which the petitioner's lawyer speaks and the interruption produced by the respondent's lawyer is almost imperceptible. Probably this is why the petitioner's lawyer seems not to notice this interruption and thus produces an overlap. Interestingly, although on the one hand the petitioner's lawyer remains insensitive to the respondent's interruption, on the other hand he considers its content when he corrects his utterance. In these three turns, the main speakers *compete* in order to express their mutual disagreement and leave no space for the interpreter to take her turn to render their utterances. Consequently, the interpreter has to wait until the petitioner's lawyer completes his turn. Because of the lawyer's argument, the interpreter, in order to comply with the principle of accuracy, intends to include in her rendition all the data "retrieved" from the original speech. She achieves it not only by summarizing the information, but also by asking the witness additional questions, which are probably supposed to help her transmit the original messages accurately. Remarkably, it could be the witness's humbling *yhm* response, which makes the interpreter ask him an additional question: *what do you mean by that*? When answering this question, the witness uses an increasing intonation with a clearly audible question mark at the end, while the interpreter's intonation when rendering the witness's answer is affirmative. Also, the fact that the interpreter adds a particle *yes* to her rendition contributes to an impression of a shift – from the witness's uncertainty to the interpreter's certainty – in the meaning of the original utterance and the interpreter's rendition. In this episode of interaction, overlapping produced by the petitioner's lawyer is competitive; the overlapper's intention is probably to upset the respondent's lawyer. Moreover, overlapping works also as a trigger for the interpreter who assumes the responsibility for asking questions in order to transmit all the information provided by the main speakers.

In the episode of interaction shown in Table 7.3, the lawyer is an overlapper, while the judge becomes an overlappee.

The aim of the overlaps produced by the lawyer is to deny the judge's question about *heating* or *cooking* and to correct the judge's question whether the witness does not cook by himself. The interpreter, although supposed to

Table 7.3 Interpreter-excluded overlapping produced by the lawyer

Speaker	*Original Polish/English talk*	*Author's verbatim translation into English*
Judge	a chodzi o ogrzewanie (.) [tak?	*This refers to heating, yes?*
Lawyer	[nie (0.2) o gotowanie.	*No, cooking.*
Judge	(.) aha::: (.) o gotowanie (0.3) rozumiem (.) że pan nie gotu[je?	*Aha, cooking. I understand that you do not cook?*
Lawyer	[czy pan gotuje samodzielnie?	*Do you cook by yourself?*
Interpreter	(xxx)	

render the utterances produced by both main speakers, evidently cannot do that. What is more, when the overlapping act of communication is completed, she remains silent. Two aspects are worth emphasizing here. First, during the overlapping, both the judge and the lawyer speak simultaneously and dynamically and leave no space for the interpreter to intervene with her rendition. Secondly, the interpreter may perceive the lawyer's behaviour towards the judge as arrogant, while the judge seems to be withdrawn and reluctant to use his power to discipline the lawyer. These two issues may contribute to the interpreter's choice not to interfere and eventually to remain silent. Consequently, an English-speaking party is linguistically absent from the act of communication. In this episode of interaction, overlapping produced by the lawyer is competitive; the overlapper probably wants to correct the judge, which misleads the interpreter, who fails to render the overlapping questions.

7.5.2 Interpreter-included overlaps

In the episode of interaction shown in Table 7.4, the judge is an overlapper, while the interpreter is an overlappee.

After the judge asks the witness whether he travelled to the US, the interpreter proceeds to render this question. She begins with a pragmatic marker *so*, the function of which may be the interpreter's subconscious intention to put a line between the judge's and her own turn. The judge, however, takes advantage of the instance the interpreter begins her turn and overlaps with a subsidiary expansion, in which he limits the defendant's answer to

Table 7.4 Interpreter-included overlapping produced by the judge

Speaker	*Original Polish/English talk*	*Author's verbatim translation into English*
Judge	czy: y::: w międzyczasie (.) pan wyjeżdżał do Stanów czy::: czy:::: czy: jest nieprzerwany (.) cały czas pobyt tutaj?	*Did you go to the States in the meantime or … or … or is there an uninterrupted stay for the whole time here?*
Interpreter	(0.5) so y:: (.) [did you go in the meantime…	
Judge	[jakieś dłuższe okresy…	*Any longer periods …*
Interpreter	(0.4) to the US in the longer periods o::r (0.3) >did you stay< in Poland permanently?	
Defendant	(1.0) y:: the only time I left Poland (.) was to go to London for 10 days.	
Interpreter	(0.2) y::: (0.3) jedynym razem (.) kiedy:: właściwie wyjechałem (.) to było do Londynu na dziesięć dni.	*The only time I actually left was to go to London for 10 days.*

the information about the longer periods of his stay in the US. The interpreter renders this information immediately as if she wanted to prevent the judge from another overlapping. Interestingly, although the interpreter does not hesitate to render the judge's subsidiary expansion, she seems to have lost her train of thought, which leads to inaccurate interpretation where *a permanent stay* instead of *an uninterrupted stay* appears in the rendition. Furthermore, when the defendant chooses not to provide a projected either *yes* or *no* answer and tells the judge where he went and for how long, the interpreter provides a precise rendition. In this episode of interaction, the judge's overlapping is cooperative; the judge rather gives the interpreter hints so that she does not forget any detail she is supposed to transmit to the defendant.

In the episode of interaction presented in Table 7.5, the witness is an overlapper and the interpreter is an overlappee.

The judge asks the witness to answer a brief question whether the witness withdraws or upholds his demand. The interpreter takes her turn immediately after the judge completes his question. Nonetheless, when she is in the middle of rendering the original message, the witness overlaps with his answer and says *it was withdrawn*. This may be due to two aspects of this act of communication. First, the witness might be nervous at appearing in court. Secondly, he might want to emphasize that he has already exercised his right to withdraw the demand. Thirdly, it may be the case that he at least partially understands Polish so he does not need to wait until the end of the interpreter's turn to understand the judge's question. What is more, as regards the overlapper's turn, the emphasis put on the verb *was* and the use itself of passive voice (*it was withdrawn*) might contribute to the interpreter's rendition of this turn. Namely, she does not echo the grammatical or pragmatic content of this answer; instead, she distances herself by deploying an indirect style which enables her to indicate a real speaker (*He states that he has already withdrawn it*). It can be speculated that in this episode of interaction, overlapping is competitive and may be aimed at showing the witness's disagreement to asking the question, the answer to which should be already known to the court. In turn,

Table 7.5 Interpreter-included overlapping produced by the witness

Speaker	*Original Polish/English talk*	*Author's verbatim translation into English*
Judge	krótko (0.2) pytanie >jest na razie< krótkie (0.2) czy cofa pan (.) czy pan je podtrzymuje? =	*Briefly, the question is brief for the time being, do you withdraw or do you uphold it?*
Interpreter	do you withdr[a::w …	
Witness	[it was withdrawn.	
Interpreter	(.) pan twierdzi (.) że już to °wycofał°.	*He states that he has already withdrawn it.*

the interpreter's rendition may covertly manifest her disagreement with the witness's behaviour before the court.

In the episode of interaction presented in Table 7.6, the interpreter is an overlapper, while the judge is an overlappee.

The judge's turn begins with three units (*yes; it's true; I was the plaintiff's chairman*) dictated in order to be included in the minutes written by the court clerk. Only the fourth unit (*What did the implementation of the agreement with X regarding the contract look like*?) is a question asked of the witness. The interpreter does not render these first three units as most probably being a repetition of what she has already interpreted in the previous episode of interaction; instead, she begins rendering only the last one. The judge – assured by the interpreter's intonation and suspended rendition that it is his turn to speak – takes the next turn to include more information in his question. Then, the interpreter overlaps perhaps when she realizes the complexity and degree of detail of the judge's question. The overlapping function is probably to enable the interpreter to keep up with the information provided by the judge. This, however, leads to inaccurate rendition of the original message that consists of the out-of-context data. In this episode of interaction, overlapping produced by the interpreter is doubly competitive. First, the interpreter probably *competes with* the judge's intention to have a long and complex turn. Secondly, she *competes with* (or, better, *struggles against*) the inherent limitations of her short-term memory capacity.

Table 7.6 Interpreter-included overlapping produced by the interpreter

Speaker	*Original Polish/English talk*	*Author's verbatim translation into English*
Judge	tak (.) to prawda (0.2) byłem prezesem strony powodowej. (0.2) jak wyglądała realizacja umowy z X dotycząca kontraktu…	*Yes, it's true, I was the plaintiff's chairman. What did an implementation of the agreement with X regarding the contract look like?*
Interpreter	(1.0) what was (0.2) the execution of the contract… =	
Judge	dotycząca kontraktu z marca dwa tysiące siódmego roku: na przygotowanie i przeprowadzenie przetargu na (.) wieloletni kontrakt e:: pilotażowy (0.2) [na zarządzanie i utrzymanie dró::g oparty na wskaźnikach…	*… regarding the contract of March 2007 for preparing and carrying out a tender for a multi-year pilot contract involving the management and maintenance of roads based on indicators …*
Interpreter	[for the performance of the proje:ct of y:: the road buildi:ng (.) based on indexes (.) that's >the name of the< who:le project (0.3) how was the settlement of this project done.	

Table 7.7 Interpreter-included overlapping produced by the interpreter

Speaker	*Original Polish/English talk*	*Author's verbatim translation into English*
Judge	Ile pan ma lat?	*How old are you?*
Interpreter	how old are you? (.) how old are you?	
Witness	((to the interpreter)) (.) wha[t?	
Interpreter	[how old are you? =	
Witness	= seventy nine. =	
Interpreter	= mam siedemdziesiąt dziewięć lat.	*I'm 79.*

Similarly, in the episode of interaction shown in Table 7.7, the interpreter is an overlapper, while the witness is an overlappee.

After the judge asks the elderly witness about his age, the interpreter renders the judge's question twice. Such a repetition may result from the interpreter's knowledge of the witness's hearing problems. However, the witness still cannot hear anything and addresses the interpreter a short question *what*? to give her to understand that she should repeat her rendition. At a time when the witness asks this question, the interpreter produces an almost imperceptible overlap to repeat *how old are you*? As a result, the overlappee is capable of answering the judge's question. In terms of the turn-taking sequence in this episode of interaction, the interpreter's overlap is competitive, as she does not let the overlappee complete his turn. Nonetheless, such a competitive overlap does not interrupt the act of communication; instead, it contributes to making it smooth. By applying an overlap, the interpreter manifests not only her competence to anticipate, but also her empathy toward the main speaker.

In the episode of interaction shown in Table 7.8, both the judge and the interpreter become overlappers and overlappees, interchangeably.

The judge and the interpreter produce overlaps interchangeably. The interpreter never waits until the judge completes his turn in this episode of interaction. First, when the judge asks the witness *What it is that his wife is not able to take care of by herself*?, as indicated, the interpreter starts interpreting before the judge completes his turn; that may be because she is able to project the ending of the judge's turn. Nonetheless, she uses an impersonal rendition *help is needed for what things*?, which triggers the judge's expansion, *But I am referring to your wife*. In other words, the judge, who presumably speaks English, overlaps to correct the interpreter's rendition. The judge's expansion makes the interpreter overlap when she starts her rendition to transmit all the details of the judge's original message.

In his next turn, the judge expands his question by giving an example of a possible activity (*planning shopping*) that could, or could not, be done by the witness's wife. When the interpreter renders this expansion, the judge overlaps twice to stress the expression *by herself*, by which he probably wants to attract

Table 7.8 Interpreter-included overlapping produced by the judge and the interpreter

Speaker	*Original Polish/English talk*	*Author's verbatim translation into English*
Judge	czego >nie jest w stanie samo[dzielnie załatwić<?	*What is it that she is not able to take care of by herself?*
Interpreter	[help is needed for [what things?	
Judge	[ale chodzi mi o żonę (0.3) czego żona nie jest w stanie zał[atwić samodzielnie?	*But I am referring to your wife, what is it that your wife is not able to take care of by herself?*
Interpreter	[what >are the activities that your wife is not able to do<? =	
Judge	na przykład planowanie zakupów… =	*For example planning shopping …*
Interpreter	= is she able [to plan shopping?	
Judge	[ale samodzielnie (0.3) czy żona może w ogóle samodzielnie wyjść na: dwór (0.2) i samodzielnie wrócić do domu?	*But by herself. Is your wife, in general, able to go outside and come back home?*
Interpreter	(.) is your wife (.) is [she…	
Judge	[sama. =	*By herself.*
Interpreter	= capable of going out and (.) coming back home independently?	

Table 7.9 Interpreter-included overlapping produced by the judge and the interpreter

Speaker	*Original Polish/English talk*	*Author's verbatim translation into English*
Judge	i czy dzisiaj (0.2) jeszcze raz (0.3) po raz trzeci (.) sąd pyta (0.2) [proszę powiedzieć.	*And today once again, for the third time, the court asks, could you say*
Interpreter	[and today (.) you are asked for the third time [if you…	
Judge	[i ostatni… =	*And the last one …*
Interpreter	= and the last (.) if you withdraw.	

the interpreter's attention to the key concept in his questions. In this episode of interaction, cooperative overlapping is produced. Even in the case of the first overlap, where the judge seems to correct the interpreter's rendition, he does so supportively. An overall impression of this particular act of communication is as if the judge's voice was in the background of the interpreter's renditions, all in order to help the interpreter's renditions be as accurate as possible.

Likewise, in the episode of interaction shown in Table 7.9, both the judge and the interpreter become overlappers and overlappees, interchangeably.

The first overlap appears when the interpreter starts her turn after the judge's words *the court asks*, which gives the interpreter a cue that it is the first possible completion of the judge's turn. However, the judge expands his sequence by adding *could you say*, which leads to the interpreter's overlap. Then, the judge, who does not let the interpreter complete her turn, produces the second overlap (*And the last one*). This overlap is to give the interpreter hints as to what information she is to transmit. In this respect, the judge is successful as the interpreter, with no gap between the judge's and her own turn, renders the judge's utterance. In this episode of interaction, two types of overlapping are produced. In the case of the interpreter being an overlapper, it is competitive. It may be, as in the previous episode of interaction, a result of the interpreter's need to maintain as short a *décalage* as possible to render the original message accurately. In the case of the judge's overlap, it is cooperative as it presumably supports the interpreter's long-term memory capacity.

In the same way, in the episode of interaction shown in Table 7.10, the witness and interpreter are both overlappers and overlappees.

The witness mentions *Operational problems* and suspends his voice, which the interpreter understands as a possible completion of his turn, thus she starts her rendition. However, the witness expands his sequence by adding further details of the problems he has referred to in his first turn. The interpreter does not let the witness complete his turn, probably because she projects that this is going to be short. Although the witness interrupts her turn to say *yes*, she continues interpretation in her next turn. It is worth emphasizing however that the interpreter modifies the original message; in her rendition, *operational problems consisting of flight delays* appear instead of *operational problems due to flight delays*. In this episode of interaction, both competitive and cooperative overlapping appear. When the interpreter is an overlapper, as in previous examples, it is due to her need to take advantage of her short-term memory capacity. In the case of the witness, overlapping is produced because of his intention to complete the utterance.

In the episode of interaction presented in Table 7.11, the judge overlaps the interpreter's turn.

Table 7.10 Interpreter-included overlapping produced by the interpreter

Speaker	*Original Polish/English talk*	*Author's verbatim translation into English*
Witness	(.) operational problems… . =	
Interpreter	= proble[my operacyjne…	*Operational problems…*
Witness	[because [of delays of flights…	
Interpreter	[z powodu::::…=	*…due to…*
Witness	= ye:s. =	
Interpreter	ta:k (0.3) problemy operacyjne polegające na: opóźnieniach lotów.	*Yes…, operational problems consisting of flight delays.*

Table 7.11 Interpreter-included overlapping produced by the judge

Speaker	*Original Polish/English talk*	*Author's verbatim translation into English*
Witness	ye:s (1.0) we've got a condominium in X… =	
Interpreter	= tak (0.3) mamy kondominium [w X.	*Yes, we have a condominium in X …*
Judge	[°mieszkanie°…	*An apartment …*
Interpreter	((gazes at the judge)) (xxx)	

The witness declares that they've got *a condominium in X*. The interpreter's rendition is accurate. A Polish *kondominium* ("a territory governed by the joint control of two or more states, or the joint control over such territory"[3]) is a calque of an English *condominium* ("an apartment building in which each apartment is owned by the person who lives there" and "one of the privately owned apartments in a condominium"[4]). However, a Polish *condominium* (not *kondominium*) is a jargon equivalent of an English condominium. The judge, probably in the assumption that the interpreter uses an incorrect calque, overlaps by saying *An apartment* to correct the interpreter's rendition. This contributes to the interpreter's silent turn, which might express her consent with the judge's correction.

7.6 Conclusion

The aim of this qualitative study was to discuss overlaps from the perspective of the interpreter's participation in the turn-taking system at institutional talk, the interpreter's renditions of institutional talk, and the interpreter complying with an ethical principle of accuracy.

The overall findings of the study prove that overlaps constitute an inherent feature of courtroom interactions, in which the interpreter renders her services. This contradicts the description of monolingual institutional talk (Atkinson and Drew, 1979, Atkinson, 1982, Heffer, 2005) as one in which spontaneous reactions of the parties to the utterances produced by other parties do not appear. Moreover, the use of an overlap by a particular speaker subject to this analysis seems to be impulsive. In legal terms, overlaps in the institutional talk of the courtroom might be described as produced *under emotional strain* instead of *with premeditation*.

As far as detailed observations are concerned, first, the results draw attention to a multi-directionality of interactions during interpreter-mediated encounters understood as communication carried out among all the speakers (including the interpreter) during a particular bilingual communicative event. In other words, both the main speakers and the interpreters have the potential to produce overlaps. Interestingly, the presumed reasons for overlapping vary according to the communicative aim of a particular interlocutor, be it the main speaker or the interpreter. This means that the main speaker's and the interpreter's overlaps can be both cooperative and competitive. The main speakers produce mutual competitive overlaps because they argue (Table 7.2), or they want to make an impression on their interlocutors, and are convinced that their viewpoint supersedes the other interlocutor's opinion (Tables 7.3, 7.5, and 7.9). When the main speakers produce cooperative overlaps, they do so in order to support the interpreter in their renditions by giving clues (Tables 7.4 and 7.8) or even correcting their renditions (Table 7.11). As regards the interpreters, they produce competitive overlaps because they strive to provide an immediate rendition of the main speaker's complex utterances (Tables 7.6 and 7.10) or they anticipate the main speaker's words (Table 7.7). In the material analysed, there have been no instances of the interpreter's cooperative overlaps, although it could be the interpreter's intention to produce such overlapping (Table 7.7). Nonetheless, this observation does not mean that court interpreters do not produce cooperative overlaps at all; it is only conducive to the recommendation to carry out further research into this aspect.

Secondly, not once in the episodes of interaction analysed does the judge use his power to instruct the main speakers not to speak at the same time. By not intervening, the judge never helps the interpreter in terms of the turn-taking system of the interaction. Instead, the judges overlap the interpreters either to support them or to correct their renditions.

Thirdly, after Roy (1990, p. 85), the analysis has confirmed that overlaps are problematic for court interpreters and thus may lead to non-compliance with the ethical principle of accuracy in court interpreting. In some cases (Tables 7.1 and 7.2), overlaps produced by the main speakers are "those mechanisms which have a potential to exclude the interpreter, and therefore the non-Polish speaking party, from the interaction" (Biernacka, 2019, p. 154). In instances where interpreter-excluded overlaps are produced, the interpreters wait until the main interlocutors stop speaking, and only then intend, or not, to intervene with their renditions (Tables 7.2 and 7.3). As regards interpreter-included overlaps, there are episodes of interaction where the interpreters are either overlappers or overlappees, or both. From the perspective of complying with the principle of accuracy, the interpreters' most precise renditions are a result of the overlaps produced collaboratively by the main speaker and the interpreter (Tables 7.8 and 7.9). Therefore, it can be concluded that such overlaps are the most efficient in terms of the ethics of court interpreting. When the interpreters are overlappers, they usually produce either supportive questions (Table 7.7) or inaccurate renditions (Tables 7.6 and 7.10). In turn, when they are overlappees, they take advantage of the information transmitted by the overlappers and therefore are able to provide more accurate renditions than before the overlapping.

Furthermore, it is worth noticing that overlaps prove that the capacity of the communication space is limited; thus, if an overlapper steps in the interaction, an overlappee has to step out. From the perspective of the principle of accuracy in court interpreting, it means that competitive overlaps produced by the main speakers or by the main speaker and the interpreter have the potential to lead to exclusion of the interpreter or of the other main speakers, respectively. Consequently, as regards the legal and ethical responsibilities of the interpreter to render everything that is said in the courtroom, the interpreter's exclusion from the communicative event results in her failure to make the other main speakers "linguistically present" (Gentile et al., 1996, p. 98).

To sum up, the results draw attention to an ambiguous nature of overlaps. Interpreter-excluded overlaps lead to the interpreter's (non-)participation in the communicative event, thus they are considerable obstacles to performing interpreting responsibilities according to the principle of accuracy. The interpreter-included overlaps have the potential to result in either accurate or inaccurate renditions. At the same time, it is worth emphasizing that further research in the role of overlaps produced in bilateral institutional talk of the courtroom is to be recommended.

Notes

1 Ustawa o zawodzie tłumacza przysięgłego z dnia 25 listopada 2004 r. *[The Act on the Profession of Sworn Translator of 25 November 2004*] (Dz. U. z 2015 r. Nr 487 ze zm.), available at: https://bip.ms.gov.pl/pl/rejestry-i-ewidencje/tlumacze-przysiegli (accessed 15 February 2021).

2 Kodeks zawodowy tłumacza przysięgłego [The Sworn Translator's Professional Code], available at: http://tepis.org.pl/wp-content/uploads/Kodeks-zawodowy-t%C5%82umacza-przysi%C4%99g%C5%82ego-2018.pdf (accessed 15 February 2021).

3 http://sjp.pwn.pl/szukaj/kondominium.html Słownik języka polskiego [Dictionary of the Polish Language] (accessed 2 February 2021).

4 www.collinsdictionary.com/dictionary/english/condominium (accessed 2 February 2021).

References

Atkinson, J. M. (1982). "Understanding Formality: The Categorization and Production of 'Formal' Interaction." *The British Journal of Sociology*, 33, 86–117.

Atkinson J. M., and Drew, P. (1979). *Order in Court. The Organisation of Verbal Interaction in Judicial Settings*. Atlantic Highlands: Humanities Press.

Bednarek, G. A. (2014). *Polish vs. American Courtroom Discourse: Inquisitorial and Adversarial Procedures of Witness Examination in Criminal Trials*. New York: Palgrave Macmillan.

Biernacka, A. (2019). *Interpreter-Mediated Interactions of the Courtroom. A Naturally Occurring Data Based Study*. Berlin: Peter Lang.

Biernacka, A. (2020). "Non-Verbal Communication as a Component of Polish–English Courtroom Talk Affecting the Accuracy and Impartiality of Interpreting." *The Interpreters' Newsletter*, 25, 95–111.

Collins Dictionary. Available at: www.collinsdictionary.com/dictionary/english/condominium (accessed on 2 February 2021).
Díaz-Campos, M., Geeslin, K. L., and Gurzynski-Weiss, L. (2017). *Introducción y Aplicaciones Contextualizadas a la Lingüística Hispánica*. Hoboken, NJ: Wiley-Blackwell.
Gentile, A., Ozolins, U., and Vasilakakos, M. (1996). *Liaison Interpreting*. Melbourne: Melbourne University Press.
Hale, S. (2007). *Community Interpreting*. Houndmills, Basingstoke, Hampshire: Palgrave Macmillan.
Heffer, C. (2005). *The Language of Jury Trial. A Corpus-Aided Analysis of Legal-Lay Discourse*. New York: Palgrave Macmillan.
Jacobsen, B. (2004). "Pragmatic Meaning in Court Interpreting: An Empirical Study of Additions in Consecutively Interpreted Question–Answer Dialogues." *Hermes. Journal of Linguistics*, 3, 237–249.
Jefferson, G. (1983). *Issues in the Transcription of Naturally Occurring Talk: Caricatures versus Capturing Pronunciational Particulars*. Tilburg: Tilburg University.
Jefferson, G. (1986). "Notes on 'Latency' in Overlap." *Human Studies*, 9, 153–183.
Jefferson, G. (2004). "Glossary of Transcript Symbols with an Introduction." In: Lerner G. H. (ed.) *Conversation Analysis: Studies from the First Generation*. Amsterdam: John Benjamins, 13–23.
Liddicoat, A. J. (2011). *An Introduction to Conversation Analysis*. London: Continuum.
Roy, C. (1990). "Interpreters, Their Role and Metaphorical Language Use." In: Wilson, L. (ed.) *Looking Ahead. Proceedings of the 31st Conference of the American Translators Association*. Medford, NJ: Learned Information, 77–86.
Sacks, H., Schegloff, E., and Jefferson, G. (1974). "A Simplest Systematics for the Organization of Turn-taking for Conversation." *Language*, 50, 696–735.
Truong Khiet, P. (2013). "Classification of Cooperative and Competitive Overlaps in Speech Using Cues from the Context, Overlapper, and Overlappee." *Interspeech*, 8, 1404–1408.
Wadensjö, C. (1998). *Interpreting as Interaction*. London: Longman.
Wardhaugh, R. (1985). *How Conversation Works*. Oxford: Basil Blackwell.

8 A Bourdieusian perspective on interpreters providing services to Syrian refugees in Turkey[1]

Aslı Polat Ulaş

8.1 Introduction

Due to the civil war that started in the Syrian Arab Republic in 2011, millions of Syrians were forcibly displaced and took shelter in neighbouring countries like Turkey, Lebanon, Egypt and Jordan. Today, with nearly 3.6 million Syrians, Turkey hosts the world's largest refugee population (UNHCR, 2019). Although refugees' basic rights to accommodation, healthcare and education have been secured through the Temporary Protection Regulation adopted in 2014, the language barrier is still one of the most important factors preventing many Syrians from accessing public services (Torun *et al.*, 2018; Yücel *et al.*, 2018). Although there are language courses sponsored by the state, municipalities and non-governmental organizations (NGOs), many Syrians cannot access these services (Nimer & Oruç, 2019; Yücel *et al.*, 2018). Hence, in meeting refugees' communication needs in public institutions, interpreting services offered on an institutional scale seem to be the most functional solution for the time being.

Currently in Turkey, interpreters provide services to Syrian refugees mainly in provincial directorates managing migration; certain NGOs, such as the Turkish Red Crescent Community Centres and the Association for Solidarity with Asylum Seekers and Migrants (ASAM); and legal and public healthcare institutions. This study focused on interpreters working in the ASAM units, legal settings such as courthouses and police stations and public healthcare institutions under the EU-funded healthcare project called SIHHAT.[2] The study aimed to explore interpreters' social, cultural, educational and professional backgrounds; their perspectives on the interpreting activities they were involved in; and their attitudes towards and expectations about public service interpreting. The interpreters were described as social actors, foregrounding the social contexts surrounding them. The aforementioned issues were discussed from a Bourdieusian perspective through the concepts of *habitus*, capital and *illusio*. Thus, it is hoped that the study will contribute to discussions revolving around the sociology of translators/interpreters, as proposed by Chesterman (2006, 2009).

DOI: 10.4324/9781003197027-11

8.2 Literature review and conceptual framework

Due to increased migration movements worldwide in the 1980s and 1990s, public service interpreting became highly important in meeting the communication needs of migrants/refugees in the host countries. In recent years, the increasing recognition of interpreting activities in various public and social settings, and the fact that interpreters perform a kind of "linguistic social work" (Bahadır, 2011, p. 264) in dynamic and complex communication processes, has led to a questioning of the norms of invisibility and neutrality, and the roles of "conduit" and "code-switcher" (Knapp-Potthoff & Knapp, 1986; Lee, 2009; Morris, 2011; Pöchhacker, 2004; Tipton, 2014) traditionally attributed to interpreters. A large number of studies addressing interpreters' roles and task boundaries and the problem of applying ethical principles in dynamic communication processes in social settings – especially in legal and healthcare contexts – have defined public service interpreters as more involved actors in communication processes, which is in contrast to what is traditionally expected of interpreters (Angelelli, 2004; Barsky, 1996; Berk-Seligson, 1990; Bot, 2003; Clifford, 2004; Hale, 2008; Hsieh, 2006; Ibrahim, 2007; Leanza, 2005; Lee, 2009; Mikkelson, 1998; Morris, 1995, 1999; Niska, 1995; Pöchhacker, 2000; Rudvin, 2007; Souza, 2016; Wadensjö, 1998). A number of researchers (Aguilar Solano, 2012; Guéry, 2014; Inghilleri, 2003, 2005; Tipton, 2014; Valero Garcés, 2012) have also highlighted the importance of the social context and the increased agency of interpreters by employing concepts from the French sociologist Pierre Bourdieu's social theory.

In a similar vein, in this study, the interpreters providing services to Syrian refugees in Turkey were treated as social actors in the light of the subfield of the sociology of translators proposed by Chesterman (2006, 2009), which deals with issues such as practitioners' status and image, and their rates of pay, working conditions, attitude towards their work, *habitus* and networks. Within this framework, the present study sought to address the following research questions:

- What are the social backgrounds of the public service interpreters? What is the influence of their backgrounds on their performing interpreting?
- What are the interpreters' perceptions of their interpreting experiences and of their agency in interpreting assignments? What are the context-dependent factors that affect their agency? To what extent do their perceptions match up with the principles prescribed in codes and standards[3] designed for public service interpreters?
- What are the interpreters' perceptions of the interpreting profession? Do they find it worth practising as a future career?
- What forms of capital are (un)available to the interpreters? Do the available forms of capital have the potential to contribute to the formation of a professional identity?

The findings of the research were discussed through Bourdieu's concepts of *habitus* (Bourdieu, 1977, 1998, 2000), capital (Bourdieu, 1986, 1989, 1991, 1998) and *illusio* (Bourdieu & Wacquant, 1992; Bourdieu, 2000).

8.3 Methodology

8.3.1 The fieldwork, data collection and data analysis

This study adopted a qualitative research method drawing on interviews with interpreters and the public officials working with them, on documents about the working conditions and work procedures for interpreters within NGO, legal and healthcare contexts. Since it involves data collection methods heavily associated with traditional ethnographic studies, this study is one of the studies "incorporating ethnographic principles" in the sense of Hale and Napier (2013, p. 95). The study also adopted the case study approach within the qualitative research paradigm, in that it examined interpreters within the specific contexts of NGO, legal and healthcare (see Creswell, 2007).

The fieldwork providing data for this study was carried out between October 2018 and June 2019 in the following four provinces where the largest Syrian populations reside in Turkey: Gaziantep, Adana, Mersin and İzmir.[4] The approval of the Ethical Board of the Faculty of Letters of Dokuz Eylül University was obtained to conduct the fieldwork. Within this scope, semi-structured interviews were conducted with nine interpreters and three officials in the ASAM units, ten interpreters and five legal professionals (two judges and three lawyers) in the legal context and ten interpreters and six healthcare professionals (four doctors and two nurses) in the healthcare context. Before the interviews, the interviewees signed consent forms indicating the information would only be used for research purposes and would be kept anonymous. The interviews conducted with the interpreters were audio-recorded. Since the public officials did not consent to the audio-recording, the researcher took notes during the interviews conducted with them.

The documents obtained for analysis were: in the NGO context, the institutional code of conduct (Ulusoy & Rezaei Osalou, 2019) and the job posting for interpreters; in the legal context, the binding law articles, the regulations for interpreters, the sample form for declaring the knowledge of the relevant interpreting language and the manual entitled *Child Friendly Interpreting in Judicial Processes* (Aydın *et al.*, n.d.) obtained during the one and only training event organized for the interpreters in cooperation with the Department of Training in the Ministry of Justice (Turkey) and UNICEF; and in the healthcare context, the materials providing information about the EU-funded SIHHAT project, the job posting for interpreters, the materials on the recruitment of the interpreters and on the training given to the interpreters within the scope of the project.

In the analysis stage, all the audio-recorded interviews were transcribed verbatim. The transcripts of the three groups of semi-structured interviews conducted with the interpreters – the major data source of the study – were manually coded and separately subjected to deductive thematic analysis (see Braun & Clarke, 2006), which was guided by the aforementioned research questions of the study. Accordingly, the emerging codes related to each research question were noted down using different-coloured pens on the interview transcripts, and then a codebook was created in Excel format. The codes for each research question, their definitions and their locations in the transcripts were entered into a separate Excel sheet. At the next stage, the codes that were similar in content and important for the relevant research question were categorized, and relationships were sought among all the emerging categories in order to derive the preliminary themes. Then the preliminary themes were reviewed to identify the overarching themes and the related sub-themes.[5] The prevalence of the themes and the sub-themes was determined based on the number of the respondents mentioning them.

The data from the complementary sources, i.e. the interviews conducted with the officials and the documents, were discussed in alignment with the findings of the thematic analyses of the interpreter interviews.

8.3.2 The interpreters' demographic profiles and social backgrounds

Within the scope of this study, nine interpreters were interviewed in the NGO context. This group included five females and four males. Their average age was 31 and their average interpreting experience was around 2.5 years. Five interpreters were Turkish citizens of Arab origin, one was a Turkish citizen of Kurdish origin and three were Syrian Kurds. Seven interpreters held a university degree, and among these, only one held a degree in translation and interpreting. Seven interpreters had previous short-term work experience in interpreting (for refugees, traders or tourists) or in service areas related to refugees, such as tutoring Syrian students. All the interpreters attended the institutional, annually organized, in-service training.

In the legal context, ten interpreters were interviewed. The interpreters were selected from interpreter lists compiled annually by the provincial justice commissions. Of the ten interpreters, five were female and five were male. Their average age was 39 and average interpreting experience was around 3.5 years. All the interpreters were Turkish citizens, as stipulated under Article 6 of the Regulation on Compiling Interpreters Lists.[6] Seven interpreters were of Arab origin and two were of Kurdish origin. Among the ten interpreters, five held a university degree. None of the interpreters held a degree in translation and interpreting. Eight interpreters were engaged in different jobs and practised interpreting as a sideline. The only training attended by eight of the interpreters was the three-day training entitled "Child Friendly Interpreting in Judicial Processes".

In the healthcare context, ten interpreters were interviewed. The interpreters were selected from among the staff recruited under the name of "patient guide"[7] within the scope of the EU-funded SIHHAT project. Of the ten interpreters, two were female and eight were male. Their average age was 28 and their average interpreting experience was around 2 years. Eight interpreters were Syrian Turkmen, one was Syrian Arab and the other was Palestinian Arab. Three interpreters were continuing their university education in Turkey when this study was being conducted, and two held a university degree received in countries other than Turkey. None of the interpreters held a degree in translation and interpreting. Seven interpreters had previous work experience in interpreting for refugees/migrants or as an interpreter in the business sector. All the interpreters attended the in-service training organized over seven rounds within the scope of the project.

Given the information above, none of the interpreters in the three groups, except for NGOI-4,[8] received education in the interpreting field. They were individuals who have mostly learned interpreting on the job. Thus, it can be suggested that the institutionalized state of cultural capital in the form of a university degree or a relevant certificate (Bourdieu, 1986, p. 245) was not a determining factor in their recruitment as interpreters. The most distinctive resource these individuals possessed in working as interpreters was their "embodied linguistic capital" (Koskinen, 2020, p. 110) acquired naturally based on ethnic origin, family background and social environment, the factors forming part of their primary *habitus*[9] (Bourdieu, 1972, cited in Bourdieu and Wacquant, 1992, p. 134; Bourdieu, 1998). In other words, the majority of the practitioners[10] had not developed a rooted belief and interest, namely *illusio*[11] (see Bourdieu, 2000, p. 11), in the field of interpreting from an early age. Nor did they possess the long-term investment, experience and preparedness required for the formation of professional *habitus*[12] in this field (see Bourdieu, 1998, 2000). Especially for the NGO and healthcare interpreters, the only investments in the field were the short-term in-service training and the sporadic interpreting experiences before their current job. In this sense, the vast majority of interpreters can be said to act in a sort of "zone of uncertainty" (see Bourdieu, 2000, pp. 157–160) characterized by the inconsistency between their positions and dispositions. And, as will be discussed later, this situation had implications for the practitioners' awareness of a professional code of conduct in interpreting and also for their attitudes towards the job they were performing.

It is also worth mentioning that, unlike the NGO and healthcare interpreters, the legal interpreters did not work as permanent staff under an institutional identity. Most of them were engaged in different jobs and interpreting was a sideline; unlike the NGO and healthcare interpreters, the legal interpreters were not offered the opportunity for regular in-service training. Furthermore, the legal interpreters did not have previous work experience in interpreting and/or in service areas related to refugees, unlike the majority of the NGO and healthcare interpreters. Hence, with their backgrounds of the least training and the least experience in the field, the legal interpreters seemed to be less disposed towards the interpreting job compared to the other two groups of interpreters.

8.4 Discussion

8.4.1 The forms of capital (un)available to the interpreters in the work trajectory

Bourdieu (1986) defined capital as "accumulated labour" in the materialized or embodied form (p. 241). It refers to the resources deployed in the struggle for dominance in social spaces. In Bourdieu's framework, capital is not reduced to only material goods. Rather, Bourdieu (1986) proposed three main forms of capital – economic, cultural and social capital – which are all convertible into each other and also into symbolic capital. Symbolic capital is manifested as status, prestige, esteem and recognition in the eyes of social agents "endowed with categories of perception" (Bourdieu, 1998, p. 47).

In general, public service interpreting is regarded as a low-prestige occupation and is mostly not considered an autonomous and established field in Bourdieu's (1984, 1993) sense. This is due to factors such as the lack of public awareness of the skills necessary for interpreting in public domains, the lack of an established system guaranteeing professional standards, the lack of status and protection of title, the scarcity of education and training opportunities and the lack of incentives – such as high pay – to encourage investment of time and money in professional development (Corsellis, 2008, pp. 56–57; Hale, 2015, pp. 67–68; Rudvin, 2015, p. 437). Being viewed as a secondary activity compared to professions in established fields such as law, medicine and other technical fields, public service interpreting does not offer substantial resources or rewards to its practitioners. Under the circumstances, the most distinct capital possessed by practitioners is usually the linguistic capital, which Bourdieu (1991) proposed as a subtype of cultural capital.

In a similar vein, the most outstanding capital owned by the interpreters in this study was their linguistic capital, mostly acquired in the family and social environment. In the face of the increased communication needs of the large number of refugees in Turkey, this linguistic capital has in fact derived a "scarcity value", according the interpreters a sort of distinction in Bourdieu's (1986) sense. However, it is worth noting that the linguistic capital mentioned has become relatively controversial in the case of legal interpreters,[13] since they were not required to submit any document or certificate proving their language proficiency in the recruitment process.

The NGO and healthcare interpreters in this study are able to transform their linguistic capital into economic capital in the form of a regular salary. The legal interpreters do not work as permanent staff in courthouses. They are only sporadically called by the relevant courthouses when needs arise. Yet there is currently no standardization in job assignments and fees paid to the legal interpreters, and the majority of the practitioners perform interpreting as a sideline. Thus, it can be argued that in Turkey, this field of interpreting is not a job that guarantees sound economic capital.

In terms of accumulation of social capital, the NGO interpreters seemed to be the most advantaged group. The NGO they work for, i.e. ASAM,[14] has been carrying out projects and activities for 25 years in cooperation with many international and national associations and organizations, particularly with the United Nations specialized agencies. Working in such an association is likely to provide interpreters with a sort of social capital in the form of institutional identity and membership. On the other hand, since the legal interpreters do not work as permanent staff in the relevant institutions, such a form of social capital is not available to them, and although the healthcare interpreters work within the scope of an EU-funded project, they do not seem to accumulate such a form of social capital, since limited-duration employment contracts[15] and their refugee background mostly prevent them from being considered as staff members in the fullest sense, as will be discussed in the following section.

Overall, the NGO interpreters seemed to accumulate more rewards in their work trajectory. The rewards available to them were economic capital in the form of a regular salary, quite high by Turkey's standards; social capital in the form of an institutional identity; and the in-service training and institutional code of conduct – the elements that could contribute to their professional development. Although the healthcare interpreters received the rewards brought by the EU-funded project, such as a regular salary and in-service training, the limited duration of their contracts and their refugee background put them on precarious ground in this sense. Lacking most of these rewards, the legal interpreters were the most disadvantaged group.[16] In the final analysis, the majority of the interpreters in each context still seemed far from accumulating symbolic capital due to their lack of professional development and dispositions required for interpreting, and/or the general lack of awareness and institutionalization of public service interpreting in Turkey.

8.4.2 The interpreters' perspectives on their interpreting activities

In terms of the practitioners' interpreting agency, the NGO interpreters seemed to have developed more awareness towards the traditional ethical principles and the framework of the interpreters' role specified in various ethical codes (The Australian Institute of Interpreters and Translators (AUSIT), 2012; California Healthcare Interpreters Association (CHIA), 2002; National Association of Judicial Interpreters and Translators (NAJIT), 2002; The National Register of Public Service Interpreters (NRPSI), 2016) and in ASAM's code of conduct (Ulusoy & Rezaei Osalou, 2019) – also highlighted by the institution officials interviewed. In this respect, the principles most frequently emphasized by the majority of the interpreters were impartiality, accuracy, the use of first-person pronouns and emotional stamina. The regular in-service training, the institutional code of conduct, the institutional identity and the supervision mechanism it brings along with it could explain how the NGO interpreters developed such awareness.

The other widely emphasized issue by the NGO interpreters was their limited authority compared to other officials equipped with higher amounts of capital. In that sense, the practitioners defined their role as only a "transmitter", using the analogies of "machine", "robot", "voice", "video", "post", "mirror" and "channel". For instance, NGOI-6 defined her role as a "mirror" in that she did not make any changes to what was spoken and she tried to reflect the parties' body language. She remarked:

> I totally view my role as a mirror. I mean, transferring what the counselee and the consultant want to convey as it is, without making any changes.[17]

As to their restricted authority, the majority of the NGO interpreters also said that they struggled to reduce refugees' high expectations of them and generally acted with a sense of responsibility towards officials. In this regard, the majority underlined that those having the main expertise, knowledge, authority and responsibility were the officials due to their educational status and institutional position. Regarding this issue, NGOI-4 stated:

> When I am with the consultants, I usually interpret whatever they say because they are already educated and experts in their fields. I try not to go beyond what they say, and I don't.

Furthermore, the NGO interpreters implied that they mostly exercised restricted agency, and in this regard, they mentioned that they avoided expressing their own opinions, taking the initiative in interpreting tasks and engaging in dialogues with refugees outside the interpreting tasks. Overall, in line with the institutional role framework projected for them, the practitioners seemed to have internalized their restricted autonomy compared to the other professional groups within the institution, and also seemed to have adopted the submissive behaviour traditionally associated with translators/interpreters (see Simeoni, 1998).

In the legal context, the thematic analysis indicated the legal interpreters' contradictory attitudes to the interpreting processes. The majority of practitioners highlighted the issues of court ethics, their legal responsibilities and their restricted authority compared to the courts and their officials equipped with more volumes of capital. Within this framework, while talking about certain behaviours they avoided when interpreting, LFI-5, LFI-6 and LFI-9 referred to the oath taken by interpreters, stipulated under Article 64 of the Turkish Code of Criminal Procedure.[18] LFI-9 stated:

> We take an oath every December. ... So additions or omissions mean not being loyal to the oath. If you take an oath, you have to be loyal to that oath.

Within the scope of their legal responsibility, while mentioning their avoidance of undertaking initiatives in interpreting situations, LFI-3, LFI-4 and LFI-9 in particular implied the risk of penalties stipulated under Article 276 of the Turkish Penal Code,[19] according to which a prison sentence from 3 to 7 years is imposed on interpreters who make false statements or do not perform interpreting as required.

On the other hand, nearly all the legal interpreters made contradictory remarks hinting at their interventions in the interpreting processes. These include modifying and summarizing messages to be interpreted, giving advice and guidance to refugees, holding dialogue with refugees and reflecting their emotions during interpreting, which are in fact deemed as violations of certain principles according to various ethical codes (JCCD, 2017; NAJIT, 2002) and the manual entitled *Child Friendly Interpreting in Judicial Processes* (Aydın *et al.*, n.d.) provided to interpreters during training under the same title. The following remarks of LFI-5, who admitted he sometimes summarized refugee statements due to time constraints, could exemplify such interventionist attitudes adopted by the interpreters:

> Actually, if we [have] time, I usually try to convey all [that is said]. Even if not exactly … I try to explain what the person means in the most basic way. … The important thing is fulfilling the need, solving the problem, removing the blockage. If I convey everything that comes out of the migrant's mouth word-for-word, the point in fact gets lost.

And LFI-10, mentioning he sometimes reflected his emotions in the courtroom, in fact implied that he was going beyond the machine role projected for interpreters:

> If I am emotionally affected, I show this through my posture and facial expressions. … Because after all, we are not robots. Although we interpret impartially, we are human beings, and I have witnessed cases where I hardly controlled my tears.

As for the healthcare context, the thematic analysis discovered that the interpreters took part as active actors in the healthcare processes involving refugees, and their job was not limited to only interpreting. It is worth noting that the interpreters in fact act in line with the job descriptions specified for them under the title of "patient guide" and with the healthcare professionals' expectations of them. Within this scope, the outstanding issues mentioned by the interpreters were the additional tasks performed, such as accompanying and guiding refugees in healthcare institutions; the relationships established with refugees external to interpreting, involving the issues of pre-interview dialogues, explanations, recommendations and advice; and interventions during interpreting involving issues such as correcting refugees' misstatements, and modifications and omissions in messages. What HI-1 mentioned regarding the additional tasks performed by the interpreters is remarkable:

> [Patients] focus on the solution. Therefore, we also deal with carrying them in the emergency unit. If there is no person to accompany them, we carry the person on the stretcher.

The remarks made by HI-9 about the pre-interview dialogues held with patients could also exemplify the interventionist roles taken by the interpreters:

> We have to make a preliminary assessment because time is limited. Not every doctor wants to wait. I learn about [patients'] main complaints. How long it has lasted, how much it hurts and so on ... So that there is no loss of time in the doctor's room. Patients' conditions may be critical. I try to understand them while they are waiting.

The practitioners in the healthcare context also explained the challenges they faced in the work setting, and the most highlighted issues were gender-related issues; shortage of interpreters leading to an increased workload; negative biases towards refugees, sometimes including the interpreters themselves; tense atmospheres; and refugees' problematic expectations. The analysis indicated that refugee patients' communication styles and their reservations about receiving service from a member of the opposite sex might cause disruption to the interpreters' daily work. Furthermore, HI-1, HI-6 and HI-9 in particular mentioned that they were offended by the negative bias and discriminatory behaviour of some Turkish people and sometimes of public officials towards Syrians. It was also reported that Turkish patients' negative reactions towards Syrians sometimes created a tense atmosphere in the work setting, leaving the interpreters in a difficult situation. In this respect, HI-1 said:

> People we work with, those we serve, Syrians, are excluded from the society. For example, we go to the doctor. The doctor hates both us and patients. ... The society is also reactive. They react, saying, "We can't receive treatment in our country." ... But actually that [Syrian] makes an appointment, comes to the appointment and waits for her/his turn. [Turkish patients] don't accept this. This time we are stuck in between.

Lastly, in the face of refugee patients' problematic expectations, stemming from their lack of understanding of medical procedures, the majority of the interpreters felt the need to undertake the initiative, and they tended to ease patients' tension, warn them to behave properly and provide proper explanations to them. Overall, the healthcare interpreters in this study seemed to lack the power to handle the aforementioned challenges in the work environment. Their concerns about losing their job, their lack of professional knowledge and experience and the lack of the institutional mechanisms to improve unfavourable conditions affecting the interpreters' performances could be considered to be the likely reasons for this situation.

On the whole, it was found that the legal and healthcare interpreters seemed to adopt a more intrusive behaviour during interpreting processes and go beyond the traditionally attributed roles of "conduit" or "machine", in parallel to the findings of the many scholarly studies mentioned earlier (see Section 8.2). In this respect, considering the practitioners' lack of professional development, it can be suggested they mostly act intuitively, rather than based on a careful analysis of the situation and on professional judgement. Besides, the unfamiliarity of both communities in the service area with the concept of interpreting as defined in Western societies, the dynamic nature of the work settings mainly not addressed by the ethical codes and standards prescribing certain behavioural patterns for interpreters, the social aspect of the interpreters' work and the absence of institutional supervision mechanisms might also explain the legal and healthcare interpreters' interventionist approaches. For the healthcare interpreters, most of whom are refugees, the sincerity developing based on common *habitus* shared with refugees also seemed to be a factor leading them to adopt an interventionist approach. Having said that, it can also be argued that the fact that the interventionist attitudes the practitioners adopt are not based on professional judgement may in fact cause disruption of public services and loss of rights in important areas such as healthcare and law.

8.4.3 The interpreters' attitudes towards and expectations about public service interpreting

The majority of the interviewed interpreters, especially those in the legal and healthcare contexts, were of the opinion that public service interpreting is not an appreciated job, and public service interpreters are an undervalued group. In this regard, the interpreters underlined the poor working conditions, the lack of professional development opportunities and the lack of motivating rewards. In the healthcare context, interpreters' belonging to the marginalized group of refugees was found to be another factor undermining the public appreciation towards them. Under the circumstances, NGOI-3, NGOI-4, NGOI-5; LFI-3; and HI-1, HI-5, HI-7, HI-8 in particular seemed to have become disillusioned and "indifferent" (see Bourdieu and Wacquant, 1992, p. 116) towards the job they were performing.

Regardless of maintaining their commitment and interest in the job, most interpreters in each context do not view public service interpreting as a job that can be performed in the long run. Those having further skills and educational background would like to invest in other areas of translation and interpreting or in areas that suit their skills, expectations and educational background. It was also revealed that in the legal context, LFI-1, LFI-9 and LFI-10, who did not have high expectations of the interpreting job they were performing, found interpreting worth practising merely based on their desire to meet refugees' needs. In the healthcare context, HI-3, HI-6 and HI-9, who had lower educational backgrounds and more limited resources, seemed to maintain their commitment and interest in the interpreting job. For these practitioners, interpreting might be the best job opportunity in the country where they live as refugees.

8.5 Conclusion

The analysis of the data obtained through the interviews and the documents in the NGO, legal and healthcare contexts showed that public service interpreting is an unrecognized and undervalued service area in Turkey. It is mostly viewed as a secondary activity compared to other established and technical professions.[20] Even most of its practitioners do not view public service interpreting as a profession with strong *habitus*, for which comprehensive and formal education, specialized knowledge and skills are required. The interpreters in general lack the power to define their positions and to form a professional identity, due to their lack of professional development and the dispositions required for interpreting, and/or the general lack of awareness towards public service interpreting and the lack of professional development opportunities, rewards and incentives.

Turkey currently hosts the world's largest refugee population, which requires public service interpreting to be an institutionalized occupation performed professionally. The interpreting services offered within the institutional framework in the NGO and healthcare contexts are positive developments. However, there is still a long way to go in the institutionalization and professionalization of public service interpreting in Turkey. To this end, a multicultural framework with developed language and interpreting services needs to be adopted at a national level. Through cooperation between the relevant institutions, academies and professional associations, strong professional standards need to be introduced, and societal awareness needs to be increased towards public service interpreting. Formal education and training programmes need to be enhanced to raise interpreters who are well equipped in linguistic, communicative and cultural matters. Furthermore, establishing permanent interpreter positions in institutions with improved working conditions, involving higher selection criteria, extensive and regular in-service training and practical training for other professional groups working with interpreters, will allow interpreters to act on a more solid basis, and will improve the quality and functioning of interpreter-mediated public services.

Acknowledgements

I would like to express my special thanks to my PhD supervisor Assoc. Prof. Dr. Atalay Gündüz for his valuable support, contributions and guidance. I would also like to thank Prof. Dr. Neslihan Kansu-Yetkiner and Assist. Prof. Dr. Şeyda Kıncal for their comments and suggestions. Lastly, I want to thank the interpreters and officials who collaborated to share their valuable opinions during this study.

Notes

1 This study was produced based on the author's doctoral thesis completed under the supervision of Assoc. Prof. Dr. Atalay Gündüz at Dokuz Eylül University (Turkey), Translation Studies PhD Programme.
2 See www.sihhatproject.org/ for project details.
3 In Turkey, there is currently no available document regulating professional standards, including ethical issues. For this reason, the interpreters' statements about their interpreting activities were discussed against the backdrop of certain ethical codes designed for public service interpreters in countries such as Australia, the United States and the United Kingdom (AUSIT, 2012; CHIA, 2002; JCCD, 2017; NAJIT, 2002; NRPSI, 2016).
4 See www.goc.gov.tr/gecici-koruma5638 for statistics on Syrian refugees in Turkey.
5 See the discussion section for an overview of the emerging themes and sub-themes.
6 The relevant regulation can be accessed at: www.resmigazete.gov.tr/eskiler/2013/03/20130305-6.htm
7 Besides giving interpreting services, the interpreters are also responsible for guiding and accompanying patients during various hospital procedures.
8 NGOI refers to "NGO interpreter", LFI refers to "legal field interpreter" and HI refers to "healthcare interpreter".
9 In the most general sense, *habitus* represents durable dispositions embodied in the individual (Bourdieu, 1977). It relates to an individual's personal trajectory, particular history, identity, gender, class, cultural background, past experiences, beliefs and values (Bourdieu, 1998). *Habitus* enables agents to be positioned in social spaces and to act in line with the rules of those social spaces (Bourdieu, 1998). Acquiring *habitus* starts in the family through both conscious and unconscious practices, and early socialization in the family forms the basis of all ensuing experiences (Bourdieu, 1972, cited in Bourdieu & Wacquant, 1992, p. 134).
10 In each context, only one or two interpreters (NGOI-3 and NGOI-4, LFI-8 and HI-1) have relatively sounder investments and experience in the interpreting field.
11 *Illusio* refers to the motives driving agents to invest in the game and to their commitment and interest in it (Bourdieu & Wacquant, 1992). It is recognizing the value of the stakes of the game and believing its stakes are "worth pursuing" (Bourdieu & Wacquant, 1992, pp. 116–117). The concept of *indifference*, i.e. "to be unmoved by the game" (Bourdieu & Wacquant, 1992, p. 116), is used as the opposite of *illusio*.
12 Through an individual's socialization process, primary *habitus* turns into professional *habitus*, being a gradual and mostly unconscious process (Bourdieu, 2000, p. 11). Professional *habitus* is formed of the dispositions instilled in individuals by the structures of professional fields during their professional trajectory (Bourdieu, 1998).
13 For the NGO and healthcare interpreters, proving language proficiency was among the requirements to be selected as interpreters. The healthcare interpreters were even required to take a language examination, albeit questionable in terms of the adequacy of the scope and content.
14 See https://sgdd.org.tr/ for details.
15 The project in question was planned to run between 2016 and 2020. See www.sihhatproject.org/proje-faaliyetleri_0-657 for details. However, the interpreters interviewed stated their contracts were extended until 2021.

16 Only LFI-4 and LFI-8, who perform interpreting as their main job and who indicated that they are called to the relevant courthouses and/or police units for a large number of interpreting tasks, mentioned that they at least generate relatively sufficient economic income.

17 The translation of all the excerpts from the interview transcripts and the other data sources into English was carried out by the author.

18 The relevant law can be accessed at: www.resmigazete.gov.tr/eskiler/2004/12/20041217.htm

19 The relevant law can be accessed at: www.resmigazete.gov.tr/eskiler/2004/10/20041012.htm

20 Although the NGO officials and some of the healthcare professionals interviewed seem to acknowledge the interpreters' significant role in meeting communication needs, the public officials ultimately project a fairly restricted autonomy and role for interpreters.

References

Aguilar Solano, M.A. (2012). *Positioning of Volunteer Interpreters in the Field of Public Service Interpreting in Spanish Hospitals: A Bourdieusian Perspective*. Unpublished doctoral dissertation. Manchester: The University of Manchester.

Angelelli, C.V. (2004). *Medical Interpreting and Cross-Cultural Communication*. Cambridge: Cambridge University Press. https://doi.org/10.1017/CBO9780511486616.

Aydın, M., Coşkun, S., Dağlı, T., Karakaya, Ş., Koçyıldırım, G., Rezaei Osalou, A., Önçırak, Y., Özdemir, D., Şener, E., Teker, N., Tezcan, E., Ulusoy, L. (n.d.). [Adli Süreçlerde Çocuk Dostu Tercüme.] Unpublished raw data. UNICEF and Republic of Turkey Ministry of Justice.

Bahadır, Ş. (2011). The task of the interpreter in the struggle of the other for empowerment: Mythical utopia or sine qua non of professionalism? In R. Sela-Sheffy & M. Shlesinger (Eds.), *Identity and Status in the Translational Professions* (pp. 263–278). Amsterdam: John Benjamins. https://doi.org/10.1075/tis.5.1.08bah.

Barsky, R. (1996). The interpreter as intercultural agent in convention refugee hearings. *The Translator*, 2(1), 45–63. https://doi.org/10.1080/13556509.1996.10798963.

Berk-Seligson, S. (1990). *The Bilingual Courtroom: Court Interpreters in the Judicial Process*. London: The University of Chicago Press.

Bot, H. (2003). The myth of the uninvolved interpreter interpreting in mental health and the development of a three-person psychology. In L. Brunette, G.L. Bastin, I. Hemlin & H. Clarke (Eds.), *The Critical Link 3* (pp. 27–35). Amsterdam: John Benjamins. https://doi.org/10.1075/btl.46.07bot.

Bourdieu, P. (1972). *Esquisse d'une théorie de la pratique. Précédé de trois études d'ethnologie kabyle*. Geneva: Droz.

Bourdieu, P. (1977). *Outline of a Theory of Practice* (R. Nice, Trans.). Cambridge: Cambridge University Press. https://doi.org/10.1017/CBO9780511812507.

Bourdieu, P. (1984). *Distinction: A Social Critique of the Judgement of Taste* (R. Nice, Trans.). Cambridge, MA: Harvard University Press.

Bourdieu, P. (1986). The forms of capital. In J.G. Richardson (Ed.), *Handbook of Theory and Research for the Sociology of Education* (pp. 241–258). New York: Greenwood Press.

Bourdieu, P. (1989). Social space and symbolic power. *Sociological Theory*, 7(1), 14–25. https://doi.org/10.2307/202060.

Bourdieu, P. (1991). *Language and Symbolic Power* (G. Raymond & M. Adamson, Trans.). Cambridge: Polity Press.

Bourdieu, P. (1993). *Sociology in Question* (R. Nice, Trans.). London: Sage Publications.

Bourdieu, P. (1998). *Practical Reason: On the Theory of Action* (R. Johnson, Trans.). Stanford, CA: Stanford University Press.

Bourdieu, P. (2000). *Pascalian Meditations* (R. Nice, Trans.). Stanford, CA: Stanford University Press.

Bourdieu, P., Wacquant, L.J.D. (1992). *An Invitation to Reflexive Sociology*. Cambridge: Polity Press.

Braun, V., Clarke, V. (2006). Using thematic analysis in psychology. *Qualitative Research in Psychology*, 3(2), 77–101. https://doi.org/10.1191/1478088706qp063oa.

California Healthcare Interpreters Association (CHIA). (2002). *California Standards for Healthcare Interpreters: Ethical Principles, Protocols, and Guidance on Roles & Intervention*. Retrieved October 31, 2018 from www.chiaonline.org/Resources/Documents/CHIA%20Standards/standards_chia.pdf.

Chesterman, A. (2006). Questions in the sociology of translation. In J.F. Duarte, A.A. Rosa & T. Seruya (Eds.), *Translation Studies at the Interface of Disciplines* (pp. 9–27). Amsterdam: John Benjamins. https://doi.org/10.1075/btl.68.03che.

Chesterman, A. (2009). The name and nature of translator studies. *Hermes*, 42, 13–22.

Clifford, A. (2004). Is fidelity ethical? The social role of the healthcare interpreter. *TTR: Traduction, Terminologie, Redaction*, 17(2), 89–114. https://doi.org/10.7202/013273ar.

Corsellis, A. (2008). *Public Service Interpreting: The First Steps*. New York: Palgrave Macmillan.

Creswell, J.W. (2007). *Qualitative Inquiry and Research Design: Choosing Among Five Approaches* (2nd ed.). Thousand Oaks, CA: Sage Publications.

Guéry, F. (2014). *Learning to be a Public Service Interpreter: Boundaries, Ethics and Emotion in a Marginal Profession*. Unpublished doctoral dissertation. Manchester: The Manchester Metropolitan University.

Hale, S.B. (2008). Controversies over the role of the court interpreter. In C. Valero-Garcés & A. Martin (Eds.), *Crossing Borders in Community Interpreting* (pp. 99–121). Amsterdam: John Benjamins. https://doi.org/10.1075/btl.76.06hal.

Hale, S.B., Napier, J. (2013). *Research Methods in Interpreting: A Practical Resource*. London: Bloomsbury Publishing.

Hale, S.B. (2015). Community interpreting. In F. Pöchhacker (Ed.), *Routledge Encyclopedia of Interpreting Studies* (pp. 65–69). London: Routledge.

Hsieh, E. (2006). Conflicts in how interpreters manage their roles in provider–patient interactions. *Social Science & Medicine*, 62(3), 721–730. https://doi.org/10.1016/j.socscimed.2005.06.029.

Ibrahim, Z. (2007). The interpreter as advocate: Malaysian court interpreting as a case in point. In C. Wadensjö, B. Englund-Dimitrova & A.L. Nilsson (Eds.), *The Critical Link 4* (pp. 205–213). Amsterdam: John Benjamins. https://doi.org/10.1075/btl.70.23ibr.

Inghilleri, M. (2003). Habitus, field and discourse: Interpreting as a socially situated activity. *Target*, 15(2), 243–268. https://doi.org/10.1075/target.15.2.03ing.

Inghilleri, M. (2005). Mediating zones of uncertainty: Interpreter agency, the interpreting habitus and political asylum adjudication. *The Translator*, 11(1), 69–85. https://doi.org/10.1080/13556509.2005.10799190

Knapp-Potthoff, A., Knapp, K. (1986). Interweaving two discourses – The difficult task of the non-professional interpreter. In J. House & S. Blum-Kulka (Eds.), *Interlingual and Intercultural Communication* (pp. 151–168). Tübingen: Gunter Narr.

Koskinen, K. (2020). *Translation and Affect: Essays on Sticky Affects and Translational Affective Labour*. Amsterdam: John Benjamins. https://doi.org/10.1075/btl.152.

Leanza, Y. (2005). Roles of community interpreters in pediatrics as seen by interpreters, physicians and researchers. *Interpreting*, 7(2), 167–192. https://doi.org/10.1075/intp.7.2.03lea.

Lee, J. (2009). Conflicting views on court interpreting examined through surveys of legal professionals and court interpreters. *Interpreting*, 11(1), 35–56. https://doi.org/10.1075/intp.11.1.04lee.

Mikkelson, H. (1998). Towards a redefinition of the role of the court interpreter. *Interpreting*, 3(1), 21–46. https://doi.org/10.1075/intp.3.1.02mik.

Morris, R. (1995). The moral dilemmas of court interpreting. *The Translator*, 1(1), 25–46. https://doi.org/10.1080/13556509.1995.10798948.

Morris, R. (1999). The gum syndrome: Predicaments in court interpreting. *Forensic Linguistics*, 6(1), 6–29. https://doi.org/10.1558/sll.1999.6.1.6.

Morris, R. (2011). Images of the court interpreter: Professional identity, role definition and self-image. In R. Sela-Sheffy & M. Shlesinger (Eds.), *Identity and Status in the Translational Professions* (pp. 209–229). Amsterdam: John Benjamins. https://doi.org/10.1075/tis.5.1.02mor.

National Association of Judicial Interpreters and Translators (NAJIT). (2002). *Code of Ethics and Professional Responsibilities*. Retrieved October 31, 2018 from https://najit.org/wp-content/uploads/2016/09/NAJITCodeofEthicsFINAL.pdf

Nimer, M., Oruç, T. (2019). *Sustainable Approaches to Humanitarian Assistance in the Field of Language Education for Adult Refugees in Turkey*. IPC-Sabanci University-Stiftung Mercator Initiative. Retrieved September 23, 2019 from https://ipc.sabanciuniv.edu/Content/Images/CKeditorImages/20200313-11034972.pdf.

Niska, H. (1995). Just interpreting: Role conflicts and discourse types in court interpreting. In M. Morris (Ed.), *Translation and the Law* (pp. 293–316). Amsterdam: John Benjamins. https://doi.org/10.1075/ata.viii.

Pöchhacker, F. (2000). The community interpreter's task: Self-perception and provider views. In R.P. Roberts, S.E. Carr, D. Abraham & A. Dufour (Eds.), *The Critical Link 2: Interpreters in the Community* (pp. 49–65). Amsterdam: John Benjamins. https://doi.org/10.1075/btl.31.07poc.

Pöchhacker, F. (2004). *Introducing Interpreting Studies*. London: Routledge.

Rudvin, M. (2007). Professionalism and ethics in community interpreting: The impact of individualist versus collective group identity on interpreting performance. *Interpreting*, 9(1), 47–69. https://doi.org/10.1075/intp.9.1.04rud.

Rudvin, M. (2015). Interpreting and professional identity. In H. Mikkelson & R. Jourdenais (Eds.), *The Routledge Handbook of Interpreting* (pp. 432–446). London: Routledge.

Simeoni, D. (1998). The pivotal status of the translator's habitus. *Target*, 10(1), 1–39. https://doi.org/10.1075/target.10.1.02sim.

Souza, I.E.T. De V. (2016). *Intercultural Mediation in Healthcare: From the Professional Medical Interpreters' Perspective*. Bloomington, IN: Xlibris.

The Australian Institute of Interpreters and Translators (AUSIT). (2012). *Code of Ethics and Code of Conduct*. Retrieved October 31, 2018 from https://ausit.org/AUSIT/Documents/Code_Of_Ethics_Full.pdf.

The Judicial Council on Cultural Diversity (JCCD). (2017). *Recommended National Standards for Working with Interpreters in Courts and Tribunals*. Retrieved October 31, 2018 from www.naati.com.au/media/1680/mca04694-national-standards-web-171025pdf.pdf.

The National Register of Public Service Interpreters (NRPSI). (2016). *Code of Professional Conduct*. Retrieved October 31, 2018 from www.nrpsi.org.uk/downloads/NRPSI_Code_of_Professional_Conduct_22.01.16.pdf.

The United Nations Refugee Agency (UNHCR). (2019). *Global Trends: Forced Displacement in 2018*. Retrieved September 23, 2019 from www.unhcr.org/statistics/unhcrstats/5d08d7ee7/unhcr-global-trends-2018.html.

Tipton, R. (2014). Perceptions of the 'occupational other': Interpreters, social workers and intercultures. *British Journal of Social Work*, 46(2), 463–479. https://doi.org/10.1093/bjsw/bcu136.

Torun, P., Mücaz-Karaaslan, M., Sandıklı, B., Acar, C., Shurtleff, E., Dhrolia, S., Herek, B. (2018). Health and health care access for Syrian refugees living in İstanbul. *International Journal of Public Health*, 63, 601–608. https://doi.org/10.1007/s00038-018-1096-4.

Ulusoy, L., Rezaei Osalou, A. (2019). [Tercümanlık ve Tercümanla Çalışma Alanlarında Açıklanması Gereken 14 Kritik Bilgi.] Unpublished raw data. ASAM.

Valero Garcés, C. (2012). A sociological perspective on TIPS. Explorations into the translator's/interpreter's (in)visibility in translation and interpreting in public services. *The Interpreter's Newsletter*, 17, 13–37.

Wadensjö, C. (1998). *Interpreting as Interaction*. London: Longman.

Yücel, A., Utas, C., Luchsinger, G., Kavlak, İ.V., Kristjansdottir, İ.B., Freizer, S. (2018). *Needs Assessment of Syrian Women and Girls under Temporary Protection Status in Turkey*. Ankara: UN Women & ASAM. Retrieved September 29, 2019 from www2.unwomen.org/-/media/field%20office%20eca/attachments/publications/country/turkey/the%20needs%20assessmentengwebcompressed.pdf?la=en&vs=3139.

9 Interpreting for the linguistic majority

A historical review of court interpreting in Hong Kong

Eva N.S. Ng[1]

9.1 Introduction

For well over 150 years, public service interpreting (PSI) in Hong Kong had all along been about interpreting in courts and in other legal settings such as the Police Force and the Correctional Services Department. It was not until after the enactment of the Racial Discrimination Ordinance (RDO) (Cap 602, Laws of Hong Kong) in 2008, which prohibits direct and indirect discrimination, harassment and vilification on the ground of race, that the Administrative Guidelines on Promotion of Racial Equality were issued by the Constitutional and Mainland Affairs Bureau in 2010 to promote racial equality and ensure equal access by ethnic minorities to public services. This was followed by the expansion of PSI to cover also interpreting services in other public sectors, including public hospitals and government clinics, as well as social welfare and housing services-related departments (Ng, Leung, & Loper, forthcoming). The expanded PSI is however targeted at ethnic minority groups, which in the context of Hong Kong refers to racial groups speaking neither English nor Cantonese. This chapter, however, addresses the issue of court interpreting, focusing specifically on interpreting services between English and Cantonese in Hong Kong courts.

Court interpreting in Hong Kong was necessitated as a result of the cession of Hong Kong to Britain in 1842 by virtue of the Nanking Treaty. Due to the British colonial background, for well over a century until 1974, English was the only official language and the language in which court proceedings were conducted in Hong Kong. On the other hand, lay litigants appearing in court, defendants and witnesses alike, are mostly Chinese and more often than not would choose to testify in Cantonese, the local vernacular spoken by about 90% of the local population (Census and Statistics Department, 2017), or occasionally in other Chinese dialects. This accounts for the ubiquity of court interpreters, whose service has been indispensable in court proceedings for bridging the communication gap between English-speaking legal professionals and local Chinese-speaking litigants. The use of English as the trial language in a Chinese society has rendered the Hong Kong courtroom a unique setting in which interpreting services are provided, ironically

DOI: 10.4324/9781003197027-12

to cater to the needs of the linguistic majority rather than that of linguistic minorities (Ng, 2013b, 2015, 2018). For this reason, the legal system in Hong Kong is dubbed "one of the most 'interpreted' legal systems in the world" (Ng 2009, p. 120).

With the handover of Hong Kong's sovereignty to China in 1997 and subsequently the increasing use of Cantonese as the trial language in the past two decades or so, court interpreters are no longer a fixture in the courtroom as they used to be, especially in the lower courts, including magistracies, tribunals and even the District Court, where most cases are now heard in Cantonese. In the High Court, however, a large proportion of criminal cases are still heard in English on a day-to-day basis (Key Figures and Statistics, 2020), because of the presence of expatriate judges and/or counsel. This chapter presents a historical review of the practice of court interpreting in Hong Kong from early colonial days to the present time. It seeks to demonstrate what makes the Hong Kong courtroom a unique bilingual setting and how this bilingual legal setting has changed over time. It explores how these changes have impacted on the role of court interpreters and illustrates with authentic data the challenges presented to court interpreters working in the present-day Hong Kong courtroom. It also highlights the limitations of *chuchotage* in the unique courtroom setting where interpreting is provided to cater to the needs of the linguistic majority, and proposes ways to address these challenges and limitations (see also Ng, 2019).

9.2 Court interpreting in early colonial days

Britain started its colonial rule over Hong Kong soon after the ratification of the Nanking Treaty in 1842. During the first 20 years of the British administration, the question of interpretation had been a matter that "caused the greatest embarrassment" to the colonial government, as very often courts either could not sit because no interpreters were available, or had to adjourn because of incorrect interpretation (Norton-Kyshe, 1971, p. 8). As trials were conducted in English, local litigants appearing in court as witnesses or defendants would not be able to participate in court proceedings without the assistance of an interpreter. While it is nowadays commonplace for educated people in Hong Kong to be bilingual in English and Chinese to varying degrees, in early colonial days, people proficient in both Chinese and English were *rare species*. Those of the few who could act as interpreters and translators between the British administrators and the local Chinese population were mostly missionaries who had learned Chinese to spread the gospel (Bickley, 2001, p. 10). Missionaries, however, devoted much of their effort to "evangelisation, conversion and education of the Chinese", and most of them were not British and were antipathetic to the colonial government (Lethbridge, 1970, p. 38). Moreover, the Chinese dialects spoken by these missionaries were mostly Cantonese or Mandarin, whereas there were other Chinese dialects spoken by at least one-quarter of the local population at that time, for which there were no competent interpreters (Eitel, 1877, p. 5).

As such, the lack of interpreters was one of the most difficult problems facing the government in its administration and maintenance of law and order, and inevitably hindered the administration of justice (Smith, 1975). Some interpreters were not sufficiently acquainted with English, while others were good at neither English nor Chinese (Eitel, 1877). To make matters worse, interpreters in those days had little understanding of their role and would often engage in lengthy private conversations with witnesses and "put at their own instigation leading questions to witnesses" (Eitel, 1877, p. 10). They were also observed to suggest to witnesses what to say, and to be in the habit of bullying, lecturing and scolding witnesses for giving absurd replies, while the absurdity might be a result of the witnesses' "incomprehensibility of the interpreter's unidiomatic speech or peculiarity of pronunciation" or their "mental incapacity or intentional evasion" (ibid.). Eitel suggested that:

> the evasions, equivocations and other subterfuges which witnesses so often indulge in, and which in the case of English witnesses are at once noted by Counsel, Jury and Judge as a significant part of the evidence, are thus entirely lost sight of in the case of Chinese witnesses.
>
> (ibid.)

Meanwhile, as the Chinese witnesses were not able to testify in the language of the court, their evidence was subject to the interpreter's "knowledge, judgment and discretion" and depended on "how much he may retranslate or entirely omit their evidence" (ibid.). As a natural consequence, the Chinese population then supposed that justice in Hong Kong depended "as much upon the good-will or knowledge of the interpreter as upon the legal acumen of the Counsel or the impartiality of the Judge" (Eitel, 1877, p. 10).

Worse still, the few Chinese interpreters who were able to bridge the communication gap between court personnel and lay participants were "frequently exposed to the temptation of bribes for giving false interpretation" (Smith, 1975, p. 71). Therefore, from time to time there were native Chinese interpreters caught indulging in corrupt practices and subsequently dismissed, and as noted by Eitel (1877, p. 3), "the cases of detection were probably few as compared with the amount of rascality carried on undetected".

The reason why interpreters in those days were able to manipulate the courtroom discourse, and to escape being caught for their malpractice or for any mistakes made, is that back then, none of the legal and court personnel, including the judges, lawyers and jury, understood a word of Chinese, although it was the language spoken by the majority of local litigants (Jarman, 1996, p. 629). Besides, what was kept in the court record was the utterances made in English and the English interpretation of the testimony given in court. What was said by the witnesses/defendants in Cantonese or any other Chinese dialects was never entered into the court record, let alone picked up by a recording system, which was something unheard of in those days. This is in stark contrast to the present-day Hong Kong courtroom, which is dominated by judges and lawyers who speak both English and Cantonese, and where court proceedings are now audio recorded.

9.3 Court interpreting from the 1970s to 1997

The entire legal and judicial landscape underwent fundamental changes from the 1970s to the 1990s. This arose primarily from Chinese being accorded its official status in 1974, the emergence of locally trained lawyers and subsequently the introduction of bilingual legislation, as well as bilingual court reporting enabled by the installation of an audio-recording system in court (Ng, 2018, 2019). This has also changed the linguistic landscape of the courtroom, and presented unprecedented challenges to the court interpreters working in it, while at the same time better safeguarding the delivery of justice.

9.3.1 The official status of Chinese and the legal arena's resistance to use it in court

The year 1974 marked a major watershed in the official language policy of Hong Kong. It was in this year that the Official Languages Ordinance was passed, establishing both English and Chinese as official languages for the purposes of communication between the government and the general public, as well as for court proceedings (Official Languages Ordinance, Cap 5, Laws of Hong Kong). Subsequent to the enactment of the Official Languages Ordinance, the requirement to use only English in courts was lifted at the Magistrates' Courts and various tribunals in the same year. This language restriction was later removed at the District Court and the High Court in stages from 1996 to 1997 (Information Paper, 13 October 1997; see also Ng, 2013b, 2018, 2019).

The freedom to use Chinese (i.e. Cantonese) as the trial language in the Magistrates' Courts from 1974 did not, however, result in an immediate switch of the court language from English to Chinese. The plan to use Cantonese as the trial language in the Magistrates' Courts met with resistance from the Hong Kong Bar Association and had thus to be postponed (Wong, 1990). Since the scheme allowed magistrates hearing a trial in Cantonese to make a record of the proceedings in English, the Bar Association expressed concerns that magistrates, not being qualified translators, would have to translate Cantonese testimony into English by themselves and that since their notes were not open to scrutiny by other parties during the trial, translation errors made would escape notice. In a trial conducted in English, however, the Bar Association argued, any mistakes made by the court interpreter would be noticed and rectified by other Chinese speakers in court (ibid.). The argument put forward by the Bar Association is indicative of the interpreting reality in the Hong Kong courtroom in the early 1990s, which remains by and large true of the status quo in the present-day bilingual Hong Kong courtroom: in a trial conducted in English, the court interpreter is, unlike his/her counterparts in early colonial days, not the only bilingual in court and his/her interpretation is open to scrutiny by the other bilinguals in court.

The other reality, which was true of the early 1990s Hong Kong courtroom, is that English was often chosen as the trial language with interpretation provided, not necessarily because there was a genuine communication barrier between lay participants and legal professionals, but because the magistrates did not wish to or, more likely, were not able to translate the court proceedings into English by themselves. Although the law does not require magistrates to keep their notes in English in a Cantonese trial, the Chinese magistrates back then all kept their notes in English.[2] The reason for this practice was twofold: first, the writing system of Chinese is far more complicated than its English counterpart and it is thus understandably more efficient to note in English than in Chinese; second, even if the record of the proceedings was kept in Chinese in a Cantonese trial, the Chinese record would have to be translated into English in case of an appeal, as Chinese was not allowed in the High Court until late 1996 (Ng, 2018). This accounts for resistance to the use of Chinese in the courts from the legal arena and thus the continued use of court interpreters so that a scrutinised official record of the proceedings could be kept.

Another reason for magistrates to shy away from the use of Chinese as the trial language despite their freedom to use it from 1974 is that English remained the language of the law until 1987, when the Official Languages Ordinance was amended to require new laws to be enacted and published in both English and Chinese. It was not until April 1989 that the first bilingual ordinance was enacted – which also marks the commencement of the bilingual legislation programme in preparation for the changeover of Hong Kong's sovereignty in 1997. Before the entire Law Book (Laws of Hong Kong) was available in a bilingual form, any reference to the statutory law for which no Chinese version was available would mean that magistrates would have to translate into Chinese the English statutes to be cited. As such, court interpreters in Magistrates' Courts continued to play their role even when their services were strictly speaking superfluous, as in the case with bilingual judges and counsel and local litigants.

9.3.2 The use of Chinese in the Magistrates' Courts and the role of the interpreter

When it later became obvious that the use of Chinese in the courts was inevitable with the imminent handover of Hong Kong's sovereignty in 1997, bilingual magistrates and counsel made no more attempt to resist the trend but chose to go with it. However, instead of releasing court interpreters, many magistrates kept the interpreters as language consultants in court and would seek help from them in a whisper when they encountered a problem in the process of silently translating the proceedings into English (Ng, 2013b, 2018). Therefore, even in Cantonese trials, the interpreters had to pay close attention to what was going on in court, as the magistrates might ask them for help, in a whisper, with any translation problem encountered at any time during a trial.

9.4 Post-colonial court interpretation in Hong Kong

9.4.1 Increasing use of Chinese in the courts and declining need for interpreters

The changeover of Hong Kong's sovereignty in 1997 has resulted in an increasing use of Cantonese as the trial language in the Magistrates' Courts as well as in the District Court since that time. In the Court of First Instance (CFI) of the High Court, however, quite a substantial percentage of criminal cases are still heard in English on a daily basis due to the presence of expatriate court personnel, judges and counsel included. Statistics from the Department of Justice of Hong Kong reveal that, in 2020, only 21.6% of criminal trials in the CFI of the High Court were heard in Chinese, while the corresponding figures in the District Court and the Magistrates' Courts were 79.3% and 84.1% respectively (Key Figures and Statistics, 31 December 2020). Unlike in the early 1990s when interpreters had to remain in court during court proceedings conducted in Chinese to assist magistrates with their translation discreetly, as was mentioned above, Chinese trials nowadays are conducted without the presence of the court interpreter, thus reducing the demand for court interpreting. The freedom to use Chinese in the High Court so that appeals from lower courts conducted in Chinese need not be translated into English, and the installation of the audio-recording system (to be explained later in this chapter), have relieved judges in the lower courts of the need to translate Chinese court proceedings into English.

9.4.2 Increasing need to work with bilingual co-participants in court

In early colonial days, the court interpreter was usually the only person speaking both the language of the lay participants and the court language, as has been mentioned above. Any interpreting mistakes would simply go unnoticed because few would be able to challenge the accuracy of the interpretation provided in court; nor was the testimony given in Chinese or the Chinese interpretation provided kept in the court record for subsequent review. Today, while interpreters continue to play their part in trials conducted in English, they are no longer the only bilinguals in the courts, which are dominated by legal professionals who are bilingual in Chinese and English. As such, it is not uncommon for a bilingual counsel to challenge the interpretation provided in court, either because the interpretation itself is not as precise, or as an advocacy strategy.

Examples 1–4 below, extracted from a High Court rape trial, serve to illustrate the challenges facing the court interpreter working with bilingual counsel. In this case, the defendant was charged with raping his younger sister's ex-girlfriend, a lesbian. The defendant did not deny having sexual intercourse with the complainant, but alleged that he had done that at the invitation of the complainant. In Example 1 below, the defendant describes how the complainant invited him to go up to bed to have sex with her by pulling his "garment/upper garment". The word in Cantonese uttered by the defendant was "*saam*1[3]" (衫), which is ambiguous in meaning and can mean clothing in general or a top (commonly rendered as garment and upper garment respectively in court). See Appendix 9.1 for the transcription symbols used.

Example 1. Examination-in-chief of defendant

Turn	Speaker	Utterance/interpretation (translation or back-translation in italics)
1	Defendant	咁喺同一時間:，(.)佢就: si:–, eh用佢嘅:左手就(.)少少彎彎地，就拉住我件衫，啫係腰度件衫。 *In the meantime, she used her left hand, (elbow) slightly at an angle, to pull my* ***saam1,*** *that is,* ***saam1*** *at my waist area.*
2	Interpreter	And then–, 你再講多一次。 *And then–, say that again.*
3	Defendant	Er佢用佢嘅左手拉我er腰度，啫係腰部份嘅件衫。 *She used her left hand to pull my waist area, that is, the garment–, piece of garment/ upper garment (ge3gin6 saam1) at my waist area.*
4	Interpreter	And then, she used her left hand to pull the um (.) garment at my eh waist area.

The use of the term *saam*1, as mentioned above, is capable of being interpreted as garment or upper garment, depending on the preceding context or the context in which the term is uttered. Since it had been established in the complainant's evidence in chief and in the defendant's earlier testimony that he was wearing only a pair of shorts on the day in question and prior to the sexual intercourse, the interpreter's choice of the word "garment" in lieu of "upper garment" in her interpretation seems to be a well-deliberated decision. In other words, she opted for an interpretation consistent with the preceding evidence. This, however, apparently goes against the will of the prosecutor, the cross-examiner, whose primary aim in cross-examination is to discredit the testimony of the witness (Salhany, 2006), and in this case to prove that the defendant has lied about the "invitation" extended to him by the complainant. The prosecutor, however, chose not to challenge the interpretation during the defendant's examination in chief, but to accuse the defendant of having invented a story about the complainant's consent in his cross-examination of him. See Example 2 below.

Example 2. Cross-examination of defendant

Turn	Speaker	Utterance/interpretation (translation or back-translation in italics)
1	Prosecutor	Alright. Now, you have made up (.) a very good story about how (.) that day developed into your going up onto (.) her bed.
2	Interpreter	咁你呢，就係呢，係作咗個好嘅古仔呢，就係話當日呢，係個事情呢，係點樣發展到呢，你呢就係上咗去佢嗰張床度喇。 *And you, you made up a good story to explain how the event on the day in question developed to the stage of you going up onto her bed.*
3	Defendant	我冇作到古仔，[我可以發誓。 *I didn't make up a story. [I can swear.*
4	Interpreter	[I didn't. I didn't eh make up any story. I can swear(.) by God.
5	Prosecutor	There was only one hitch though. You were not wearing any upper garment that day.
6	Interpreter	咁但係呢，有一點就係話當時呢，你係冇着到任何嘅上衫個噃，係咪呀？ *But there is one thing, that is, you were not wearing any upper garment (soeng6saam1). Is that right?*
7	Defendant	係。 *Right.*
8	Interpreter	Yeah.
9	Prosecutor	So, how could she have pulled (.) you by the upper garment (.) at the waist position?
10	Interpreter	咁佢當時又點樣係扯你嗰件上衫–, 係eh腰部嘅衫呀？ *So how could she have pulled your upper garment (soeng6saam1), that is, eh, garment (saam1) at the waist position?*

Although the interpreter had rendered *saam*1 as "garment" in the defendant's evidence in chief, not "upper garment", when referring to the defendant's earlier evidence, the prosecutor used "upper garment" (turn 5), which in his opinion, was what *saam*1 should have been taken to mean. In her interpretation of the prosecutor's comment, the interpreter had to add the word *soeng6* (upper) to the word *saam1* to differentiate it from the more ambiguous word *saam1* and of course her earlier rendition of it as "garment". However, since the actual word uttered by the defendant was *saam1*, not *soeng6saam1*, the interpreter must have realised the need to reconcile the discrepancy in her Cantonese interpretation in turn 10 when she hesitated after rendering "upper garment" as *soeng6saam1* and finally settled on *saam1*, in an obvious attempt to make her interpretation consistent with the actual word used by the defendant, and presumably her interpretation of it as "garment" as well. It must also be noted that the term *soeng6saam1* is marked and not an ordinary or idiomatic expression.

The prosecutor's comment about the inconsistency in the defendant's evidence prompted the judge, an expatriate who did not speak Cantonese, to review his notes, which however showed no such discrepancy as the judge's notes were based on the interpretation provided in court. At this point, the prosecutor flagged an interpretation mistake and informed the court that the word "garment" was the interpreter's rendition, whereas the word from the mouth of the defendant was *saam1*, which he understood to be "upper garment" – a result of his de-contextualisation of the word. (See Example 3 below.)

Example 3. Interaction between judge and prosecutor

Turn	Speaker	Utterance/interpretation
1	Prosecutor	*Saam1*, the Chinese used by the accused himself was *saam1*, and it was translated (.) as "garment"=
2	Judge	=Yes, you say that the translation is incorrect. It should be "upper garment"?
3	Prosecutor	To be eh, to be exact, it should be "upper garment".

Being not conversant with Cantonese and thus not equipped with the bilingual skill to decide if the prosecutor's allegation was valid, the judge could only leave the matter in the hands of the interpreter, as indicated in turn 1 of Example 4 below.

Example 4. Interaction between judge and interpreter

Turn	Speaker	Utterance/interpretation
1	Judge	Well, I suppose insofar as the first one is concerned, the question is whether my interpreter is happy with the interpretation she's uh, she's given, or whether she wants to er qualify that in any way.
2	Interpreter	< whispering >Yeah, I am happy with that=
3	Judge	=You are happy with interpretation just "garment"?
4	Interpreter	Er with er "upper".
5	Judge	"upper garment", okay. <sighs > Right.

The interpreter's decision to adopt the prosecutor's suggestion may be regarded as a reflection of her loss of linguistic power in the presence of a bilingual counsel.

The above examples show that interpreting between English and Cantonese in present-day Hong Kong courts is very much a transparent process, and the interpreters no longer enjoy the monopolistic linguistic power that their counterparts did in the old days.

In addition to the presence of bilingual co-participants in court, another factor contributing to the transparency of court interpreting in Hong Kong is the use of the consecutive mode of interpreting arising from the need to interpret for the linguistic majority. As was mentioned earlier, in a trial conducted in English, not only the defendant, but also most, if not all, of the witnesses require interpretation services. The use of consecutive interpreting makes it easier for bilingual counsel and judges, or even local witnesses with English proficiency to varying degrees to scrutinise and to challenge the interpretation during the court proceedings.

9.4.3 Implementation of the bilingual court reporting system

The installation of the Digital Audio Recording and Transcription System (DARTS) in the courts in the late 1990s further enhanced the transparency of the court interpreting process in Hong Kong and enabled a bilingual court reporting system. Before that, only utterances made in English and the English interpretation were kept in the court record. What was said by the witnesses/defendants in Chinese and the Chinese interpretation of English utterances vanished into thin air once spoken. Even if an appeal should ensue at a later stage on the grounds of an alleged interpreting error, verification was impossible in the absence of any record of the original testimony in Cantonese. What the court relied on for its verdict was the English version of the court proceedings. With the introduction of DARTS, any mistake allegedly made by the interpreter can be checked against the record. Interested parties can apply for access to the bilingual record in case of an appeal.

The appeal case between the Hong Kong Special Administration Region (HKSAR) and Ng Pak Lun (HKSAR v. Ng Pak Lun, 2011) is an example of DARTS serving as evidence of misinterpretation by the interpreter, which eventually led to the conviction being set aside by the Court of Appeal and to a retrial of the case. In this case, the interpreter twice rendered "really serious bodily harm" in the judge's questions to the defendant into "some degree of harm". Interestingly, misinterpretation did not constitute grounds for the appeal application in this case, as counsel for both parties and the trial judge were all non-Cantonese-speaking expatriates and were unaware of the inaccuracy in interpretation. It was during the examination of the DARTS transcript necessitated by the appeal that the interpretation problem was uncovered. As a result, the appeal was allowed and a fresh trial was ordered by the judge of the Court of Appeal.

9.4.4 The limitations of chuchotage *and of the recording system*

The transparency of the interpreting process refers, however, only to the process of consecutive interpreting, which is provide in open court, audible to everyone present in court, and as a result, is picked up by DARTS. Interpretation in a whisper (i.e. *chuchotage*) provided for the defendant in the dock is, however, intended only for the defendant, and is thus not recorded by DARTS. This includes interpretation of interactions between the judge and the jury (as in jury instructions and summings-up) and of counsel's opening/closing speeches or mitigation. Therefore, if a defendant lodges an appeal on the grounds of inadequate interpretation provided to him/her during this process and argues that the inadequacy compromises his/her right to a fair trial, in the absence of a record of the interpretation, it would be difficult to substantiate the claim, or for the court to make a ruling on the allegation. It would be at the discretion of the appellate court on a case-by-case basis. For example, in HKSAR *v.* Moala Alipate (2019), the accuracy of interpretation provided in *chuchotage* was challenged and the Tongan interpreter admitted in his affidavit that he had been able to interpret only around 20–30% of what was said by the judge in his jury instructions and summing-up, as the judge was allegedly speaking too fast for him to keep up. The appeal was allowed and the conviction of the defendant was set aside, with a trial de novo ordered by the court. In HKSAR *v.* Gutierrez Alvarez Keishu Mercedes (2020), however, the appeal raised on a similar ground was dismissed by the appellate court. Although in the two aforementioned cases, the interpretation was not between English and Cantonese, but between English and ethnic minority languages, i.e. Tongan and Spanish, the limitations of *chuchotage* apply also to day-to-day interpretation between English and Cantonese.

For example, in HKSAR *v.* Chan Hon Wing (2020), the quality of interpretation provided in *chuchotage* was once again called into question and raised as grounds for appeal. At trial, the jury informed the court of an immense difficulty in understanding the judge's instructions given in English and asked for the interpretation provided in *chuchotage*, otherwise audible only to the defendant, to be made available to them through headphones during the subsequent case summing-up by the judge. The request was granted by the court, which, however, later was advanced as grounds for appeal. It was submitted by counsel for the appellant that the *chuchotage* provided primarily for the defendant could not be a full and complete interpretation of what the judge said in her summing-up; yet the jury was expected to have a full comprehension of it in order to be able to follow the instructions given by the judge and to return a true verdict. Again, in the absence of a record of the interpretation provided in *chuchotage*, there is no basis for a sound judgement to be made about the quality of the interpretation. The interpreter involved in this case was a full-time employee of the Judiciary, not a freelance interpreter, unlike in the previous two cases.

She was asked to provide a written statement about her qualifications and experience in interpreting, and about the quality of her interpretation. The appeal was eventually dismissed.

As a matter of fact, jurors selected to sit in an English-medium trial are presumed to have a sufficient level of English proficiency to enable them to follow court proceedings conducted in English, although this presumption is ill grounded as research findings have demonstrated otherwise (see Duff et al., 1992; Ng, 2013b, 2016, 2018). This appeal case provides further evidence about the questionable ability of Chinese jurors in Hong Kong to hear cases conducted in English and highlights the pressing need to make the Hong Kong courtroom fully bilingual to all, not just to the defendant. As has been noted above, the day-to-day court interpretation between Chinese and English is to cater to the needs of the linguistic majority, including the jury, whose ability to hear a case in English without the assistance of the court interpreter cannot be taken for granted, as evidenced in *HKSAR v. Chan Hon Wing* (2020), cited above.

9.5 Recommendations

In view of the limitations of *chuchotage*, and that day-to-day interpreting services in the Hong Kong courtroom are provided to cater to the linguistic majority, the need to make the courtroom fully bilingual is apparent. This will make the interpretation provided in court accessible to anyone in need of the service, including but not limited to the defendant and the jury. To assist the appellate court in their decision in times of appeals advanced on the grounds of inadequate interpretation provided in *chuchotage*, it is equally important for a full record of the interpretation to be kept for later review. To this end, the following recommendations, among others, are made to address these issues specifically.

9.5.1 Implementation of an electronic mode of simultaneous interpretation system in lieu of chuchotage

The implementation of an electronic mode of simultaneous interpretation system will enable the access of all parties in court to the interpretation currently provided in *chuchotage*. This is particularly important for jurors, whose ability to understand legal instructions in court without the assistance of a court interpreter is questionable (Duff et al., 1992; Ng, 2013b, 2016, 2018). The drug trafficking case cited above (HKSAR *v.* Chan Hon Wing, 2020) provides further evidence on this aspect. Simultaneous interpretation provided in the electronic mode will enable both the defendant and the jury as well as anyone in court in need of the service to access it. This includes interpretation not only of jury instructions and summings-up by judges and speeches by counsel, but also of testimony given in English, as in the case of expert witnesses testifying in English (Ng, 2018, 2020). However, to ensure accuracy in interpretation, the consecutive mode for witnesses testifying in Cantonese should stay and should not be replaced by simultaneous interpreting.

9.5.2 Maintaining a full record of the interpretation provide in court

The installation of DARTS was to enable a bilingual reporting system of court proceedings. For this reason, it is important for DARTS to record not only interpretation provided in the consecutive mode, but also the interpretation provided in the simultaneous mode (now in a whisper and not able to be picked up by the system). This is to ensure a full record of the proceedings and of the interpretation provided, and in the event of an appeal raised on the grounds of defective interpretation, the record can be used as an essential reference for evaluation of the interpretation. In the long run, this may also help prevent the use of inaccurate or inadequate interpretation as a convenient ground of appeal.

9.5.3 Quality in interpreting as a shared responsibility

Interpreting in the highly charged legal setting is particularly demanding and challenging, and accuracy cannot be comprised. On the other hand, simultaneous interpreting itself is a cognitively challenging process. Fast speech delivery rates have an adverse impact on the accuracy and completeness of the rendition (Barghout, Rosendo, & García, 2015; Seeber, 2017), and omissions seem unavoidable in extremely difficult conditions whether as a mistake, a technique or a pragmatic strategy on the part of the interpreter in conference interpreting (Gile, 1995; Korpal, 2012; Pym, 2008; Setton, 1999). In court interpreting, however, any inadequacy in interpretation may be raised as grounds for appeal and arguably lead to a miscarriage of justice. For this reason, it is important for the court to keep a record of everything said and of the interpretation provided in both modes, and to assume shared responsibility for ensuring the quality of interpretation, especially in simultaneous interpretation, which by default would not be accurate without the required conditions under which it is performed. To facilitate the work of the interpreter, in the first place, speakers in court must speak slowly, clearly and loudly enough for the interpreter to hear them. In the Nuremburg Court trial in 1945, in which simultaneous interpreting was used in court for the first time in history, speakers were instructed to speak at a dictation rate of not higher than 60 words per minutes in order to ensure accuracy in interpretation (Gaiba, 1998), when the average speech delivery rate at conferences is around 150 words per minute.

Interpreters must also be allowed access to relevant court documents, including speaker scripts, if any, for preparation. It is important to recognise that quality in interpreting should not be regarded as the sole responsibility of the interpreter (Ozolins & Hale, 2009), but one that should be adequately shared by all those involved in the court proceedings.

9.6 Conclusion

Court interpreting is an essential subset of public service interpreting with the longest history in Hong Kong. In early colonial days, it was a service provided chiefly by ad hoc interpreters, who might not even possess the required language proficiency in both Chinese and English, let alone proper training in translation and interpreting skills and ethics. Today, those serving in the Hong Kong Judiciary as full-time court interpreters are mostly university graduates, with some even holding a Master's degree or law qualifications (Judiciary Administration, 2004). However, the increasingly transparent process of interpreting, arising from the presence of bilingual court participants, the use of the consecutive mode of interpreting, as well as the implementation of the audio-recording system, while ensuring better administration of justice, inevitably subjects interpreters working in the process to immense external pressure as their output is constantly scrutinised by other bilinguals in court and picked up by the recording system. To better equip interpreters for the challenge, concerted efforts must be made to ensure the quality of interpreting, which should be made a shared responsibility among all the participants in court.

On the other hand, the uniqueness of the Hong Kong courtroom, where day-to-day interpretation services are provided to cater to the needs of the linguistic majority, renders *chuchotage* as a mode of interpreting largely inappropriate and inadequate. This study highlights an urgent need to make the Hong Kong courtroom fully bilingual with the implementation of an electronic mode of simultaneous interpreting system and a truly bilingual court reporting system which records everything said and interpreted in court.

Notes

1 The author of this chapter served in the Judiciary as a court interpreter before the handover of Hong Kong's sovereignty to China in 1997, and was given permission to access authentic recordings of court proceedings of some criminal trials for academic purposes. Some contents of this paper have previously appeared in Ng (2013a, 2013b, 2018 and 2019).

2 This was commonplace when the author served in the courts from 1994 to 1995.

3 Romanisation of Cantonese characters in this chapter is based on *Jyutping*, a Cantonese Romanisation system developed by the Linguistic Society of Hong Kong. This system distinguishes six tones in Cantonese and the number at the end of a syllable is a tone marker.

References

Barghout, A., Rosendo, L. R., & García, M. V. (2015). The influence of speed on omissions in simultaneous interpretation: An experimental study. *Babel, 61*(3), 305–334.

Bickley, G. (2001). The student-interpreters' scheme and the Chinese teacher's allowance: Translator education in nineteenth-century Hong Kong. In S.W. Chan (Ed.), *Translation in Hong Kong: Past, Present and Future* (pp. 9–19). Hong Kong: The Chinese University Press.

Census and Statistics Department. (2017, February 27). *Population Aged 5 and Over by Usual Spoken Language and Year*. 2016 Population By-Census. Retrieved from: https://www.bycensus2016.gov.hk/en/bc-mt.html (accessed 21 February 2021).

Duff, P., Findlay, M., Hawarth, C., & Chan, T. F. (1992). *Juries: A Hong Kong Perspective*. Hong Kong: Hong Kong University Press.

Eitel, E. J. (1877). Chinese studies and official interpretation in the colony of Hongkong. *The China Review, or Notes & Queries on the Far East*, *6*(1), 1–13.

Gaiba, F. (1998). *The Origins of Simultaneous Interpretation (Perspectives on Translation)*. Ottawa: University of Ottawa Press.

Gile, D. (1995). *Basic Concepts and Models for Interpreter and Translator Training*. Amsterdam: John Benjamins.

Information Paper (1997, 13 October). *Use of Chinese in Courts*. Provisional Legislative Council: Panel on Administration of Justice and Legal Services. Retrieved from: www.legco.gov.hk/yr97-98/english/panels/ajls/papers/aj13104a.htm (accessed 5 October 2021).

Jarman, R. L. (Ed.). (1996). *Hong Kong Annual Administration Reports, 1841–1941*. Farnham Common: Archive Editions.

Judiciary Administration (2004). *Performance of Court Interpreters*. Panel on Administration of Justice and Legal Services – LC Paper No. CB(2)1592/03-04(01). Retrieved from: www.legco.gov.hk/yr03-04/english/panels/ajls/papers/aj0322cb2-1592-1e.pdf (accessed 5 October 2021).

Key Figures and Statistics (2020, 31 December). *Percentage of Criminal Cases Conducted in Chinese*. Department of Justice. Retrieved from: www.doj.gov.hk/en/about/stat.html (accessed 5 October 2021).

Korpal, P. (2012). Omission in simultaneous interpreting as a deliberate act. In A. Pym, & D. Orrego-Carmona (Eds.), *Translation Research Projects 4* (pp. 103–111). Tarragona: Intercultural Studies Group Universitat Rovira i Virgili.

Lethbridge, H. J. (1970). Hong Kong cadets, 1862–1941. *Journal of the Hong Kong Branch of the Royal Asiatic Society, 10*, 36–56.

Ng, K. H. (2009). *The Common Law in Two Voices: Language, Law, and the Postcolonial Dilemma in Hong Kong*. Stanford, CA: Stanford University Press.

Ng, E. N. S. (2013a). Garment, or upper-garment? A matter of interpretation? *International Journal for the Semiotics of Law –Revue internationale de Sémiotique juridique*, *26*(3), 597–613. doi: 10.1007/s11196-012-9290-9.

Ng, E. N. S. (2013b). *The Atypical Bilingual Courtroom: An Exploratory Study of the Interactional Dynamics in Interpreter-Mediated Trials in Hong Kong*. Doctoral dissertation, Aston University. Retrieved from: http://publications.aston.ac.uk/20908/1/Studentthesis-2013.pdf (accessed 22 February 2021).

Ng, E. N. S. (2015). Judges' intervention in witness examination as a cause of omissions in interpretation in the Hong Kong courtroom. *International Journal of Speech Language and the Law, 22*(2), 203–227. https://doi.org/10.1558/ijsll.v22i2.17782.

Ng, E. N. S. (2016). Do they understand? English trials heard by Chinese jurors in the Hong Kong courtroom. *Language and Law / Linguagem e Direito*, *3*(2), 172–191.

Ng, E. N. S. (2018). *Common Law in an Uncommon Courtroom: Judicial Interpreting in Hong Kong*. Amsterdam: John Benjamins. https://doi.org/10.1075/btl.144.

Ng, E. N. S. (2019). A historical review of court interpreting in Hong Kong and the way forward. In E.S.K. Cham, & E.K.H. Lee (Eds.), *Bilingual Legal System in Hong Kong: Language and Translation* (pp. 1–19). Hong Kong: Hong Kong University Press. [<香港法庭傳譯之回顧與前瞻>，載湛樹基，李劍雄：《香港雙語法制：語言與翻譯》。香港：香港大學出版社。]

Ng, E. N. S. (2020). Linguistic disadvantage before the law: When non-native English speakers waive their right to an interpreter. In E.N.S. Ng, & I.H.M. Crezee (Eds.), *Interpreting in Legal and Healthcare Settings: Perspectives on Research and Training* (pp. 21–43). Amsterdam: John Benjamins. https://doi.org/10.1075/btl.151.01ng.

Ng, E. N. S., Leung, J., & Loper, K. (forthcoming). *A Study on a Potential Model for Accreditation and Regulation of Interpreters and Translators in Ethnic Minority Languages in Hong Kong*. Hong Kong: Equal Opportunities Commission.

Norton-Kyshe, J. W. (1971). *The History of the Laws and Courts of Hong Kong from the Earliest Period to 1898: Volume II*. Hong Kong: Vetch and Lee (original work published 1898).

Ozolins, U., & Hale, S. (2009). Quality in interpreting: A shared responsibility. In S. Hale, U. Ozolins, & L. Stern (Eds.), *The Critical Link 5: Quality Interpreting – A Shared Responsibility* (pp. 1–10). Amsterdam: John Benjamins. https://doi.org/10.1075/btl.87.01ozo.

Pym, A. (2008). On omission in simultaneous interpreting: Risk analysis of a hidden effort. In G. Hansen et al. (Eds.), *Efforts and Models in Interpreting and Translation Research: A Tribute to Daniel Gile* (pp. 83–105). Amsterdam: John Benjamins.

Salhany, R. E. (2006). *Cross-Examination: The Art of the Advocate*, 3rd ed. Markham, Ontario: LexisNexis Canada.

Seeber, K. (2017). Interpreting at the European institutions: Faster, higher, stronger. *CLINA*, *3*(2), 73–90. https://doi.org/10.14201/clina2017327390.

Setton, R. (1999). *Simultaneous Interpretation: A Cognitive-Pragmatic Analysis*. Amsterdam: John Benjamins.

Smith, C. T. (1975). English-educated Chinese elites in nineteenth-century Hong Kong. In M. Topley (Ed.), *Hong Kong: The Interaction of Traditions and Life in the Towns* (pp. 65–96). Hong Kong: Hong Kong Branch of the Royal Asiatic Society.

Wong, V. (1990, April 1). Cantonese in courts scheme postponed. *South China Morning Post*.

Legal references

Laws

Racial Discrimination Ordinance (RDO), Cap 602, Laws of Hong Kong.

Official Languages Ordinance, Cap 5, Laws of Hong Kong.

Cases cited

HKSAR *v.* Moala Alipate, HKCA 537 (2019). Retrieved from: https://hklii.org/cgi-bin/sinodisp/eng/hk/cases/hkca/2019/537.html (accessed 20 September 2021).

HKSAR *v.* Gutierrez Alvarez Keishu Mercedes, HKCA 184 (2020) HKEC 440. Retrieved from: https://hklii.org/cgi-bin/sinodisp/eng/hk/cases/hkca/2020/184.html (accessed 20 September 2021).

HKSAR *v.* Ng Pak Lun, HKCA 441 (2011). Retrieved from: https://hklii.org/cgi-bin/sinodisp/eng/hk/cases/hkca/2011/441.html (accessed 20 September 2021).

HKSAR *v.* Chan Hon Wing, HKCA 938 (2020). Retrieved from: https://hklii.org/cgi-bin/sinodisp/eng/hk/cases/hkca/2011/441.html (accessed 20 September 2021).

Appendix 9.1 Transcription keys

key	*Meaning*
(.)	A brief pause of less than a second
:	Prolonged sound, indicated by the length of the row of colons
–,	Incomplete word or false start
[	Start of an interruption and the utterance interrupted
<word>	Transcriber's description

Part III

Education and training

10 Preparing informed users of language services in public service interpreting courses

Differentiated learning outcomes for a diverse student population

Christopher D. Mellinger

10.1 Introduction

Many courses on community or public service interpreting (PSI) are skills-based courses that aim to prepare students for future work in a range of contexts, including legal, medical/healthcare, and educational settings (Bao, 2015; Stern & Liu, 2020). Increasing societal needs for interpreting services and efforts to organise the provision of such services have been cited as motivations for interpreter training in higher education (e.g., Bao, 2015; Rudvin & Tomassini, 2011), and there is greater interest in bridging the professional–academic divide (Way, 2020). A market-oriented pedagogy has led to course designs and curricula that focus on how to work as interpreters, including the modes of interpreting, the various codes of ethics and professional standards of practice, and the boundaries within which these future interpreters may operate (Angelelli, 2004, 2006; Stern & Liu, 2020). There is growing recognition that these courses ought to adopt a more research-based pedagogy in order to achieve learning objectives that are professionally oriented and skill-specific while also providing room for reflective and situated practice (Angelelli, 2017; González-Davies & Enríquez-Raído, 2016; Tipton & Furmanek, 2016; see also Cirillo & Niemants, 2017). In some instances, interpreting courses align with research conducted on interpreting behaviour in professional contexts, insofar as questions of accuracy (Ng & Crezee, 2020), employability and professionalism (Rodríguez de Céspedes et al., 2017), and occupational concerns and ethics (Mikkelson, 2017) regularly figure into course materials.[1] This emphasis on skill development is often reinforced when pass rates for professional interpreting exams or placement in degree-related positions are used as metrics to determine the overall success of interpreting programmes (Godfrey, 2010).

Despite a growing body of scholarship advocating for the inclusion of a range of professional practice issues in PSI courses,[2] Hale (2007) recognises the inherent tension between the scope of a programme and the content and

DOI: 10.4324/9781003197027-14

skills included in the curriculum. As Hale (2007) suggests, time restrictions limit what may be possible to include, requiring instructors to emphasise specific elements or aspects of interpreting. Additionally, PSI training programmes vary considerably in profile, with some authors conceptualising these programmes as being professional or basic training (Sandrelli, 2001) and others typifying them by means of national approaches to interpreter preparation (Niska, 2005).

Angelelli (2017, 2019) provides further nuance to different types of interpreting programmes, distinguishing between interpreter training and education – whereas training primarily emphasises the skills required to function as an interpreter, education encompasses both these skills and research-based skills and knowledge about the task itself. Nevertheless, most programmes offered by educational institutions focus primarily on training students how to interpret (Angelelli, 2019), perhaps due to such training existing primarily to meet the pragmatic needs of the language industry (Angelelli, 2006). In many respects, this distinction aligns with the idea of a competency-based approach to interpreter education (Tipton & Furmanek, 2016), in that the aspects that comprise professional interpreter behaviour can be specifically targeted as part of an interpreter's preparation. Moreover, institutions that initially developed conference interpreting programmes did not include courses or modules on PSI. While this situation has begun to change, the primary emphasis on conference settings has led to slower development of PSI education (Stern & Liu, 2020).

These issues are further compounded when interpreting courses are offered as freestanding courses or modules within a language programme rather than as part of a multi-course interpreting programme that allows concentrated study of the profession as a primary goal. Short courses, certificates, and non-degree programmes enable flexible configurations to provide training of specific skills or languages; however, these programmes are often limited in duration and scope in their ability to provide greater flexibility and more targeted instruction (Bao, 2015). In the United States, for instance, there are relatively few, if any, interpreting programmes dedicated to either interpreting training or education in specific settings such as the judiciary (Matthews & Ardemagni, 2013). Instead, interpreting courses are typically offered as elective courses or as part of a more general language degree programme or within language for specific-purpose courses (e.g., Hardin, 2015).[3] Increasing recognition of the interplay among courses on language for specific purposes, translation, and interpreting has led to calls for additional programme development in the United States (Mellinger, 2017).

While students undoubtedly develop a range of interpreting skills in short courses and elective modules that span several months, the time constraints of academic calendars limit the extent to which students can more fully develop their interpreting skills and abilities (Hale, 2007; Stern & Liu, 2020). Additionally, heterogeneous student populations require courses to address varying levels of language proficiency and exposure (Mellinger &

Gasca Jiménez, 2019), particularly in courses that cannot require entrance examinations or aptitude testing. The same could be said of students who may have differing backgrounds in a domain-specific area (for more on the importance of having domain knowledge, see Crezee et al., 2015 or Tipton & Furmanek, 2016). Therefore, this confluence of both academic constraints and varied demographics in the PSI classroom may not sufficiently position students for success despite the professionally oriented learning outcomes established in these programmes.

This chapter explores how PSI courses can be designed and conceptualised to account for a diverse student body with unique learning goals and objectives. Mellinger (2017, p. 243) suggests that the integration of translation and interpreting (TI) into language curricula can "help prepare well-informed consumers of language services" as well as those who may interact with interpreters in varied settings by including basic TI skills. Moreover, the integration of TI coursework into language programmes allows graduates of these programmes "to recognize the necessary skillsets required, to understand how to work with professional translators and interpreters, and to identify contexts in which their use is appropriate" (ibid., p. 244). These ideas have since been termed TI literacy (Takeda & Yamada, 2019), which speaks to the important role that community interpreting courses can play to prepare students to live and work in an increasingly multilingual society. In line with Angelelli's (2017) grounding of interpreter education in the extant literature on teaching and learning, this chapter examines how differentiated learning allows students with varied career paths and degree specialisations to engage with interpreting professionals in a range of settings. This multi-pronged approach to interpreter education allows students to begin developing the requisite skillset to become professional interpreters or to recognise when and how to engage with professional interpreters as they assume roles in other capacities. In doing so, these courses can help redress disparities of populations who rely on interpreting services to engage with public services and positively impact stakeholders in different capacities (Angelelli, 2019; Hsieh, 2016; Mellinger, 2021).

10.2 Preparing informed users of language services

Defined as "foundational knowledge of the practice of translation and interpreting," the concept of TI literacy is introduced and explored in Takeda and Yamada's (2019, p. 53) proposal for introductory survey-type courses in which students are exposed to multiple settings in which TI are conducted. As these researchers describe, this approach not only helps to prepare students for further study and training as professional translators and interpreters, but also "to foster effective users of translation and interpreting services and tools" (ibid., p. 53). For introductory community interpreting courses, a TI literacy-based approach is useful insofar as it allows for greater awareness of TI practice and the profession and is likely to reduce misconceptions about these services. Likewise, students who are unsure of a particular area or interest in interpreting can explore the field, to decide later if they wish to pursue further studies in interpreting or choose a different career path.

Takeda and Yamada (2019) examine this idea in Japan; however, the utility of this type of awareness-raising curriculum is more broadly applicable. In the United States, for example, the relatively low number of degree-granting TI programmes coupled with a lack of legal recognition of international standards for PSI may lead to misunderstandings with respect to TI services similar to those reported in Japan by Takeda and Yamada (2019). Moreover, one need not look much further than misconceptions about translation technologies or machine translation to see the utility of a literacy that focuses on its appropriate use (e.g., Bowker & Ciro, 2019). In a similar vein, non-professional or ad hoc interpreting occurs regularly among family members and friends, such that even basic instruction on how to interpret may provide valuable skills for people serving in this capacity (Antonini et al., 2017; Colina & Lafford, 2017).

Teaching practices in community interpreting have received increasing attention in the interpreting studies pedagogy literature, and efforts have increased to reach a broad range of students in recognition of the varied goals of students enrolled in these courses. Much like the broad, less-standardised approach to translation teaching in the United States (Venuti, 2017), PSI courses are uniquely configured based on programmatic and student needs in their institution. Language proficiencies vary in foreign-language classrooms in higher education (Cerezo, 2017; Winke et al., 2019), and the ability to tailor TI courses to the needs of second-language learners and heritage-language speakers is challenging (Hubert, 2017; Mellinger & Gasca Jiménez, 2019). Moreover, many students enrolled in language programmes no longer have a single major, instead favouring multiple majors with the language major as a complement to another area of study (Winke et al., 2019). Consequently, the varied language skills and interests of students coupled with institutional and curricular constraints lead to a heterogeneous student population in many PSI courses.

Diverse classrooms raise questions of how best to approach the task of teaching community interpreting, in terms of the instructional methods and teaching strategies, the overarching focus of courses or modules, and the selection of content and materials. Whereas much of the literature on interpreting pedagogy has focused on skill acquisition – which indeed is crucial to our understanding of how we can prepare students for professional work in the language industry and public services – Mellinger (2017) and Takeda and Yamada (2019) suggest an additional course goal of preparing students enrolled in TI courses to be informed users of language services. This holistic view of interpreting education perhaps aligns with Pym's (2018) argument that translation courses need not align exclusively with the translation professions, favouring instead broader training of language learners. Nevertheless, a TI literacy-oriented approach to introductory coursework ultimately requires instructors of these courses to be mindful of the diverse populations present in these courses and, as argued here, requires differentiated instruction and learning outcomes.

10.3 Differentiated instruction and learning outcomes

Scholarship on differentiated instruction and learning outcomes in TI studies is somewhat limited; however, some authors have claimed that a natural differentiation occurs in TI courses as a result of independent learning (Lakhtikova, 2015). A student-centred approach to pedagogy is one that often aligns with a social constructivist approach to translator education (Colina & Venuti, 2017; Kiraly, 2000), in that students are encouraged or empowered to engage with course material, their classmates, and the instructor to learn about the task. One area that has recognised the potential for differentiated learning is in the polylingual translation classroom (Lowe, 2016), in which translation courses are not confined to a specific language combination. Students enrolled in such courses use their own language combinations as entry points to the concepts under discussion, allowing them to socially construct new knowledge within a structure created by the instructor.

Many of these translation pedagogy approaches may also be useful in the interpreting classroom – particularly if the course were to be a multilingual interpreting course – and some work has begun to recognise differentiated instruction to accomplish similar aims. For instance, Nelson's (2019) dissertation focuses on differentiated instruction for Deaf-parented individuals enrolled in American Sign Language–English interpreting courses, and Mellinger and Gasca Jiménez (2019) suggest this approach to account for differences between L1, L2, and heritage-language speakers in interpreting courses. In both cases, the researchers aim to reconcile diverse student populations in courses while recognising the potential advantages afforded by these unique perspectives being present in the same classroom.

Differentiated instruction, though, should not be reduced simply to a student-centred approach to teaching that allows individualised instruction. In fact, Tomlinson (2001) specifically defines what differentiated instruction is, and what it is not. For instance, the tenets of differentiated instruction do include student-centredness and proactive education that is guided and structured to enable learning. However, this pedagogical approach eschews individualised instruction pedagogies from the 1970s, instead favouring qualitative differences in instruction and a combination of whole-class, group, and individual instruction (ibid.). Moreover, differentiated instruction requires multiple approaches to the content, process, and product while emphasising the role that assessment plays to enhance learning for mixed-ability classrooms. As Tomlinson (2001) suggests, this multi-pronged pedagogy accounts for increasingly diverse classrooms and allows students to access the same content and material in a course by providing unique points of entry to learning.

10.3.1 Student readiness

In a later review of the literature on differentiated learning, differentiated learning is presented as a response to address three aspects of learning: student readiness, student learning profiles, and student interest (Tomlinson et al., 2003). This first area is associated with a student's readiness or ability to learn material. Drawing on Vygotsky's (1978, 1986) concept of the zone of proximal development, Tomlinson et al. (2003) discuss student readiness with respect to a specific task, such that a student cannot be successful independently, but with structure and support, the student can meet with success. This Vygotskian concept is well known in TI studies (Kiraly, 2000), as is the need to scaffold learning for students (Colina & Venuti, 2017). The varied student profiles in each class will naturally require different levels of attention and multiple approaches to content, process, and product in order to remain within the various ability levels of the students while sufficiently challenging their progress.

PSI courses that have both prospective interpreters and users of language services enrolled in the course can benefit from an emphasis on student readiness in course development. Whereas their language skills may differ, students approaching a task or discussion from different vantage points can provide fruitful discussions. As Kaczmarek (2012) describes, differing expectations of what constitutes ethical behaviour or codes of ethics in community interpreting may ultimately lead to ethical dilemmas that are not easily resolved. Students working from different points of departure and at different levels can bring unique perspectives to bear on discussions and role plays based on these topics, allowing students to access the material in different ways based on their skillsets.

The same holds true in simulated encounters between an interpreter and the various parties. Much in the same way as Dunne (2011) demonstrates the utility of students assuming different roles of stakeholders in learning how to manage translation and localisation projects, so too can students in this setting assume different roles to understand how interpreted interaction occurs. Whereas students interested in a career in interpreting can take on the role of the interpreter, others can assume the role of an attorney or physician needing interpreting services (e.g., Hale, 2007; Kadrić, 2014). This type of activity differentiates instruction so that students can work within their abilities while also exploring the challenges inherent in working with an interpreter.

As noted above, assessment is a key feature of differentiated instruction and is intrinsically linked to student readiness for a task. In skill-building courses, PSI students require individualised feedback to help identify specific areas of improvement and support their learning. Formative feedback is often discussed in the interpreting studies pedagogy literature (e.g., Sawyer, 2004), and this type of feedback can be provided not only to students who assume the role of interpreter in role play scenarios, but also to the other speakers as well. For instance, training on how to specifically work with interpreters has been discussed outside of interpreting studies (e.g., Jacobs et al., 2010; Tribe & Raval, 2002), and interpreting studies would do well to contribute to these conversations.

Before proceeding, it should be noted that the argument here is not to advocate for individualised instruction in which there is a unique course of study or series of assignments for every student in the course. Nor should it be assumed that all students should be grouped into a single space in an effort to avoid differentiated tracks or learning for students in a language programme or interpreting course. In fact, Tomlinson (2001) explicitly argues that this is not differentiated learning. Instead, instructors ought to recognise the simultaneous goals that can be achieved in a PSI course by educating students on how interpreting is done alongside how interpreting services are used. Providing multiple points of entry to the process of interpreting allows students to simultaneously develop skills that can serve as the foundation for future training or for constructively engaging with professional interpreters in the future.

10.3.2 Student learning profiles

The second way in which differentiated instruction responds to diverse student populations – namely, student learning profiles – addresses individual differences in the classroom beyond current knowledge or ability levels, focusing on variation in student learning preferences (Tomlinson et al., 2003). Research on learning styles in conference interpreting trainees has been conducted in relation to cognitive flexibility and motivation (Timarová & Salaets, 2011), but work on PSI is more limited. Interpreting studies researchers have addressed individual differences, which merit careful consideration in the TI classroom, with studies investigating a range of topics including emotional intelligence (Hubscher-Davidson, 2013), personality (Bontempo et al., 2014), and self-efficacy (Jiménez Ivars et al., 2014). Efforts to identify a specific aptitude for interpreting have also been undertaken to predict success in interpreting coursework (e.g., Russo, 2014).

Yet despite recognition of the cognitive diversity found in potential interpreting trainees, discussions on these unique profiles tend to diminish once enrolled in an interpreting course or programme. In some respects, the need for these discussions in formal interpreting programmes with entrance or aptitude exams is somewhat lessened as the student body may be more homogeneous as a result of this screening. Nevertheless, PSI courses embedded in language programmes may not be able to rigorously screen for aptitude or proficiency for various reasons. In addition, the need for interpreting services across many languages and settings may preclude programmes from establishing thresholds that allow a presupposed mastery of both languages prior to admission. In light of the varied student profiles, PSI courses are prime candidates for differentiated instruction to support learning.

One way to address these unique learning profiles in PSI settings is to employ a dialogic pedagogy, as described by Angelelli (2017, p. 35), in which students and instructors can critically engage with a theme or topic. As discussed previously, students with varying degree or career aspirations provide multiple voices to address a topic, enriching discussions by bringing together different disciplinary traditions in a single space. Regardless of their degree or career path, students are likely to benefit from these discussions – interpreting students are likely to be more aware of the professional issues encountered by the clients for whom they will interpret, and the ultimate users of language services will be more attuned to the challenges faced by interpreters.

Angelelli (2017) also suggests problem-based learning as a means to enable and enhance learning in the TI classroom. By drawing on these social constructivist approaches to learning, students with diverse profiles are empowered to utilise different points of entry and bring to bear their experiences and perspective on the topic. Researchers have advocated for problem-based learning in TI pedagogy scholarship to leverage unique voices in the classroom to solve novel problems that are often ill defined and unique (e.g., Inoue, 2005). This same argument can be made for PSI, in that questions of language access, power differentials, professionalism, or ethical and moral dilemmas rarely have clear-cut, singular answers.

10.3.3 Student interest

The ability for differentiated instruction to address the first two aspects of learning – i.e., student readiness and learning profiles – is, in many respects, interrelated. Students may be more ready as a result of specific learning profiles or individual differences than others, and the interplay between both aspects can make it difficult to differentiate the two areas. Student interest is the third aspect of learning identified by Tomlinson et al. (2003) to which differentiated instruction speaks. While student interest, and by extension, student motivation, can certainly influence the first two aspects, it is more easily separated for study and is particularly salient for discussions of PSI courses.

In the education literature, student interest has been linked to motivation, and studies have shown how increased interest in a topic can lead to greater outcomes in student achievement and productivity (e.g., Krapp, 1999; Kriegbaum et al., 2018).[4] Interpreting studies scholars have also tried to understand student interest and motivation in conference interpreting training (e.g., Timarová & Salaets, 2011) as well as factors that can lead to demotivation (Wu, 2016). These ideas have since been extended to look at what motivates students upon completion of interpreting programmes (Horváth & Kálmán, 2020).

The notion of interest is particularly salient to differentiated instruction in PSI classroom, insofar as students with diverse interests will likely require different pedagogical approaches to achieve the learning objectives in the course. Tomlinson's (2001) tenets of differentiated instruction speak to the student-centredness of the approach. By tailoring content and allowing students to engage with various aspects of PSI, instructors can leverage intrinsic preferences for a particular area of study or extrinsic motivation to seek a particular career path. Research has suggested that creating an enjoyable learning environment and fostering self-reflection can positively impact student learning in interpreting courses (Horváth & Kálmán, 2020). In a similar vein, the environment needs to be sufficiently structured – akin to the previous discussions of student readiness – to avoid students becoming demotivated with learning to interpret (Wu, 2016).

When taken together, the current scholarship on differentiated instruction and its ability to respond to the three aspects of student learning – namely, student readiness, learner profiles, and student interest – presents a case for its inclusion in PSI courses. Not only do these approaches recognise the diverse student population that can be enrolled in these courses, but they also help to foster what Takeda and Yamada (2019) term TI literacy. Whereas their comments focused on courses that integrate both translation and interpreting into introductory overview courses, the same TI literacy can be developed in courses exclusively dedicated to PSI. A differentiated approach to instruction in introductory courses allows instructors to reach a broad range of students and lays the foundation for future interpreting training while also contributing to the professionalisation of other career paths that will ultimately rely on interpreting services.

10.4 Conclusion

This chapter has sought to outline the various aspects of differentiated instruction which align with instructional goals in PSI classrooms in order to advocate for its inclusion in the pedagogical repertoire of interpreting studies faculty. This approach recognises the diverse student body that is often encountered in these courses, not only as a result of the languages with which they work or the settings in which they perform their services, but also as a result of unique learning goals that students may have. Whereas more formal interpreting programmes can more easily screen potential students for interpreting aptitude, PSI courses embedded in language programmes or as non-degree-granting programmes are somewhat limited in their ability to homogenise their student population. As a result, differentiated learning provides an approach to reach a broader range of students enrolled in the courses, allowing different avenues for exploration and further study.

This approach, however, does not seek to replace interpreting training courses that provide training that helps prepare students for professional work as interpreters. These skills-based courses help to develop professional interpreters for a broad range of settings and serve an important role in redressing disparities and inequities that result from language barriers or limited access to language services. Nevertheless, many of the ideas of differentiated instruction are still applicable to these training configurations, insofar as there are likely to be individual differences across students in these courses. As a result, the ability to tailor courses to student readiness, learning profiles, and interest can still aid student learning in these training programmes. In doing so, interpreting courses and programmes can help develop TI literacy in their students, serving multiple constituencies at the same time, be they future interpreters or users of their services.

Notes

1 The concepts and skills listed here are by no means exhaustive, but instead are illustrative of many of the professionally oriented topics that are incorporated into community interpreting courses. For a more complete review of the skills needed to work effectively as a community interpreter, see Hale (2007).

2 In this chapter, the term *public service interpreting* (PSI) will be used synonymously and interchangeably with *community interpreting*.

3 The pedagogical role of translation and interpreting in the language classroom has been addressed by a number of researchers (e.g., Biasetti, 2016; Colina, 2002; Cook, 2010; Laviosa, 2014); however, extensive treatment lies outside the scope of this chapter. Here, the discussion remains on courses dedicated specifically to interpreting, while recognising that there is potential overlap in how differentiated learning outcomes can be applied in the language learning classroom.

4 The construct of *interest* has been defined in several ways, from being a personality-specific trait to being situation-specific. A discussion of these distinctions lies outside the scope of this chapter. For more on these topics, see Hidi and Renninger (2006), Krapp (1999), and Kriegbaum et al. (2018).

References

Angelelli, C. V. (2004). *Revisiting the Interpreter's Role: A Study of Conference, Court, and Medical Interpreters in Canada, Mexico, and the United States*. Amsterdam: John Benjamins.

Angelelli, C. V. (2006). Designing curriculum for healthcare interpreting education: A principles approach. In C. Roy (Ed.), *New Approaches to Interpreter Education* (pp. 23–46). Washington, DC: Gallaudet University Press.

Angelelli, C. V. (2017). Anchoring dialogue interpreting in principles of teaching and learning. In L. Cirillo & N. Niemants (Eds.), *Teaching Dialogue Interpreting: Research-based Proposals for Higher Education* (pp. 30–44). Amsterdam: John Benjamins. https://doi.org/10.1075/btl.138.01ang.

Angelelli, C. V. (2019). *Healthcare Interpreting Explained*. New York: Routledge.

Antonini, R., Cirillo, L., Rossato, L., & Torresi, I. (Eds.). (2017). *Non-professional Interpreting and Translation*. Amsterdam: John Benjamins.

Bao, C. (2015). Pedagogy. In H. Mikkelson & R. Jourdenais (Eds.), *The Routledge Handbook of Interpreting* (pp. 400–416). New York: Routledge.

Biasetti, G. (2016). Benefits of an interpretation course for foreign language learning and development. *Hispania*, *99*(4), 615–634. https://doi.org/10.1353/hpn.2016.0107.

Bontempo, K., Napier, J., Hayes, L., & Brashear, V. (2014). Does personality matter? An international study of sign language interpreter disposition. *Translation & Interpreting*, *6*(1), 23–46.

Bowker, L., & Ciro, J. (2019). *Machine Translation and Global Research: Towards Improved Machine Translation Literacy in the Scholarly Community*. Bingley, UK: Emerald.

Cerezo, L. (2017). Always together or alone first? Effects of type of collaborative translation on Spanish L2 development. *Journal of Spanish Language Teaching*, *4*(2), 152–167. https://doi.org/10.1080/23247797.2017.1411678.

Cirillo, L., & Niemants, N. (Eds.). (2017). *Teaching Dialogue Interpreting: Research-based Proposals for Higher Education*. Amsterdam: John Benjamins.

Colina, S. (2002). Second language acquisition, language teaching and translation studies. *The Translator*, *8*(1), 1–24. https://doi.org/10.1080/13556509.2002.10799114.

Colina, S., & Lafford, B. (2017). Translation in Spanish language teaching: The integration of a 'fifth skill' in the second language curriculum. *Journal of Spanish Language Teaching*, *4*(2), 110–123. https://doi.org/10.1080/23247797.2017.1407127.

Colina, S., & Venuti, L. (2017). A survey of translation pedagogies. In L. Venuti (Ed.), *Teaching Translation: Programs, Courses, Pedagogies* (pp. 203–215). New York: Routledge.

Cook, G. (2010). *Translation in Language Teaching*. Oxford: Oxford University Press.

Crezee, I., Mikkelson, H., & Monzon-Storey, L. (2015). *Introduction to Healthcare for Spanish-speaking Interpreters and Translators*. Amsterdam: John Benjamins.

Dunne, E. (2011). Project as a learning environment: Scaffolding team learning in translation projects. In K. J. Dunne & E. S. Dunne (Eds.), *Translation and Localization Project Management: The Art of the Possible* (pp. 265–287). Amsterdam: John Benjamins.

González-Davies, M., & Enríquez-Raído, V. (2016). Situated learning in translator and interpreter training: Bridging research and good practice. *The Interpreter and Translator Trainer*, *10*(1), 1–11. https://doi.org/10.1080/1750399X.2016.1154339.

Godfrey, L. (2010). *Characteristics of effective interpreter education programs in the United States*. Unpublished doctoral dissertation. Chattanooga: University of Tennessee at Chattanooga.

Hale, S. (2007). *Community Interpreting*. London: Palgrave Macmillan.

Hardin, K. (2015). An overview of medical Spanish curricula in the United States. *Hispania*, *98*(4), 640–661.

Hidi, S., & Renninger, K. A. (2006). The four-phase model of interest development. *Educational Psychologist*, *41*(2), 111–127. https://doi.org/10.1207/s15326985ep4102_4.

Horváth, I., & Kálmán, C. (2020). Motivational disposition of translation and interpreting graduates. *The Interpreter and Translator Trainer.* https://doi.org/10.1080/1750399X.2020.1838180.

Hsieh, E. (2016). *Bilingual Health Communication: Working with Interpreters in Cross-cultural Care*. New York: Routledge.

Hubert, M. D. (2017). Teaching translation to foreign-language majors. In L. Venuti (Ed.), *Teaching Translation: Programs, Courses, Pedagogies* (pp. 55–62). New York: Routledge.

Hubscher-Davidson, S. (2013). Emotional intelligence and translation studies: A new bridge. *Meta*, *58*(2), 324–346. https://doi.org/10.7202/1024177ar.

Inoue, I. (2005). PBL as a new pedagogical approach for translator education. *Meta*, *50*(4). https://doi.org/10.7202/019865ar.

Jacobs, E. A., Diamond, L. C., & Stevak, L. (2010). The importance of teaching clinicians when and how to work with interpreters. *Patient Education and Counseling*, *78*(2), 149–153. https://doi.org/10.1016/j.pec.2009.12.001.

Jiménez Ivars, A., Pinazo Catalayud, D., & Ruiz i Forés, M. (2014). Self-efficacy and language proficiency in interpreter trainees. *The Interpreter and Translator Trainer*, *8*(2), 167–182. https://doi.org/10.1080/1750399X.2014.908552.

Kaczmarek, Ł. (2012). Addressing the question of ethical dilemmas in community interpreting training. In S. Hubscher-Davidson & M. Borodo (Eds.), *Global Trends in Translator and Interpreter Training: Mediation and Culture* (pp. 217–239). London: Bloomsbury.

Kadrić, M. (2014). Giving interpreters a voice: Interpreting studies meets theatre studies. *The Interpreter and Translator Trainer*, *8*(3), 452–468. https://doi.org/10.1080/1750399X.2014.971485.

Kiraly, D. (2000). *A Social Constructivist Approach to Translator Education: Empowerment from Theory to Practice*. Manchester: St. Jerome.

Krapp, A. (1999). Interest, motivation and learning: An educational-psychological perspective. *European Journal of Psychology of Education*, *14*(1), 23–40.

Kriegbaum, K., Becker, N., & Spinath, B. (2018). The relative importance of intelligence and motivation as predictors of school achievement: A meta-analysis. *Education Research Review*, *25*, 120–148. https://doi.org/10.1016/j.edurev.2018.10.001.

Lakhtikova, A. (2015). Differentiated instruction and language-specific translator training textbooks. *Translation and Interpreting Studies*, *10*(1), 153–160. https://doi.org/10.1075/tis.10.1.08lak.

Laviosa, S. (2014). *Translation and Language Education: Pedagogic Approaches Explored*. New York: Routledge.

Lowe, E. (2016). Translation without borders: International perspectives on changing practices in translation theory and pedagogy. *Cadernos de Tradução*, *36*(3), 17–33. http://dx.doi.org/10.5007/2175-7968.2016v36n3p17.

Matthews, G., & Ardemagni, E. (2013). Judicial interpretation education in U.S. colleges and universities: The path to academic recognition. *Translation and Interpreting Studies*, *8*(1), 73–93. https://doi.org/10.1075/tis.8.1.04mat.

Mellinger, C. D. (2017). Translation, interpreting, and language studies: Confluence and divergence. *Hispania*, *100*(5), 241–246. https://doi.org/10.1353/hpn.2018.0059.

Mellinger, C. D. (2021). Interpreting and language access: Spoken language interpreters in U.S. educational contexts. In E. A. Winston & S. Fitzmaurice (Eds.), *Advances in Educational Interpreting* (pp. 44–67). Washington, DC: Gallaudet University Press.

Mellinger, C. D., & Gasca Jiménez, L. (2019). Challenges and opportunities of heritage language learners in interpreting courses in the U.S. context. *Revista Signos: Estudios de Lingüística*, *52*(101), 950–974. https://doi.org/10.4067/S0718-09342019000300950.

Mikkelson, H. (2017). *Introduction to Court Interpreting*, 2nd ed. New York: Routledge.

Nelson, H. (2019). *A qualitative study on differentiated instruction for deaf-parented ASL-English interpreting students*. Unpublished doctoral dissertation. Capella University.

Ng, E. N. S., & Crezee, I. H. M. (2020). Interpreting in legal and healthcare settings: Perspectives on research and training. In E. N. S. Ng & I. H. M. Crezee

(Eds.), *Interpreting in Legal and Healthcare Settings* (pp. 1–18). Amsterdam: John Benjamins. https://doi.org/10.1075/btl.151.int.

Niska, H. (2005). Training interpreters: Programs, curricula, practices. In M. Tennent (Ed.), *Training for the New Millennium: Pedagogies for Translation and Interpreting* (pp. 35–64). Amsterdam: John Benjamins. https://doi.org/10.1075/btl.60.07nis

Pym, A. (2018). Where Translation Studies lost the plot: Relations with language teaching. Translation and Translanguaging in *Multilingual Contexts*, *4*(2), 203–222. https://doi.org/10.1075/ttmc.00010.pym.

Rodríguez de Céspedes, B., Sakamoto, A., & Berthaud, S. (2017). Introduction to the special issue on employability in the translation and interpreting curriculum. *The Interpreter and Translator Trainer*, *2*(3), 103–106. https://doi.org/10.1080/1750399X.2017.1339980.

Rudvin, M., & Tomassini, E. (2011). *Interpreting in the Community and Workplace: A Practical Teaching Guide*. London: Palgrave.

Russo, M. (2014). Testing aptitude for interpreting: The predictive value of oral paraphrasing, with synonyms and coherence as assessment parameters. *Interpreting*, *16*(1), 1–18. https://doi.org/10.1075/intp.16.1.01rus.

Sandrelli, A. (2001). Teaching liaison interpreting: Combining tradition and innovation. In I. Mason (Ed.), *Triadic Exchanges: Studies in Dialogue Interpreting* (pp. 173–196). Manchester: St. Jerome.

Sawyer, D. (2004). *Fundamental Aspects of Interpreter Education*. Amsterdam: John Benjamins.

Stern, L., & Liu, X. (2020). Interpreting studies. In S. Laviosa & M. González-Davies (Eds.), *The Routledge Handbook of Translation and Education* (pp. 226–244). New York: Routledge.

Takeda, K., & Yamada, M. (2019). "TI literacy" for general undergraduate education. In D. Sawyer, F. Austermühl, & V. Enríquez Raído (Eds.), *The Evolving Curriculum in Interpreter and Translator Education: Stakeholder Perspectives and Voices* (pp. 53–73). Amsterdam: John Benjamins. https://doi.org/10.1075/ata.xix.03tak.

Timarová, S., & Salaets, H. (2011). Learning styles, motivation and cognitive flexibility in interpreter training: Self-selection and aptitude. *Interpreting*, *13*(1), 31–52. https://doi.org/10.1075/intp.13.1.03tim.

Tipton, R., & Furmanek, O. (2016). *Dialogue Interpreting: A Guide to Interpreting in Public Services and the Community*. New York: Routledge.

Tomlinson, C.A. (2001). *How to Differentiate Instruction in Mixed-ability Classrooms*. Alexandria, VA: Association for Supervision and Curriculum Development.

Tomlinson, C.A., et al. (2003). Differentiated instruction in response to student readiness, interest, and learning profile in academically diverse classrooms: A review of the literature. *Journal for the Education of the Gifted*, *27*(2/3), 119–145. https://doi.org/10.1177/016235320302700203.

Tribe, R., & Raval, H. (Eds.). (2002). *Working with Interpreters in Mental Health*. New York: Routledge.

Venuti, L. (Ed.). (2017). *Teaching Translation: Programs, Courses, Pedagogies*. New York: Routledge.

Vygotsky, L. (1978). *Mind in Society*. Cambridge, MA: Harvard University Press.

Vygotsky, L. (1986). *Thought and Language* [A. Kozulin, Trans. & Ed.]. Cambridge, MA: MIT Press.

Way, C. (2020). Training and pedagogical implications. In E. Angelone, M. Ehrensberger-Dow, & G. Massey (Eds.), *The Bloomsbury Companion to Language*

Industry Studies (pp. 179–207). London: Bloomsbury. http://dx.doi.org/10.5040/9781350024960.0013.

Winke, P., Gass, S. M., & Heidrich, E. S. (2019). Modern-day foreign language majors: Their goals, attainment, and fit within a twenty-first century curriculum. In P. Winke & S. Gass (Eds.), *Foreign Language Proficiency in Higher Education* (pp. 93–113). Cham, Switzerland: Springer.

Wu, Z. (2016). Towards understanding interpreter trainees' (de)motivation: An exploratory study. *Translation & Interpreting*, *8*(2), 13–25. https://doi.org/10.12807/ti.108202.2016.a02.

11 Non-language-specific health interpreter education

Challenges and solutions

Ineke H.M. Crezee

11.1 Introduction and background

Migrants and refugees are increasingly making New Zealand their home, with some bringing in their (often non-English-speaking) parents. New Zealand has undertaken to resettle 1500 refugees per year. Many refugees rely on interpreters during their first years after arrival in New Zealand. Others who might need interpreting services include overseas workers who have come to New Zealand under the Registered Seasonal Employment (RSE) scheme. Employers in the horticultural and wine-growing sectors are heavily dependent on such workers – and to this end, the New Zealand government is allowing in RSE workers from nearby Pacific nations to work in the country thinning apple trees (Sharpe, 2020)[1] and harvesting other fruit, including grapes. The government is also allowing overseas tourists who were unable to leave New Zealand as a result of the Covid-19 pandemic response, in particular the March 2020 lockdown, to work in these sectors. Some of these RSE workers and tourists rely on interpreters during interactions with health professionals.

As a result, the linguistic makeup of the New Zealand community is in a state of flux, and this affects both demand for and supply of translation and interpreting (T&I) services (Eser, 2020). According to the 2018 New Zealand Census (Statistics New Zealand, 2018) the most common languages spoken at that time were English, Te Reo Māori, Samoan, northern Chinese languages (including Mandarin) and Hindi. According to Statistics New Zealand (N 2020),

> [s]ince 2001, the total number of responses for people able to speak an international language has grown from 481,314 responses to 720,039 by 2013. The OEC (2018) provides notes that the term "international languages" refers to "those languages that are not official New Zealand Languages". New Zealand has two official languages: New Zealand Sign Language and Te Reo Māori, with English being a de facto official language. The growth in the number of people able to speak an international language has largely been driven by the increasing number of people speaking Hindi, Northern Chinese and Sinitic.[2]

DOI: 10.4324/9781003197027-15

In 2016, interpreting services manager Kim de Jong (Magill & de Jong, 2016) commented that she employed 21 permanent interpreters based on language utilisation, listing the most in-demand languages as Mandarin and Cantonese, Hindi, Punjabi, Samoan, Tongan, Arabic, Vietnamese, Cambodian and Cook Island language (Magill & de Jong, 2016). A 2016 report commissioned by the New Zealand government says: "[w]hile English remains the language most commonly spoken in New Zealand, more than 150 languages are now spoken here. At the time of the 2013 Census, more than 87,000 people could not have an everyday conversation in English" (MBIE, 2016, p. 5).

Many of these language users would not be able to access health or other public services without quality T&I services. In New Zealand, use of interpreters in the healthcare setting was mandated by law from the 1990s onwards: Right 5 of the Code of Health and Disability Services Consumers' Rights (Health and Disability Commissioner, 1996) mentions the *Right to effective communication* (Right 5):

> (1) Every consumer has the right to effective communication in a form, language, and manner that enables the consumer to understand the information provided. Where necessary and reasonably practicable, this includes the right to a competent interpreter.

This right was enshrined in law (Health and Disability Commissioner, 1996) following a government inquiry into a cervical cancer research project in which the absence of interpreters contributed to cervical cancer patients having treatment withheld without their informed consent.

Government policies on immigration obviously impact the diverse nature of the community. Moreover, the 2020 Covid-19 pandemic prompted many New Zealand citizens and residents to return from overseas, where returnees may have included people needing interpreting services. Conversely, the pandemic response also reduced the number of new immigrants (New Zealand Immigration, 2021) and new chain migrants and therefore potentially a further increase in the demand for T&I services. Hospitals discouraged non-urgent appointments, and court hearings were deferred, further reducing demand. Overall, however, the demand for T&I services in a diverse range of languages remains strong (Magill & de Jong, 2016).

11.1.1 Interpreter education

Auckland University of Technology (AUT) in Auckland, New Zealand, has offered non-language specific health interpreter education since 1990. This chapter will start by discussing the New Zealand context which includes legislation on the use of interpreters in certain settings and the Code of Ethics of the Sign Language Interpreters Association of New Zealand (SLIANZ, 2012) and the New Zealand Society of Translators and Interpreters (NZSTI, 2013). Classes consist of students working both towards qualification as spoken-language interpreters and as New Zealand Sign Language interpreters (Magill, 2017). Both signed and spoken-language student interpreters are familiarised with the appropriate ethical guidelines in a special introductory course, prior to students taking specialised legal and health interpreting courses.

Care is taken to ensure that student health interpreters are familiarised with the workings of the human body and the most common conditions in an interesting and engaging way (Crezee, 2013). This includes providing students with a foundational knowledge of anatomy and pathology, through lectures, audiovisual clips and realia. Students also engage in simulated roleplay scenarios with speech pathologists and reflect on these (Crezee, 2015). The speech pathology setting was chosen because it forces students to rethink the interpreter role advocated through the SLIANZ (2012) and NZSTI (2013) code of ethics and students reflect on this in reflective written assignments.

This chapter will discuss some of the challenges of non-language-specific interpreter education, especially as they relate to the need to provide students with feedback on their interpreting practice. Students use VoiceThread to self-reflect and to provide feedback to same-language peers. The author will discuss health interpreting students' feedback on simulated roleplay scenarios as well as students' reflections on their own interpreting practice and on that of their language peers. The chapter will conclude by discussing the challenges involved in (successfully) moving interpreter training and assessment online as part of the Covid-19 pandemic response.

This chapter will start by outlining the background to healthcare interpreter training in New Zealand, followed by an overview of the literature on public service interpreting before moving to healthcare interpreting. It will then review the challenges of offering non-language-specific approaches to health interpreter education, including assessment.

11.1.2 Development of interpreter training in New Zealand

Different countries have developed health interpreter training at different points in time, prompted by a variety of reasons. In New Zealand, it was a series of medical misadventures where treatment was withheld (without informed consent) from a group of women with cervical cancer stage CIN3. This series of medical misadventures was jointly referred to as "the unfortunate experiment" (Coney & Bunkle, 1988) following exposure by two journalists in a New Zealand magazine (Coney, 2020). Their article resulted in a judicial inquiry led by Judge Silvia Cartwright (Cartwright, 1988; Coney, 2020) and held in 1987–1988. The Cartwright inquiry concluded amongst other things that "the study was unethical because treatment was withheld without consent" (McCredie, 2008), p. 425). Recommendations included the utilisation of trained healthcare interpreters henceforth where practicable. In 1990 the first healthcare interpreter training course was set up at Auckland Institute of Technology (now Auckland University of Technology) in 1990, and the first health interpreting service was established at Middlemore Hospital (South Auckland) in 1991 (Crezee, 2009). Training was non-language-specific from the outset, which brought with it its own set of challenges – these will be discussed in more detail below. The 1990 training course took place over two semesters of the academic year, with the first module focusing on the code of ethics,[3] notetaking and public speaking, and the second module focusing on different healthcare settings. Interpreting assessments consisted of prerecorded bilingual dialogues related to the healthcare setting. That first (1990) class comprised 17 students (including Ineke Crezee, the author of this chapter), representing 13 different languages. The author taught and developed the healthcare component of this course from 1991 onwards, benefiting from her knowledge as a registered nurse.

Over the years, the author developed special health interpreting courses which were run at Middlemore Hospital in 1995, a large tertiary teaching hospital in South Auckland, and at Manukau Institute of Technology, in South Auckland, from 1997 to 1999. At the request of the 1995 student cohort, she developed a guide to healthcare settings and healthcare terminology (Crezee, 1997), which became the basis for her 2013 book (Crezee, 2013). From 1999 onwards, the author became programme leader of the T&I programmes at AUT. Here she became involved in the development of undergraduate degree programmes in T&I as well as a Diploma of T&I, and Graduate Certificates and Diplomas in T&I. All these qualifications offer students the opportunity to undertake introductory courses on interpreter role, ethics and practice, followed by specialised legal and health interpreter training, taught by a legal and a health professional respectively. At the time of writing AUT was the only New Zealand university offering specialised legal or medical/healthcare interpreter training.

Before looking at the specifics of non-language-specific health interpreter education, I need to point out that the two health interpreting courses are combined with a course entitled *Interpreter role, ethics and practice*, which students take either prior to or concurrently with their health interpreting studies. Ethical concepts are reinforced during the health interpreting course, by way of class discussions in relation to health topics – in particular relating to oncology, bad news interviews, diabetes, pregnancy and childbirth. The first health interpreting course aims for students to become familiar with anatomy, physiology and pathology, and for students to be able to interpret dialogues relating to a number of common conditions discussed. Priority is given to common conditions such as strokes, heart attacks, diabetes, fractures, joint replacement surgeries, gastroscopy, colonoscopy and hepatitis. The subsequent health interpreting courses builds on the first one and explores specialist topics, such as oncology, pregnancy, assisted reproductive technology, neonatal intensive care and a range of commonly encountered mental health issues. The second course aims to develop students' ability to interpret longer passages either consecutively or simultaneously, in line with the interpreting assessments held by the National Accreditation Authority for Translators and Interpreters (NAATI) in Australia. This is particularly important since the New Zealand government aims to see all New Zealand-based interpreters NAATI-accredited by 2024, as will be explained later in this chapter.

11.2 Literature review

11.2.1 Public service interpreting

The most common form of interpreting in Aotearoa New Zealand[4] is public service interpreting, also called community interpreting (cf. Eser, 2020)) or liaison interpreting (Gentile et al., 1996). Healthcare interpreting (also known as medical interpreting; see Mikkelson, 2020) developed as a form of public service interpreting. Mikkelson (2020, p. 2) writes that:

> [a]lthough in the 1970s Australia had been the first country to establish a service to provide interpreting (over the telephone) in a variety of community settings, including medical facilities, interpreters did not tend to specialize in a particular setting at that time.

In recent times, the NAATI has developed special credentialling for medical and legal interpreters, responding to some of the recommendations of a 2012 report by Professor Sandra Hale and colleagues (Hale et al., 2012). Crezee (2013) also argues that interpreting in settings such as healthcare requires special training.

Public service interpreting has been the subject of scholarly interest for many decades (Corsellis, 2008; Ozolins, 2010; Hale, 2011; D'Hayer, 2012; Eser, 2020). Setton and Dawrant (2016, p. 23) define both community-based interpreting and public service interpreting as "interpreting services to facilitate communication between public service personnel (medical and social services, law enforcement, etc.) and members of linguistic minorities in the community". Interpreters commonly work as freelance practitioners and are usually registered with a number of language service agencies, both private and public.

11.2.1.1 Challenges of public service interpreting provision

Eser (2020, p. 43) combines a multifocal interpreting studies/management studies lens to provide an overview of the challenges and issues affecting the provision of community interpreting services in Australia and beyond. According to Eser (2020 p. 43), the "challenges are mainly related to the use of technology, quality, supply and demand, sustainability and work-specific issues". Eser holds that "the industry needs to take on quality issues like credentialing, the recognition from clients, and training" (2020, p. 43). In Australia, the Commonwealth Government established NAATI in 1976 following a recommendation of the Working Party of the Committee on

Overseas Professional Qualifications (Martin, 1978). Other countries (and states) vary in the extent to which they have outlined requirements for the utilisation and training of public service interpreters, including in the healthcare setting.

11.3 Healthcare interpreting

Roat and Crezee (2015, p. 237) define healthcare interpreting and medical interpreting as "interpreting that takes place during interactions related to health care". They add that "healthcare interpreting is a later term recognizing that the field covers interactions that are not strictly medical in nature, such as rehabilitation and mental health" (Roat & Crezee, 2015, p. 237). Mikkelson (2020) traces the development of healthcare interpreting internationally, pointing that, although in the 1980s a few hospitals in Canada and the US started to employ paid interpreters, these interpreters were professional only in the sense that they were paid and "received little or no training and were hired based on self-reported bilingual proficiency" (Mikkelson, 2020, p. 2). Likewise the interpreters referred to in an article by Vranjes and Bot (2021) were professional only in the sense that they were paid (NZSTI, 2013).

11.4 Challenges of healthcare interpreter education

In this chapter I will outline some of the challenges of healthcare interpreter training, starting from the general, before focusing on the demands of teaching attendees in mixed-language classes. Health interpreter educators have to prepare their students for the realities of interpreting in a wide range of healthcare settings, across cultural barriers, involving a range of health professionals, health consumers and family members. This means that health interpreter educators have to ensure trainees possess a very sound knowledge of the body, its structure and workings (anatomy and physiology) and the most common conditions affecting different organ systems (pathology). This may be a challenge when health interpreter educators do not have a health professional background themselves. Teaching vocabulary without putting it in context may be doing students a disservice. Ideally, health interpreter education should involve lectures by health professionals who have the ability to unpack complex concepts in a straightforward manner, without giving so much detail as to make students feel overwhelmed. Educators also have to ensure trainees get ample opportunity to practise semi-authentic dialogues using either audiovisual or audio material – in the computer lab or with their same-language peers – and that trainees receive language-specific feedback on their practice. Ideally students receive language-specific feedback from experienced health interpreter tutors.

Lastly, trainees need to be skilled at turn-taking management and aware of the wide range of dilemmas they may encounter. Some of these dilemmas may stem from confusion on the part of health providers, patients and relatives as to the interpreter role (Crezee et al., 2020). Bad news interviews, including end-of-life discussions (Rhodes et al., 2021), may pose additional problems for interpreters.

11.4.1 General challenge: Knowledge underpinning skills

As indicated above, the first challenge of healthcare interpreter training will be shared by other trainers: how to ensure students have the foundational health knowledge that will enable them to work in a range of healthcare settings. The author's background as a health professional and translator and interpreter significantly influenced her approach to health interpreter training. Her main aim has always been to ensure that student interpreters achieved a foundational knowledge of how the body works and the most common conditions together with most commonly asked questions by health professionals, diagnostic studies and suggested treatment options. This is in contrast to the approach by other linguists who seem to advocate that a knowledge of vocabulary will suffice. The author argues (Crezee, 2013) that you cannot interpret what you do not understand. This is particularly important for student interpreters working with languages which do not have a broad lexicon of medical terms (Burn & Wong Soon, 2020). This includes signed languages, and languages which were not the language of education (LE) for its speakers (Burn et al., 2014). Speakers of refugee languages may have been unable to either complete schooling at all, or to complete schooling with their home language as the medium of instruction (Burn et al., 2014). A lack of medical vocabulary makes it imperative that speakers are able to unpack medical terms in simple language and this is only possible if they really understand what a medical concept entails. Samoan healthcare interpreter Hoy Neng Wong Soon provides an excellent example in her interview with Jo Anna Burn (Burn & Wong Soon, 2020), when she unpacks "malignant pleural effusion" as "[t]he condition of the illness that you have now, you have water/fluid at the part where your lungs are located at and the reason why this thing has happened/is happening is because of the seriousness of your lung cancer" in Samoan (Burn & Wong Soon, 2020, p. 63).

11.4.1.1 Solutions

Students' knowledge is built up gradually over the course of 12 weeks, starting with a general overview of the healthcare system, how body cells behave and an introduction to Greek and Latin terminology. Common Greek suffixes such as *-itis* (inflammation), *-scopy* (looking at) and *-ectomy* (cutting out/removing) are discussed and body parts such as *gastro* (stomach), *broncho* (bronchus) and *arthro* (joint) are added over the course of the semester. In the first semester, weekly sessions focus on different organ systems and the most common conditions associated with those (Crezee, 2013; Crezee & Ng, 2016). Authentic audiovisual material taken from reality television documentaries and realia such as heart catheters and peak flow meters are used to bring the world of medicine into the classroom, as part of a situated learning approach (Crezee, 2015). Weekly Kahoot quizzes are used as a fun way to encourage students to revise and test their knowledge. Students take a live interpreting exam representing an interaction between an English-speaking health professional, an interpreter and a language other than English (LOTE)-speaking client.

The second semester of the health interpreting course focuses on specialist areas such as oncology, pregnancy issues, neonatal intensive care unit and mental health conditions. The second semester also involves practice with audiovisual clips on VoiceThread in order to prepare students for long consecutive and simultaneous interpreting assessments. This semester also includes a shared pre-professional session involving students working with qualified speech language therapists (Crezee, 2015), and they are asked to reflect on this session in a written assignment (Crezee and Marianacci, under review).

11.4.2 Challenge: Interpreter role

Healthcare interpreting takes place in interactions which may involve health professionals, patients and their family members. Issues may arise from health professionals or patients and relatives not being aware of the health interpreter role and professional ethics (Crezee, 2020, 2020b). Roat and Crezee (2015, p. 246) write that "the most persistent and difficult debate in healthcare interpreting has been and continues to be the scope of the interpreter's role". The fact that different countries have adapted different guidelines for practice has only contributed to the complexity of the debate. As stated above, New Zealand-trained interpreters undertake to abide by the (2012) Code of Ethics and Code of Conduct of the New Zealand Society of Translators and Interpreters (NZSTI, 2013). The precepts of the NZSTI (2013) Code of Ethics hold (among other things) that interpreters are impartial and do not take sides, give advice or advocate for patients.

11.4.2.1 Solutions

Students are asked to reflect on their own role as healthcare interpreters in two situations in particular. Firstly, they are shown an audiovisual clip from a real-life television documentary which shows a bad news interview. There is a class discussion around the stages of grieving and crosscultural differences. Students are asked to imagine that they might be the interpreter in the audiovisual scenario in real life and how this would impact on them – in a reflective written assignment. Crosscultural issues come to the fore, in particular the contrast between doctors using the Calgary–Cambridge framework (Kurtz et al., 2003; Munson & Wilcox, 2007) for establishing rapport with the patient and asking the patient what treatment options they would prefer. Some students report that doctors tend to use an authoritative tone and tell patients what to do, rather than adopting a consultative approach. Students also report that family members may be told that a patient is terminally ill, rather than the patients themselves. This reflects the differences between more traditional and more individualistic societal attitudes (Meyer, 2016). In practice, graduate interpreters often report being approached by family members who ask them to censor any bad news the health professional may give the patient. Crezee and Marianacci (under review) report that the majority of issues reflected on by student participants ($n = 22$) involved the development of new knowledge through the shared pre-professional sessions, with students revealing that they had developed unexpected insights "through being" in a new situation. This aligns with Li's (2018) findings about students developing metacognition.

Students also reflected on the role of the therapist in trying to uncover speech and language issues and how this impacted on their own (Merlini & Favaron, 2005). This then led them to reflect on the friction between the (general) ethical guidelines for interpreters (NZSTI, 2013) and the expectations in a speech language therapy context in particular. During the scenarios, the author often heard student interpreters tell SLTs that they were not allowed to provide any metalinguistic comments. Without this commentary, SLTs cannot really assess the speech and language issue that a LOTE-speaking client presents with. Making the reflective written assignment part of the compulsory assessments contributed to student interpreters developing the habit of self-reflection. The author agrees with Bernardini (2004) that educators should prepare students to become aware, resourceful and reflective practitioners.

11.4.3 Challenge: Language-specific feedback

Traditionally interpreter education has involved language-specific teaching where teaching staff are able to provide student interpreters with language-specific feedback. From the outset, interpreter training programmes at the author's universities have involved mixed-language student cohorts, with languages as diverse as Mandarin, Samoan, Tuvalu, Kiribati, Farsi, Russian and Hungarian – to name but a few. Most academic years, classes comprise speakers of up to 17 different and usually very diverse languages. This has presented staff with the need to come up with creative approaches to ensure that students receive language-specific feedback which is so important for them to reflect on. This type of feedback helps student interpreters become aware of weaknesses such as a tendency to omit or amplify or a failure to use the correct specialist terminology or appropriate register.

11.4.3.1 Solutions

Over a number of years, the author managed to secure funding for projects which involved students receiving language-specific feedback on their interpreted renditions. Students in liaison interpreting (we borrow the term from Gentile et al., 1996), health and legal interpreting courses received language-specific feedback on their interpreted renditions (Burn & Crezee, 2017; Crezee & Grant, 2016; Crezee et al., 2017). In more recent years, the author and her colleague Jo Anna Burn introduced assessments involving students reflecting on their own interpreted renditions and on feedback received from same-language peers.

11.4.4 Challenge: Preparing to transition to NAATI credentialling

While there is no national credentialling authority for translators and interpreters in New Zealand, the government is moving towards requiring NAATI certification for all those providing interpreting services in Aotearoa New Zealand. In 2016 the Ministry of Business Innovation and Employment (MBIE) published a report on the use of interpreter services in New Zealand (MBIE, 2016). The report said that: "[i]n 2013, one-quarter of the national population was born overseas, while in Auckland this was higher at 39 percent" (MBIE, 2016, p. 2). In 2017, the New Zealand Government started its Language Assistance Services (LAS) project (Enríquez Raído, 2020; New Zealand Immigration, n.d.), which set out to improve the quality of public service interpreting. The LAS programme comprises three inter-related projects: the first of these aims to develop a cross-government policy and service guidelines on LAS; the second one aims to develop new procurement models to deliver LAS more effectively and efficiently; while the third project aims to work towards new standards and certification for language practitioners working in the public sector (New Zealand Immigration, n.d.). It was perhaps natural that those involved with the LAS project should look to Australia and its NAATI.

NAATI was established in Australia in 1977 (Martin, 1978) and has played a major role in the testing and accreditation of T&I practitioners there. More recently, however, NAATI has been criticised for providing a "snapshot" test, without requiring that applicants first complete relevant training. NAATI was also critiqued for the fact that accredited practitioners could retain that accreditation for years without providing evidence of ongoing practice or professional development (Eser, 2020). In 2012 Professor Sandra Hale and colleagues completed a NAATI-commissioned report which recommended some important changes to NAATI's testing and accreditation system. The first recommendation (Hale et al., 2012, 7) reads that: "all candidates complete compulsory education and training in order to be eligible to sit for the accreditation examinations".

NAATI had never offered specialist accreditation for medical and legal interpreters, and upon passing the general NAATI test interpreters could present themselves straight to the health or legal setting, without having received specialist training in those areas. Recommendations number 6 and 7 require "[t]hat the current levels of accreditation be replaced by a Generalist level (for both Interpreting and Translation) and Specialist accreditations for Interpreting" and "[t]hat the following specialisations be established for Interpreter accreditations: Legal, Medical, Conference and Business, with Legal and Medical having priority over the other two" (Hale et al., 2012, p. 7). This recommendation reflects the fact that most interpreting practitioners in Australia (and New Zealand) work in medical or legal settings, both of which are types of public service interpreting.

The 2012 report authors (Hale et al., 2012) also recommended important changes to testing protocols. Similarly, where NAATI previously used prerecorded "frozen" exams to test interpreting candidates, the report recommended that "[i]nterpreting tests be conducted live, as much as possible. Where this is not possible, that candidates be provided with video recorded interactions and that their performance be video recorded for marking" (Hale et al., 2012, p. 8). The report also recognised the growing importance of telephone interpreting, recommending that "[i]nterpreting tests at the Generalist level for both spoken and signed languages include a telephone interpreting component consisting of protocols for identification of all interlocutors, confidentiality assurances and dialogue interpreting only". In terms of developing the specialist medical and legal interpreting programmes which candidates must complete before taking specialist interpreting tests, the report recommended that "NAATI establish a new Expert Panel, with subpanels for the specialisations, to design the curricula for the compulsory training modules and provide guidelines for the final assessment tasks". NAATI accepted some – although not all – of the recommendations of the 2012 report (NAATI, 2016).

Under the new system, practitioners must apply for recertification every 3 years, undergo professional development and keep a log of any T&I assignments they undertake – with evidence. In terms of non-language-specific health interpreter education, the move to compulsory NAATI credentialling requires the author and her colleagues to ensure student interpreters are prepared for NAATI assessments.

11.4.4.1 Solutions

With regard to the first recommendation (Hale et al., 2012, p. 7), that "all candidates complete compulsory education and training in order to be eligible to sit for the accreditation examinations", LAS representatives have been in conversation with NAATI to discuss the training required before New Zealand-based T&I practitioners may sit a NAATI certification test. The author is involved in the academic working group for the LAS programme, and the working group was advised that New Zealand-based language access professionals would be able to sit the NAATI test after completing an induction course. This induction course involves an introduction to interpreter role and ethics and familiarising attendees with a range of New Zealand public service settings where interpreters are commonly used. The Centre for Translation and Interpreting at AUT offers two semester-long courses which meet the description of the desired induction course. The first of these two courses is called *Interpreter role, ethics and practice* (TRIN603), while the second one is called *Societal contexts for interpreters and translators* (TRIN604) and covers a range of settings in which New Zealand-based interpreters are commonly employed. Consultation with LAS programme representatives confirmed that completion of TRIN603 and TRIN604 would equate to eligibility to sit a NAATI accreditation test.

Recommendations number 6 and 7 (Hale et al., 2012) relating to specialist medical and legal interpreting programmes have been addressed since AUT offered its first health interpreter training course in 1990 and its first legal interpreter training course in 1998. Teaching staff have continued to finetune both health and legal specialist training programmes since then. They have continued to update teaching materials, very importantly adding in compulsory observation of an interpreter-mediated courtroom trial/speech language interpreting scenario to enable students to develop the life-long habit of reflecting on their performance as professional interpreters.

Report (Hale et al., 2012) recommendations as to the desirability of having live rather than prerecorded frozen exams were first implemented by the author in 2020, when three health interpreting students took their exams live through the Microsoft Teams modality. Since the language assessors and the students were in different remote locations at the time of the exam, assessors were able to mark student renditions on the script without the students being aware of this at the time. The assessors then had a brief post-assessment meeting where they agreed on the final grade for the live interpreting exams. The plan for 2021 is to conduct such live interpreting exams in person, on campus, depending on New Zealand continuing to eliminate Covid-19 community transmission.

11.4.5 Moving teaching and assessment online: Challenges and solutions

The 2020 Covid-19 pandemic necessitated two lockdowns in New Zealand: the first one came into force on 26 March 2020 and resulted in all interpreting classes and assessments being moved online. On 8 June 2020 New Zealand had returned to Alert Level 1[5], which allowed for students to come back on campus for their "frozen" prerecorded language-specific interpreting assessments. Three students were unable to attend and were instead given live interpreting exams at a later date (July 2020). The live exams were conducted remotely online, as described in the previous section. These exams were a success; however management asked the author and her colleagues to streamline the interpreting exams due to the high number of assessors and invigilators involved, as well as the cost-intensive nature of these tests (in turn due to the high number of language pairs and invigilators involved). The solution was prerecorded language-specific interpreting exams being played to students remotely at the end of the second semester, in October 2020. Technical issues, such as the repetition of sound through students' headphones during their simultaneous health and legal interpreting exams, led to the decision to conduct interpreting exams on campus again henceforward.

For 2021, the plan is to conduct and record all interpreting exams live, on campus, circumstances permitting.[6] Conducting live exams will enable students to also engage in turn-taking management (asking for repetition, managing the flow of the conversation) – another essential skill they need to develop. Exams will still need to be recorded, deidentified and made available online to language assessors. Based on the results of the exams, students will receive a recommendation from teaching staff as to whether they are considered ready for the NAATI interpreting tests or whether they need more preparation time. The nature of these exams means that only a few students can be assessed at any one time, which means other exam candidates will need to be supervised in a safe "waiting room". The organisation of exams in mixed-language classrooms remains a logistically complex process, which is not only expensive, but also labour- and personnel-intensive.

11.5 Concluding remarks

This chapter set out to sketch an overview of non-language-specific healthcare interpreter education in New Zealand, starting with the historical backdrop to non-language-specific interpreter education. It then set out the challenges of public service interpreting in general, and health interpreting in particular. The challenges of (mixed-language) health interpreter education were described, with a particular focus on the need to develop students into aware, resourceful and reflective practitioners. Creative solutions to the need for language-specific feedback were discussed, and it is hoped that these may be of use to interpreter educators in similar settings, in other areas of the world. The author feels that self-reflection and reflection on feedback received from same-language peers need to be a compulsory part of graded assessment. In her experience, most students will only invest time in those parts of assessments that count towards their final grade – although there is always a small group of dedicated trainees who are the exception to this "rule". The need to prepare students for NAATI certification was also discussed, and with it the move to live interpreting exams.

Notes

1 Working on an orchard – how hard could it be? Retrieved December 21, 2020 from: www.stuff.co.nz/business/300179644/working-on-an-orchard--how-hard-could-it-be
2 The 2018 Census had low response rates, which is why this chapter instead presents the 2013 Census data on languages spoken in New Zealand.
3 Focusing on eight tenets: professional conduct, confidentiality, competence, impartiality, accuracy, employment, professional development, and professional solidarity.

4 "Aotearoa" is the original name for New Zealand, literally meaning "land of the long white cloud" in Te Reo Māori. Aotearoa New Zealand is how New Zealanders are increasingly referring to their country.
5 www.beehive.govt.nz/speech/new-zealand-moves-alert-level-1
6 Indeed, all exams were run live on campus as outlined above at the end of Semester 1 2021, with everyone involved – students, teaching staff, assessors – very happy with the process.

References

Bernardini, S. (2004). The theory behind the practice: Translator training or translator education? In K Malmkjær (Ed.), *Translation in Undergraduate Degree Programmes* (pp. 17–29). Amsterdam: John Benjamins.

Burn, J. A., & Crezee, I. (2017). "That is not the question I put to you, officer": An analysis of student legal interpreting errors. *International Journal of Interpreter Education, 9*(1), 40–56.

Burn, J. A., Crezee, I., Hastwell, K., Brugh, E., & Harison, R. (2014). 'I study long, long time in my language, so I never forget it': Reading and first language maintenance. *Intercultural Education, 25*(5), 377–390.

Burn, J. A., & Wong Soon, H. N. (2020). Interview with Samoan-English specialist mental health interpreter Hoy Neng Wong Soon. *International Journal of Interpreter Education, 12*(1).

Cartwright, S. (1988). *The Report of the Committee of Inquiry into Allegations Concerning the Treatment of Cervical Cancer at National Women's Hospital and into Other Related Matters.* Wellington: Government Printing Office.

Coney, S. (2020). Letter to the editor: Women's experience of 'the unfortunate experiment' at National Women's Hospital, New Zealand. *Journal of Clinical Epidemiology, 127,* 232–234. https://doi.org/DOI:10.1016/j.jclinepi.2020.09.009

Coney, S., & Bunkle, P. (1988). An unfortunate experiment at National Women's. Hospital. *Bioethics News, 8*(1), 3–30.

Corsellis, A. (2008). *Public Service Interpreting: The First Steps*. London: Palgrave Macmillan.

Crezee, I. (1997). *A Brief Guide to Healthcare Terminology and Healthcare Settings–for Interpreters and Other Professionals.* Auckland: New Horizons Advisory Services.

Crezee, I. (2009). Development of the interpreting profession. In D. Clark & C. McGrath (Eds.), *Interpreting in New Zealand: The Pathway Forward* (pp. 74–79). Wellington: Department of Internal Affairs, Office of Ethnic Affairs.

Crezee, I. (2013). *Introduction to Healthcare for Interpreters and Translators*. Amsterdam: John Benjamins.

Crezee, I. (2015). Semi-authentic practices for student health interpreters. *Translation and Interpreting, 7*(3), 50–62.

Crezee, I., & Grant, L. (2016). Thrown in the deep end: Challenges of interpreting informal paramedic language. *Translation and Interpreting, 8*(2), 1–12. https://doi.org/DOI: 10.12807/ti.108202.2016.a01

Crezee, I., & Ng, N. S. (2016). *Introduction to Healthcare for Chinese-speaking Interpreters and Translators.* Amsterdam: John Benjamins.

Crezee, I., Teng, W., & Burn, J. A. (2017). Teething problems? Chinese student interpreters' performance when interpreting authentic (cross-) examination questions in the legal interpreting classroom. *Interpreter and Translator Trainer, 11*(4), 337–356.

Crezee, I., Zucchi, E., & Jülich, S. (2020). Getting their wires crossed? Interpreters and clinicians' expectations of the role of professional interpreters in the Australian health context. *New Voices in Translation Studies, 23*, 1–30. https://www.iatis.org/index.php/new-voices-in-translation-studies/item/2335-new-voices-in-translation-studies-23-2020

Crezee, I. & Marianacci, A. (under review). "How did he say that?" Interpreting students' written reflections on interprofessional education scenarios with speech language therapists. *Interpreter and Translator Trainer, (29),* 1. DOI: 10.1080/1750399X.2021.1904170

D'Hayer, D. (2012). Public service interpreting and translation: Moving towards a (virtual) community of practice. *Meta: Journal des Traducteurs/Meta: Translators' Journal, 57*(1), 235–247.

Enríquez Raído, V., Crezee, I., & Ridgeway, Q. (2020, 17 February). Professional, ethical, and policy dimensions of public service interpreting and translation in New Zealand. *Translation and Interpreting Studies, 15*(1), 15–35. https://doi.org/10.1075/tis.20007.enr

Eser, O. (2020). *Understanding Community Interpreting Services Diversity and Access in Australia and Beyond.* London: Palgrave Macmillan. https://doi.org/10.1007/978-3-030-55861-1

Gentile, A., Ozolins, U., & Vasilakakos, M. (1996). *Liaison Interpreting: A Handbook.* Melbourne: Melbourne University Press. .

Hale, S. B. (2011). Public service interpreting. In K. Malmkjær (Ed.), *The Oxford Handbook of Translation Studies* (pp. 343–356). Oxford: Oxford University Press.

Hale, S. B., Garcia, I., Hlavac, J., Kim, M., Lai, M., Turner, B., & Slatyer, H. (2012). *Improvements to NAATI Testing. Development of a Conceptual Overview for a New Model for NAATI Standards, Testing and Assessment.* www.naati.com.au/PDF/INT/INTFinalReport.pdf.

Health and Disability Commissioner (1996). Code of Health and Disability Services Consumers' Rights Regulations 1996.

Kurtz, S., Silverman, J., Benson, J., & Draper, J. (2003). Marrying content and process in clinical method teaching: Enhancing the Calgary–Cambridge guides. *Academic Medicine, 78*(8), 802–809.

Li, X. (2018). Self-assessment as 'assessment as learning'in translator and interpreter education: Validity and washback. *The interpreter and Translator Trainer, 12*(1), 48–67.

Magill, D. (2017). *Healthcare Interpreting from a New Zealand Sign Language Interpreters' Perspective.* Master's thesis, Auckland University of Technology.

Magill, D., & de Jong, K. (2016). Interview with Kim de Jong, Interpreting and Translation Service Manager. *International Journal of Interpreter Education, 8*(1), 57–66.

Martin, J. (1978). *The Migrant Presence: Australian Responses 1947–1977.* London: Routledge.

MBIE. (2016). *Fair And Accessible Public Services: Summary Report on the Use of Interpreters and Other Language Assistance in New Zealand.* www.immigration.govt.nz/documents/about-us/summary-report-fair-and-accessible-public-services.pdf https://www.mbie.govt.nz/dmsdocument/12344-fair-and-accessible-public-services-summary-report-on-the-use-of-interpreter-services-and-other-language-assistance-in-new-zealand

McCredie, M., Sharples, K., Paul, C., Baranyai, J., Medley, G., Jones, R., & Skegg, D. (2008). Natural history of cervical neoplasia and risk of invasive cancer in women with cervical intraepithelial neoplasia 3: A retrospective cohort study. *The Lancet Oncology, 9*(5), 425–434. https://doi.org/10.1016/S1470-2045(08)70103-7

Merlini, R., & Favaron, R. (2005). Examining the "voice of interpreting" in speech pathology. *Interpreting in Legal and Healthcare Settings: Perspectives on Research and Training, 7*(2), 262–302.

Meyer, E. (2016). *The Culture Map: Decoding How People Think, Lead, and Get Things Done Across Cultures.* New York: PublicAffairs.

Mikkelson, H. (2020). Development of the medical interpreting profession in the US: A case study. In *Handbook of Research on Medical Interpreting* (pp. 1-25). Hershey, PA: IGI Global.

Munson, E., & Wilcox, A. (2007). Applying the Calgary-Cambridge model. *Practice Nursing, 18*(9), 464–468.

NAATI. (2016). *NAATI Interpreter Certification: Knowledge, Skills and Attributes. Review Process and Outcomes* www.naati.com.au/wp-content/uploads/2020/02/Knowledge-Skills-and-Attributes_Interpreter.pdf

New Zealand Immigration (2021). *Visa Programme Information.* www.immigration.govt.nz/about-us/covid-19/border-closures-and-exceptions/migrant-information

New Zealand Immigration. (n.d.). *The Language Assistance Services Programme.* www.immigration.govt.nz/about-us/what-we-do/our-strategies-and-projects/the-language-assistance-services-project

NZSTI (2013). *Code of Ethics and Code of Conduct.* https://nzsti.org/Pages/SYSTEM/Utility/Download.aspx?id=976832ed-a16a-46f7-b22f-c7050caae1a8&newtab=1

OEC. (2018). *Languages Spoken in New Zealand.* www.ethniccommunities.govt.nz/resources-2/our-languages-t/languages-in-new-zealand/.

Ozolins, U. (2010). Factors that determine the provision of public service interpreting: Comparative perspectives on government motivation and language service implementation. *The Journal of Specialised Translation, 14*(1), 194–215.

Rhodes, M., Fletcher, K., Blumenfeld-Kouchner, F., & Jacobs, E. (2021, January). Spanish medical interpreters' management of challenges in end of life discussions [semi-structured interviews with professional Spanish medical interpreters]. *Patient Education and Counseling,* https://doi.org/10.1016/j.pec.2021.01.018.

Roat, C., & Crezee, I. (2015). Healthcare interpreting. In H. Mikkelson & R. Jourdenais (Eds.), *Routledge Handbook of Interpreting* (pp. 236–253). London: Routledge.

Setton, R., & Dawrant, A. (2016). *Conference Interpreting – A Complete Course.* Amsterdam: John Benjamins.

Sharpe, M. (2020). Working on an orchard - how hard could it be? *Stuff.* www.stuff.co.nz/business/300179644/working-on-an-orchard--how-hard-could-it-be.

SLIANZ. (2012). *Code of Ethics.* https://slianz.org.nz/working-with-interpreters/code-of-ethics-code-of-conduct/

Statistics New Zealand (2018). *Data Quality for 2018 Census.* www.stats.govt.nz/2018-census/data-quality-for-2018-census

Statistics New Zealand (2020). *Ethnicity Cartograms of New Zealand: The Proportion of Ethnic Populations by Territorial Authority and Auckland Local Boards (TALB)*

from the 2018 Census. https://storymaps.arcgis.com/stories/8c8c82cfc2a6406f97951 9a382d0b81b

Vranjes, J., & Bot, H. (2021). Optimizing turn-taking in interpreter-mediated therapy: On the importance of the interpreter's speaking space. *Translation & Interpreting. The International Journal for Translation & Interpreting Research, 13*(1), 17.

12 Case-based learning for public service interpreting

Designs and procedures

Zhiwei Wu

12.1 Introduction

Public service interpreting (PSI) (or alternatively "community interpreting" and "liaison interpreting"[1]) refers to "oral and signed communication that enables access to services for people who have limited proficiency in the language of such services" (ISO13611, 2014). PSI usually takes place in schools, hospitals, courts, police stations, community service centres, and churches (Tipton & Furmanek, 2016). While there is an increasing demand for PSI prompted by greater worldwide mobility, PSI training has been deemed insufficient (De Pedro Ricoy, 2010), with a much smaller number of stand-alone programmes or courses compared to those in conference interpreting. This is one of the reasons why public service interpreters have not achieved a professional status comparable to conference interpreters (Vargas-Urpi, 2016; Wu, 2016). As such, D'Hayer (2013) aptly pointed out that "[t]he curriculum design strategies, the teaching and learning approaches are the initial key to the professionalization" of PSI (p. 327).

A survey of existing literature on PSI education shows that scholarly interests revolve around three themes, corresponding to the tripartite distinction of *approaches*, *designs*, and *procedures* in a pedagogy (Kiraly, 2000). An *approach* reflects the fundamental conceptualisation of a subject domain (e.g., what is a language?) and the learning of the subject domain (e.g., what is language learning?). For instance, in the context of PSI education, a "discourse-analytical approach to interpreting" (Niemants & Cirillo, 2017, p. 6) sees meaning as being co-constructed by participants within the interpreter-mediated communication. Thus, the pedagogies undergirded by this approach do not give primacy to the cognitive skills (e.g., short-term memory), but rather to the analytical skills that help capture and negotiate interactional dynamics in PSI (Valero-Garcés, 2008).

Guided by the fundamental conceptualisations of a subject domain, a pedagogical *design* more concretely deals with learning goals, curricula, syllabi, teaching methods, teacher and learner roles, and teaching materials. For instance, De Pedro Ricoy (2010) described the PSI curriculum designs in the UK, explaining the component skills and topics in the training programmes.

DOI: 10.4324/9781003197027-16

In PSI classrooms, teachers are advised to assume the role of a facilitator (D'Hayer, 2013), "guiding the students in their interactions and shared knowledge building" (Skaaden, 2017, p. 330).

Informed by the approaches and designs, teaching *procedures* (such as teaching practices, techniques, and activities) are orchestrated and enacted in PSI classrooms. Some commonly used teaching activities include role playing (e.g., Angelelli, 2017), teacher-facilitated discussion (e.g., Davitti & Pasquandrea, 2014), and analysis of discourse markers (Major, Napier, & Stubbe, 2012).

In light of existing literature, this chapter focuses on the *design* and *procedure* of a PSI course at a university in Hong Kong. While previous studies have stressed the importance of using authentic materials (e.g., transcript of interpreter-mediated communication) in PSI education (D'Hayer, 2013; Major et al., 2012), more information is needed to guide teachers to present these materials in a principled way in order to develop the target skills (e.g., analytical and critical thinking) necessary for professional development. To this end, this chapter introduces a case-based learning (CBL) design so that real-life PSI cases are presented to students in a four-stage sequence (see Section 12.2 for details). Additionally, this chapter explains three types of metacognitive scaffolds that can potentially help students become "discourse analysts" (Roy, 2000, p. 22). These scaffolds are integrated into teacher-facilitated classroom discussion (see Section 12.4 for details) as concrete instantiations of the CBL design.

In the following sections, I will first explain the notion of "case-based learning" and then delineate the four stages of implementing this design in PSI education. I will describe the contextual particularities of the focal PSI course and explain how the CBL design is materialised in the course. Building on this, I will demonstrate how three metacognitive scaffolds are deployed to engage students in critical discussions of "rich points" (Ribas & Vargas-Urpi, 2017), i.e., potential issues that challenge students to propose and deliberate different solutions in PSI settings.

12.2 Case-based learning

CBL is a pedagogical approach that uses authentic, real-life cases to develop students' professional skills and knowledge (Thistlethwaite et al., 2012). CBL engages students in an active inquiry process of making sense of a case that promises pedagogical values, theoretical possibilities, and real-life implications. Typically, in CBL, instructors assume the role of a facilitator and guide students to conceptualise and analyse issues inherent in cases. The purpose of CBL is not to find out correct answers to case issues, but to develop students' abilities to discern and disengage the complex intricacies inherent in real-life cases so that they are prepared for similar and/or dissimilar situations in their professional life. Previous studies have shown that CBL contributes to student engagement, critical thinking skills, learning motivation, and learning outcomes (McMellon, 2013; Raza, Qazi, & Umer, 2019). Because of these benefits, CBL is widely used in medical education (Thistlethwaite et al., 2012) and business education (McMellon, 2013). In fact, CBL has great potential to be applied to PSI education because PSI skills and knowledge are simultaneously contextualised and abstract. That is, CBL can engage students in both inductive and deductive reasoning processes (e.g., from contextual particularities to generalised solutions and from professional norms to specific practices). In this way, students are guided to think about PSI issues from multiple perspectives and develop a sophisticated, systematic understanding of PSI across service settings.

Hansen and Dohn (2019) propose a four-stage design for CBL: (1) gain access to a case; (2) define an issue of inquiry; (3) engage in inquiry; and (4) develop understanding. In the first stage, the teacher directly provides students with a case or offers instructions for students to locate a case. In the context of PSI education, a case can come from transcripts in academic publications (as will be exemplified in this chapter), audio or video-recorded PSI events (e.g., Davitti & Pasquandrea, 2014), and publicly accessible contents (e.g., Pope Francis' homily in the Philippines as a featured case study in Tipton & Furmanek, 2016). These real-life cases guarantee the authenticity of training materials and tasks (D'Hayer, 2013; Major et al., 2012) and offer students rich opportunities to observe and reflect on "naturally-occurring instances of interpreter-mediated interaction [that] may allow [them] to compare actions which favour participant communication with ones that may impede it" (Gavioli, 2017, p. xii).

In addition to providing access to a case, as a second stage, the teacher needs to define an issue or issues of inquiry relevant to training goals. These issues should challenge students to think deeply about the focal case and connect experiential knowledge with conceptual knowledge. In PSI education, there are multiple issues that are worthy of inquiry and students should be made aware of them. For instance, Ribas and Vargas-Urpi (2017) identify different types of problems or what they call "rich points", including, inter alia, lexical issues (e.g., terminology), pragmatic issues (e.g., register), cultural issues (e.g., culture-specific reference), management of the conversation (e.g., long segments), and ethical issues (e.g., interpreters being requested to act outside the conventional role boundaries). The inclusion of "rich points" is motivated by the teaching goals and course contents of the PSI training. In this way, rich points can be the experiential-conceptual linkage between case particulars and professional norms.

In the third stage, students are engaged in teacher-facilitated inquiry. Teachers should guide students to approach the issues of inquiry from multiple, at times conflicting, perspectives so that they are sensitised to the complexities of professional practices. In PSI education, a dialogic pedagogy has been proposed to treat teacher–student classroom dialogues as sites of inquiry, where "teachers and learners jointly engage in observing and responding to interactional and professional dilemmas" (Niemants & Stokoe, 2017,

p. 296) and where a set of problems, solutions, and choices are considered and contested. In a simple but effective form, teacher–student dialogues can be conducted in a Socratic fashion, in which "assumptions and beliefs" are examined "in a systematic and logical way, primarily by asking searching questions" (Atkinson, 2014, p. 16). In more elaborate forms, teacher–student dialogues can be facilitated by alternative metacognitive scaffolds, defined as "tools, strategies, and guides that engage students in a higher level of regulating their thinking" (Kim & Pedersen, 2011, p. 1781). In Section 12.4, three metacognitive scaffolds (i.e., question prompts, decision matrixes, and Toulmin's model of argumentation) will be explained and illustrated with PSI cases.

In the fourth stage, at the end of the inquiry, students develop a sophisticated understanding by (re)organising and conceptualising their case experiences. In PSI education, after teacher–student dialogues in the classroom, a debriefing session can be conducted so that students have the opportunity to summarise the perspectives and solutions explored in the case study and verbalise the implications for their future learning and practices. This step can help students take stock of their learning and encourage them to translate what they have learned into practices in their (future) professional careers. In the next section, I will elucidate how the CBL design is applied to a PSI course.

12.3 Context of the course

This chapter features a course called *Advanced Liaison Interpreting* at a university in Hong Kong. It is a postgraduate, elective course, subsequent to two prerequisite courses that focus on basic interpreting skills (e.g., use of short-term memory, note-taking). As such, the focal course does not prioritise language skills or cognitive skills (because they have been dealt with in the prerequisite courses). Instead, the course exposes students to real-life PSI cases and guides them to reflectively and critically analyse these cases. The class meets in a 3-hour weekly session for a total of 13 weeks. The course contents are "segmented according to the different public service areas" (De Pedro Ricoy, 2010, p. 105), covering PSI in educational, medical, and legal settings. A discourse-analytical approach is adopted to go beyond mere linguistic features (e.g., accurate and idiomatic rendition) and look deeper into the contextual particularities and participants' roles in PSI. More specifically, the discourse-analytical approach is reflected in the four-stage CBL design. As explained in Section 12.2, the first two stages involve gaining access to cases and defining issues of inquiry. Table 12.1 summarises the issues of inquiry covered in the course as part of the course content. These issues are of great interest to PSI practice, research, and training (as illustrated by the supporting literature in Table 12.1).

To contextualise these issues, cases (in the form of PSI transcripts) are provided to students before each teaching session. Additionally, to make the

Table 12.1 Issues of inquiry in case-based learning design

Issues of inquiry	*Explanation*	*Related literature*
Pronoun shifts	Interpreter's (non-)renditions of pronouns that are deviated from the ones in the source utterance	Diriker (2004); Ng (2018)
Terminologies	Domain-specific vocabularies	Leung (2020); Vargas-Urpi (2016)
Norms	Professional norms are "performance instructions appropriate for and applicable to particular situations" (Toury, 1999, p. 14). They represent expectations about "what is conventionally right and wrong, adequate and inadequate" (Toury, 1999, p. 14) for practitioners to "serve prevailing values" (Chesterman, 2001, p. 141)	Downie (2017); Skaaden (2019)
Role boundaries	What a public service interpreter is expected to do in professional norms as compared to what he/she actually does in practice	Baixauli-Olmos (2017); Vargas-Urpi (2016)
Communicative goals	A teleological (or outcome-based) perspective that facilitates decision making to deliver the intended outcome(s) of the interpreter-mediated communication	Dean and Pollard (2011); Downie (2017)
The principle of impartiality	The interpreter's stance is expected or perceived not to align with any participant in the event.	Baixauli-Olmos (2017); Hale (2008)
The principle of transparency	"The interpreter should … interpret his or her own utterances whenever he or she has to intervene and speak as the interpreter" (García-Beyaert et al., 2015, p. 9); "the interpreted encounter must be transparent so that everyone knows what is happening at any time" (García-Beyaert et al., 2015, p. 18)	Chesterman (2001); Ribas and Vargas-Urpi (2017)

issues of inquiry more accessible, a set of question prompts are also provided to draw students' attention to specific instances/issues in the transcripts. Cases are selected from publications featuring varying language combinations (e.g., English–Italian) not limited to the students' A or B languages (Chinese–English). This is done to expose students to the diversity and possible universality across cases and milieus. The design of question prompts purports to draw out the "rich points" (Ribas & Vargas-Urpi, 2017) in the focal cases (see Section 12.4 for details).

During teaching sessions, students are engaged in active inquiry revolving around the rich points inherent in and/or emergent from the question prompts. The inquiry is conducted in the form of teacher-facilitated discussions (Skaaden, 2017). Importantly, the goal of teacher–student dialogues is not to find out the right answers to the questions. In fact, the questions do not have simple, clear-cut answers and thus need to be approached "as a set of dilemmas to consider, concepts to think about, commitments to pursue and balance, and practices to add to students' current repertoires" (Angelelli, 2017, p. 36). To facilitate students' inquiry, metacognitive scaffoldings are used so that students can grapple with the complexities of PSI cases and develop a sophisticated understanding of the issues of inquiry. These are the final two stages of the CBL design. In the following sections, three metacognitive scaffolds are exemplified.

12.4 Metacognitive scaffolds in the case-based learning design

As explained in Section 12.2, metacognitive scaffolds are pedagogical "tools, strategies, and guides" to facilitate students in the process of higher-level thinking (Kim & Pedersen, 2011, p. 1781). Carefully designed metacognitive scaffolds can draw students' attention to specific issues and guide them to think deeper about these issues. In PSI education, students may be overwhelmed by the contextual particularities and lose sight of a bigger issue at hand. Thus, in the following subsections, three metacognitive scaffolds are exemplified to facilitate students' analytical and critical thinking of PSI issues.

12.4.1 Question prompts

To assume the role of a facilitator in the PSI classroom, a teacher should ask, not answer, questions (Skaaden, 2013). Open-ended questions create problem spaces for students' reflection. The design of question prompts for the case analysis is based on three types of reflection: *descriptive*, *comparative*, and *critical* (Jay & Johnson, 2002). Questions that focus on *descriptive* reflection draw students' attention to a particular instance or instances and ask them to think about the rhetorical function and/or significance in the triadic communication. Questions that prompt *comparative* reflection require students to compare different instances, renditions, and scenarios so that they are aware of the complex, dynamic nature of PSI. Questions that promote *critical* reflection challenge students to evaluate the solution presented in the case and propose their own solutions to further the communicative goals in the featured PSI setting.

To illustrate, Extract 1 (teacher–parent meeting) is included here. Students are given the transcript, adapted from Davitti (2013). Additionally, they are provided with three sets of questions to reflect on the case from multiple perspectives:

1 In Turn 3, what pronoun does the mother use? In Turn 4, what pronoun does the interpreter use? Do these pronouns have any impact on the communication?
2 The interpreter does not interpret the mother's utterance for the teacher, but instead takes the initiative to respond to it (Turn 4). What do you think of this (non-)rendition?
3 At the end of Turn 4, the interpreter adds something not found in the teacher's original utterances. Is this acceptable to you? Why?

The three sets of question prompts feature varied combinations of descriptive, comparative, and critical reflections on the issues of inquiry (i.e., the first group of questions on communicative goals, the second group on the principle of transparency, and the third on the principle of impartiality). To elaborate further, within the first group of questions, students are asked to describe and compare the rhetorical effects of the pronoun shift (from "one" to "he"). Based on this, they are invited to come up with critical solutions to this potential communication issue.

Extract 1. Teacher-parent meeting in Italian and English (adapted from Davitti, 2013, p. 182)

1	Teacher	there's no penalty for having done the exams and then doing them again next year so
2	Interpreter	*sicuramente non c'è una una penale una una punizione per aver fallito all'esame e aver e ridarli'anno prossimo* surely there is not a penalty a punishment for failing the exam and having and trying them again next year
3	Mother	*si può ripetere* **one** can repeat it
4	Interpreter	*può ripeterli tranquillamente poi li passa* **he** can repeat it **easily then he passes them**

In addition to designing questions prompts for one single case (transcript), descriptive, comparative, and critical questions can be raised across multiple cases. For instance, Extracts 2–4 (healthcare interpreting in the contexts of Italy and Hong Kong) are provided to students, along with the following question prompts:

1 In Extracts 2 and 3, the interpreters interpret the doctor's questions and then ask some more questions. What purposes do these extra questions serve? Do you find these extra questions acceptable? Why?
2 In Extract 2, Turn 2, the interpreter renders the doctor's utterance more explicitly ("tell me now" vs. "what's your problem now?"). In Extract 3, Turn 2, the interpreter uses a more general term ("doctor") versus a

specific term ("paediatrician" in Turn 1). In Extract 4, Turn 4, the interpreter uses "sugar" rather than the original technical term in the doctor's utterance ("glucose" in Turn 1). To what extent are these instances of register shift justified?

3 What are the interpreters' roles in these three cases? To what extent are they similar with (or different from) each other? Do you think the interpreters in these cases are professional? Why?

The design of these three sets of questions is closely related to the issues of inquiry. Specifically, the first set of questions is about communicative goals and role boundaries. The second set focuses on terminologies, and the third set prompts students to reflect on professional norms versus practices.

Extract 2. Healthcare interpreting in Italian and English (adapted from Baraldi & Gavioli, 2014, pp. 341–342)

1	Doctor	*allora dimmi adesso* so tell me now
2	Interpreter	so what's your problem now?
3	Patient	my heart is worrying me, my heart
4	Interpreter	how is it worrying you?
5	Patient	ehm, my heart is
6	Interpreter	beating faster?
7	Patient	yes, yes, beat fast, fast, fast.
8	Interpreter	or you feel pain?
9	Patient	ye-yes, I feel pain.
10	Interpreter	it beats faster?
11	Patient	Yes
12	Interpreter	*eh, ha il cuore che batte forte. Ha anche dolore dice.* erm, he's got his heart beating fast. He also feels pain he says.
13	Doctor	*da quanto?* since when?

Extract 3. Healthcare interpreting in Italian and English (adapted from Baraldi & Gavioli, 2014, p. 346)

1	Doctor	*il pediatra ce l'hanno già?* have they already got their **paediatrician**?
2	Interpreter	have you chosen any **doctor** already?
3	Patient	yeah
4	Interpreter	OK. What's the name?
5	Patient	I don't know
6	Interpreter	but you have the card with you?
7	Patient	no it is at home

8	Interpreter	at home. OK. *L'hanno già scelto* they have chosen that already.
9	Doctor	*comunque l'hanno già scelto* anyway they have chosen that
10	Interpreter	*sì sì* yes yes
11	Doctor	OK

Extract 4. Healthcare interpreting in Punjabi and English (adapted from Leung, 2020, p. 276)

1	Doctor	He had his blood checked on 9th May. We checked **glucose**, lipids and also his adrenal function. The adrenal function test was normal.
2	Interpreter	*Twahdda inhan ne may noo laiya ni test nau may noo wo thik hai* *'twahdda* They took a blood test on 9th May; it is all right.
3	Patient	*Sugar thik hai sara?* Sugar is all right all?
4	Interpreter	*Thik hai sugar thik hai.* It's all right; **sugar** is OK

In the later stage of the *Advanced Liaison Interpreting* course, question prompts can guide students to think about PSI cases across settings. For instance, when Extract 5 (court interpreting) is provided to students, the following questions are designed to critically compare PSI contexts:

1 In Extract 1, Extract 2, and Extract 5, what pronouns are used by the interpreters to represent the speakers?
2 In these three extracts, pronoun shifts are noticeable. How do they differ from each other? Think about the possible motivations and consequences of the pronoun shifts.
3 It is a widely held professional norm to interpret in the first person. To what extent do you think this norm can be more flexible in the three cases?
4 Building on the analysis of pronouns, how do you think the power structures and communicative goals differ across the educational, medical, and legal settings? What implications can be drawn for interpreters navigating these PSI settings?

These four sets of questions are in common with the previous ones outlined above in that they are descriptive (question 1), comparative (question 2), and reflective (questions 3 and 4). However, they are less specific because students are not told where and how pronouns are shifted. Thus, they need to locate specific instances on their own and describe the patterns across the educational, medical, and legal settings. This design at the later stage of the course is to provide opportunities for students to apply what they have learned in new PSI cases.

Extract 5. Court interpreting in English and Cantonese (adapted from Ng, 2018, p. 155)

1	Judge	Er well, you are eligible for the Duty Lawyer Scheme. And I would as you are pleading not guilty, er I would uh advise you uh to retain the services for the trial.
2	Interpreter	*其實你呢係有資格可以用當值律師嘅服務㗎，既然你宜家不認罪吓，法官就話你最好都係呢，係審訊嘅時候，聘請當值律師代表你。* In fact, you are eligible for the duty lawyer service. Since you have pleaded not guilty, the judge said it's better for you to hire a duty lawyer to represent you at the trial.
3	Defendant	*Er我自己搵律師。* Uh I'll find a lawyer myself.
4	Interpreter	I'll get a lawyer myself.

12.4.2 Decision matrix

A decision matrix is a tool to evaluate different aspects (decision points) of several options. A decision matrix has two typical forms: unweighted and weighted. In the unweighted form, equal weighting is assumed for all decision points. For instance, in Table 12.2, four PSI contexts and their exemplar events are compared to determine the level of difficulty of these PSI contexts. Three aspects are considered: public (the extent to which the event is publicly accessible), technical (the extent to which terminologies are opaque), and interactive (the extent to which interaction is back and forth). It is important to note that the values in the cells are subjective and relative. A student may think legal terms are more technical than medical terms, so she assigns value "2" to the legal context and "3" to the medical context. Others may disagree and have different perceived levels of technicality for legal and medical terms. Regardless of the particular values, Table 12.2 offers a way to describe and compare different PSI contexts from three aspects, the sum of which indicate the difficulty of possible job assignments.

In a weighted form, a decision matrix specifies the weighting of each decision point (Table 12.3). Again, weightings are subjective and relative. Comparing Table 12.2 and Table 12.3, we find that the results are somewhat different. In Table 12.2, legal and religious contexts are considered most difficult. In Table 12.3, after weightings are factored, legal contexts are considered most difficult. It is important to reiterate that these numeric values are for illustrative purposes only. In this way, students can articulate their feelings and

Table 12.2 A decision matrix (equal weightings assumed) about the difficulty of job assignments across public service interpreting (PSI) settings

Context (PSI event)	*Public*	*Technical*	*Interactive*	*Difficulty*
Educational (teacher–parent meeting)	1	1	2	4
Legal (recorded session of police interview)	2	2	3	7
Medical (pre-operation information session)	1	3	2	6
Religious (mass)	3	3	1	7

Table 12.3 A decision matrix (with different weightings) about the difficulty of job assignments across public service interpreting (PSI) settings

Context (PSI event)	*Public*	*Technical*	*Interactive*	*Difficulty*
Weighting	*2*	*1*	*3*	*Total*
Educational (teacher–parent meeting)	1×2=2	1×1=1	2×3=6	9
Legal (police investigation recording session)	2×2=4	2×1=2	3×3=9	15
Medical (pre-operation information session)	1×2=2	3×1=3	2×3=6	11
Religious (mass)	3×2=6	3×1=3	1×3=3	12

opinions about PSI contexts and see how contexts can influence interpreters' decision making.

In addition to the two typical forms presented previously, a decision matrix can do without numeric values. For instance, Salisbury, Goff, and Blitz (2019) proposed a decision matrix with three components (i.e., decision points, underlying concepts, and guiding questions) to compare two assessment tools for school leadership. In PSI education, this alternative form has two advantages. First, it is integrated with the metacognitive scaffold (i.e., question prompts) demonstrated in Section 12.4.1, thus providing additional metacognitive support for students. Second, it maps questions to decision points and to underlying issues of inquiry, which enables students to develop systematic ways of reflecting on PSI cases. For instance, in relation to Extracts 1, 2, and 5 (corresponding to educational, healthcare, and legal settings), students are asked to think about the professional norm of interpreting in the first person. During the classroom discussion, the teacher can further guide students' analysis with the help of a decision matrix (Table 12.4) that approaches the issue from three aspects (i.e., decision points). In the matrix, relevant underlying issues of inquiry and more detailed guiding questions are presented to help

Table 12.4 A decision matrix evaluating pronoun shifts in public service interpreting (PSI)

Decision points	*Underlying issues of inquiry*	*Guiding questions*
Referential clarity	Norms	Does the pronoun shift cause referential confusion? Does the deictic shift lead to better referential clarity than sticking to the first-person professional norm?
Visibility of the interpreter	Role boundaries	Does the pronoun shift unnecessarily project the voice of the interpreter? Would the projection of the interpreter's voice overstep his or her expected role boundaries?
Perceived alignment	The principle of impartiality	Does the pronoun shift lead to an impression that the interpreter is aligning with one party in the communication? Does the pronoun shift make both parties' voices better recognised and thus fully and equally represented?

students evaluate pronoun shifts in the light of professional norms and contextual practices. The decision matrix engages students in active inquiry of the relationship between practices as they are and as they should be, thus allowing students to deliberate how "rules or standards" might not be independent "from one situated practice to another … or from one setting to another" (Angelelli, 2020, p. 117).

Whether in typical or alternative forms, the primary purpose of a decision matrix is to engage students in a systematic, structured decision-making process. Instead of solely relying on either their intuition or inflexible standards of practice, students can use a decision matrix as a metacognitive scaffold to explore and reflect on the "fluidity and dynamism" in a variety of PSI contexts (Tipton & Furmanek, 2016, p. 10). In this way, students will be able to understand that professional PSI practices shall not be subjected to intuitive responses or dictated by rigid norms, but shall be the result of a series of informed and balanced decision making.

12.4.3 Toulmin's model of argumentation

Toulmin's model of argumentation contains three primary elements: data, warrant, and claim (Toulmin, 2003). Data are facts, grounds, and evidence to support a claim (which can be an assertion, an argument, or a thesis). Warrant is the justification that links data to the claim. To use a daily-life example, the evidence ("Jack was born into the Smith family") can be used to support the claim that "Jack is red-haired" because of the warrant ("Red hair is the trademark of the Smiths"). Toulmin's model has three other elements: backing, rebuttal, and qualifier (Toulmin, 2003). Backing offers additional support to establish the relevance and validity of the warrant. Rebuttal explores exceptions that might undermine the claim. Qualifier modifies the claim to avoid absolute statements. To continue with the previous example, the backing to further support the warrant can be "All Jack's brothers are red-haired". However, a rebuttal may be "Jack has dyed his hair or has gone white", which leads to the qualifier ("so, almost certainly") (Table 12.5, cf. Toulmin, 2003).

After students familiarise themselves with Toulmin's model of argumentation, the teacher can exploit its heuristic values in discussing PSI cases. For instance, in relation to Extract 1 (parent–teacher meeting), students are asked to deliberate on the extra comments made by the interpreter. Students may offer various opinions and statements. The teacher can ask them to organise their observation, reasoning, and propositions around the six components. Table 12.6 offers a possible line of argument to critically evaluate the acceptability (i.e., the claim) of the interpreter's additional comments (i.e., the data) in light of the principle of impartiality (i.e., the warrant) and consequence of non-compliance of the principle (i.e., the backing). Importantly, the model also prompts students to consider possible scenarios in which the interpreter's behaviours are justified (i.e., the rebuttal) so that the claim is made in relative, not absolute, terms (i.e., the qualifier).

Table 12.5 An example of Toulmin's model of argumentation (adapted from Toulmin, 2003, p. 117)

Element	*Item*
Data	Jack was born into the Smith family
Warrant (*because*)	Red hair is the trademark of the Smiths
Backing (*since*)	All Jack's brothers are red-haired
Rebuttal (*unless*)	Jack has dyed his hair or has gone white
Qualifier	*so, almost certainly*
Claim	Jack is red-haired

Table 12.6 Acceptability of public service interpreters adding extra comments

Element	*Item*
Data	The interpreter adds some comments about the boy, trying to comfort the mother
Warrant (*because*)	Interpreters are bound by the principle of impartiality
Backing (*since*)	Aligning with one participant may affect the trust of the other
Rebuttal (*unless*)	In the previous part of the conversation, the teacher has made comments about the boy's ability to pass exams easily
Qualifier	*so, probably*
Claim	The additional comments are unacceptable

Table 12.7 Acceptability of public service interpreters asking extra questions

Element	*Item*
Data	The interpreter asks additional questions to solicit information from the patient
Warrant (*because*)	These questions increase the "doctorability" of the patient's answers
Backing (*since*)	The interpreter controls the flow of turn-taking and saves time
Rebuttal (*unless*)	The questions are not routine ones
Qualifier	*so, chances are that*
Claim	The interpreter's intervention contributes to the communicative goals

As a second example, we refer to Extracts 2 and 3 (healthcare interpreting) and the related issues about the interpreter asking additional questions. Students can be asked to organise and synthesise their thoughts around the six components of the model. Table 12.7 presents one way to structure the critical reflection on the interpreter's taking initiative to ask extra questions (i.e., the data) in light of the increased "doctorability"[2] of the patient's answers (i.e., the warrant), which is made possible by saving unnecessary back-and-forth turns (i.e., the backing). Hence, the increased "doctorability" can justify the interpreter's behaviours as facilitative in furthering the communicative goals (i.e., the claim). However, students are also urged to think about situations in which asking additional information may overstep the interpreter's role boundaries (i.e., the rebuttal).

These two examples show that Toulmin's model of argumentation offers a useful set of heuristics for students to connect their case experience with issues of inquiry inherent in the cases (e.g., the principle of impartiality and the communicative goals). The model, as a metacognitive scaffold, can enable students to approach PSI issues from multiple perspectives and formulate sound, balanced arguments about interpreters' strategies in dealing with PSI issues. An expected outcome of using this model in the PSI classroom is the development of students' analytical and critical thinking skills. Such skills are important for them to consider contextual particularities relative to professional norms and to avoid "the uncritical transfer of codes of conduct and standards of practice across interpreting settings" (Niemants & Cirillo, 2017, p. 2).

12.5 Conclusion

As Turner (2005) aptly pointed out, "the ability to reflect critically when we encounter complexity and unfamiliarity is a vital component of professional practice" (p. 48). To train students' reflective and critical thinking skills to grapple with the complexity in PSI, this chapter proposes a CBL design in PSI education. The design features four stages: selecting real-life PSI cases, defining issues of inquiry, engaging students in active inquiry, and developing a sophisticated understanding of PSI. Additionally, three metacognitive scaffolds (i.e., question prompts, decision matrixes, and Toulmin's model of argumentation) are integrated into the CBL design so that students are sensitised to contextual particularities and guided to reflect on various issues emergent from PSI cases. Hopefully, the pedagogical designs and procedures described in this chapter will function as a set of heuristics for PSI educators to orchestrate their course contents and teaching practices that enable students to become "discourse analysts". As a positive and promising outcome, they will be keenly aware and critical of the "room for manoeuvre and [the] amount of freedom to make professional decisions" (Hammer & van den Bogaerde, 2017, p. 69).

Notes

1 In this chapter, the three terms are used interchangeably as they are widely used in the literature (Niemants & Cirillo, 2017).

2 Heritage and Robinson (2006) pointed out that "a doctorable problem is one that is worthy of medical attention, worthy of evaluation as a potentially significant medical condition, worthy of counseling and, where necessary, medical treatment" (p. 58). An interpreter can increase the doctorability of a patient's utterances by soliciting more information that is medically relevant (Baraldi & Gavioli, 2014).

References

Angelelli, C. V. (2017). Anchoring dialogue interpreting in principles of teaching and learning. In L. Cirillo & N. Niemants (Eds.). *Teaching Dialogue Interpreting* (pp. 30–44). Amsterdam: John Benjamins.

Angelelli, C. V. (2020). Community/public-service interpreting as a communicative event: A call for shifting teaching and learning foci. *Translation and Translanguaging in Multilingual Contexts*, 6(2), 114–130.

Atkinson, D. P. (2014). Developing psychological skill for the global language industry: An exploration of approaches to translator and interpreter training. *Translation Spaces*, 3(1), 1–24.

Baixauli-Olmos, L. (2017). Ethics codes as tools for change in public service interpreting: Symbolic, social and cultural dimensions. *The Journal of Specialised Translation*, 28, 250–272.

Baraldi, C., & Gavioli, L. (2014). Are close renditions the golden standard? Some thoughts on translating accurately in healthcare interpreter-mediated interaction. *The Interpreter and Translator Trainer*, 8(3), 336–353.

Chesterman, A. (2001). Proposal for a hieronymic oath. *The Translator*, 7(2), 139–154.

D'Hayer, D. (2013). Public service interpreter education: A multidimensional approach aiming at building. In C. Schäffner, K. Kredens, & Y. Fowler (Eds.). *Interpreting in a Changing Landscape: Selected Papers from Critical Link 6* (pp. 321–337). Amsterdam: John Benjamins.

Davitti, E. (2013). Dialogue interpreting as intercultural mediation: Interpreters' use of upgrading moves in parent–teacher meetings. *Interpreting*, *15*(2), 168–199.

Davitti, E., & Pasquandrea, S. (2014). Enhancing research-led interpreter education: An exploratory study in Applied Conversation Analysis. *The Interpreter and Translator Trainer*, 8(3), 374–398.

De Pedro Ricoy, R. (2010). Training public service interpreters in the UK: A fine balancing act. *Journal of Specialised Translation*, *14*, 100–120.

Dean, R. K., & Pollard Jr, R. Q. (2011). Context-based ethical reasoning in interpreting: A demand control schema perspective. *The Interpreter and Translator Trainer*, *5*(1), 155–182.

Diriker, E. (2004). *De-/Re-contextualizing Conference Interpreting: Interpreters in the Ivory Tower?* Amsterdam: John Benjamins.

Downie, J. (2017). Finding and critiquing the invisible interpreter – A response to Uldis Ozolins. *Interpreting*, *19*(2), 260–270.

García-Beyaert, S., Bancroft, M. A., Allen, K., Carriero-Contreras, G., & Socarrás-Estrada, D. (2015). *Ethics and Standards for the Community Interpreter. An International Training Tool*. Accessed December 22, 2020. https://ddd.uab.cat/pub/recdoc/2015/218104/Garcia-Beyaert_et_al_2015_TCii_Ethics_and_Standards.pdf

Gavioli, L. (2017). Foreword. In L. Cirillo & N. Niemants (Eds.). *Teaching Dialogue Interpreting* (pp. xi–xii). Amsterdam: John Benjamins.

Hale, S. (2008). Controversies over the role of the court interpreter. In C. Valero-Garcés & A. Martin (Eds.). *Crossing Borders in Community Interpreting: Definitions and Dilemmas* (pp. 99–121). Amsterdam: John Benjamins.

Hammer, A., & van den Bogaerdei, B. (2017). Sign language interpreting education: Reflections on interpersonal skills. In L. Cirillo & N. Niemants (Eds.). *Teaching Dialogue Interpreting* (pp. 63–81). Amsterdam: John Benjamins.

Hansen, J. J., & Dohn, N. B. (2019). Design principles for professional networked learning in "Learning Through Practice" designs. In A. Littlejohn, J. Jaldemark, E. Vrieling-Teunter & F. Nijland (Eds.). *Networked Professional Learning: Emerging and Equitable Discourses for Professional Development* (pp. 129–146). Cham: Springer.

Heritage, J., & Robinson, J. (2006). Accounting for the visit: Giving reasons for seeking medical care. In J. Heritage & D. Maynard (Eds.). *Communication in Medical Care: Interactions Between Primary Care Physicians and Patients* (pp. 48–87). Cambridge: Cambridge University Press.

ISO 13611. (2014). Interpreting – Guidelines for Community Interpreting. Geneva: ISO.

Jay, J. K., & Johnson, K. L. (2002). Capturing complexity: A typology of reflective practice for teacher education. *Teaching and Teacher Education*, *18*(1), 73–85.

Kim, H. J., & Pedersen, S. (2011). Advancing young adolescents' hypothesis-development performance in a computer-supported and problem-based learning environment. *Computers & Education*, *57*(2), 1780–1789.

Kiraly, D. (2000). *A Social Constructivist Approach to Translator Education: Empowerment from Theory to Practice*. Manchester: St. Jerome.

Leung, E. S. (2020). Medical interpreting as an emerging profession in Hong Kong. In E. Ng and I. Crezee (Eds.). *Interpreting in Legal and Healthcare Settings: Perspectives on Research and Training* (pp. 263–286). Amsterdam: John Benjamins.

Major, G., Napier, J., & Stubbe, M. (2012). "What happens truly, not textbook!" Using authentic interaction in discourse training for healthcare interpreters. In L. Swabey & K. Malcolm (Eds.). *In our Hands: Educating Healthcare Interpreters* (pp. 27–53). Washington: Gallaudet University Press.

McMellon, C. (2013). New advantages and insights into the living case teaching method: An exploratory study. *Journal of Academy of Business and Economics*, 13(1), 17–24.

Ng, E. N. (2018). *Common Law in an Uncommon Courtroom: Judicial Interpreting in Hong Kong*. Amsterdam: John Benjamins.

Niemants, N., & Cirillo, L. (2017). Dialogue interpreting: Research, education and professional practice. In L. Cirillo & N. Niemants (Eds.). *Teaching Dialogue Interpreting* (pp. 1–28). Amsterdam: John Benjamins.

Niemants, N., & Stokoe, E. (2017). Using the conversation analytic role-play method in healthcare interpreter education. In L. Cirillo & N. Niemants (Eds.). *Teaching Dialogue Interpreting* (pp. 293–322). Amsterdam: John Benjamins.

Raza, S. A., Qazi, W., & Umer, B. (2019). Examining the impact of case-based learning on student engagement, learning motivation and learning performance among university students. *Journal of Applied Research in Higher Education*, *12*(3): 517–533.

Ribas, M. A., & Vargas-Urpi, M. (2017). Strategies in public service interpreting: A roleplay study of Chinese–Spanish/Catalan interactions. *Interpreting*, *19*(1), 118–141.

Roy, C. (2000). *Interpreting as a Discourse Process*. Oxford: Oxford University Press.

Salisbury, J., Goff, P., & Blitz, M. (2019). Comparing CALL and VAL-ED: An illustrative application of a decision matrix for leadership feedback instruments. *Journal of School Leadership*, *29*(1), 84–112.

Skaaden, H. (2013). No set answers? Facilitating interpreter students' learning in an experiential approach. In C. Wadensjö (Ed). *Training the Trainers: Nordic Seminar on Interpreter Education* (pp. 12–24). Stockholm: Tolk-och översättarinstitutet, Stockholms universitet.

Skaaden, H. (2017). "That we all behave like professionals" – An experiential–dialogic approach to interpreter education and online learning. In L. Cirillo & N. Niemants (Eds.). *Teaching Dialogue Interpreting* (pp. 323–340). Amsterdam: John Benjamins.

Skaaden, H. (2019). Invisible or invincible? Professional integrity, ethics, and voice in public service interpreting. *Perspectives*, *27*(5): 704–717.

Thistlethwaite, J. E., Davies, D., Ekeocha, S., Kidd, J. M., MacDougall, C., Matthews, P., ... & Clay, D. (2012). The effectiveness of case-based learning in health professional education. A BEME systematic review: BEME guide no. 23. *Medical Teacher*, *34*(6), 421–444.

Tipton, R., & Furmanek, O. (2016). *Dialogue Interpreting: A Guide to Interpreting in Public Services and the Community*. London: Routledge.

Toulmin, S. E. (2003). *The Uses of Argument*. Cambridge: Cambridge University Press.

Toury, G. (1999). A handful of paragraphs on 'translation' and 'norms'. In C. Schäffner (Ed.). *Translation and Norms* (pp. 9–31). Clevedon: Multilingual Matters.

Turner, G. (2005). Toward real interpreting. In M. Marschark, R. Peterson, & E. A. Winston (Eds.). *Sign Language Interpreting and Interpreter Education: Directions for Research and Practice* (pp. 29–56). New York: Oxford University Press.

Valero-Garcés, C. (2008). Hospital interpreting practice in the classroom and the workplace. In C. Valero-Garcés & A. Martin (Eds.). *Crossing Borders in Community Interpreting: Definitions and Dilemmas* (pp. 165–185). Amsterdam: John Benjamins.
Vargas-Urpi, M. (2016). Problems and strategies in public service interpreting as perceived by a sample of Chinese–Catalan/Spanish interpreters. *Perspectives*, *24*(4): 666–678.
Wu, Z. (2016). Towards professionalizing public service translators in China: Education and certification. *New Voices in Translation Studies*, *14*, 164–189.

13 Delivering the first MA/PGDip Business and Public Service Interpreting programme in the UK

Experience from the University of Leeds

Binhua Wang and Lihong Pan

13.1 Introduction

In almost every nation, there are groups of people who are linguistic minorities, such as migrants and ethnic minorities, who do not speak the language of the majority. Whether and how they access public services constitute significant issues for both themselves and society not only due to the language barriers faced by migrants and ethnic minorities, but also because the language in healthcare, legal and social services is often highly specialised, and it usually takes several years of learning to attain native-speaker fluency in the language of the majority. "The ability to communicate accurately and reliably in such contexts as the police station and the doctor's consulting room requires a native speaker fluency that would be measured at postgraduate level in academic terms" (Corsellis, 2008: 2). Therefore, linguistic minorities often need to rely on public service interpreters to access public policies and public services, such as healthcare, legal, education and social services (e.g. housing, social security, welfare, etc.). Public service interpreting (PSI) is essential for members of linguistic minorities who wish to exercise their right to communicate and access public services (ISO 13611-2014: v).

In its development as a social practice, PSI has carried different denominations, including: "liaison interpreting" (Gentile, Ozolins and Vasilakakos, 1996), "dialogue interpreting" (Mason, 1999), "community interpreting" (Hale, 2007) and "public service interpreting" (Corsellis, 2008). Their definitions as follows highlight different aspects of the same social practice (italics by the present author):

> We use the term "liaison interpreting" to refer to a growing area of interpreting throughout the world: in business settings, where executives from different cultures and languages meet each other; in meetings between a society's legal, medical, educational and welfare institutions and its immigrants who speak a different language; in relations

DOI: 10.4324/9781003197027-17

> between a dominant society and indigenous peoples speaking different languages; in a whole host of less formal situations in tourism, education and cultural contacts. Liaison interpreting is the style adopted in these varied settings – a style where the interpreter is physically present in an interview or meeting, and *usually uses the consecutive mode of interpreting*.
>
> (Gentile et al., 1996: 1)

> "Dialogue interpreting" includes what is variously referred to in English as Community, Public Service, Liaison, Ad Hoc or Bilateral Interpreting – *the defining characteristic being interpreter-mediated communication in spontaneous face-to-face interaction*. Included under this heading are all kinds of professional encounters: police, immigration and welfare services interviews, doctor–patient interviews, business negotiations, lawyer–client and courtroom interpreting, and so on. Dialogue interpreting is thus to be distinguished from Conference Interpreting (both simultaneous and consecutive), which is typically monologic and does not involve face-to-face interaction (although dialogue encounters do take place on the fringe of conference activity).
>
> (Mason, 1999: 147–148)

> Community Interpreting [is] the overarching term for the type of interpreting that takes place *within one country's own community, and between residents of that country, as opposed to Conference Interpreting*, which takes place between delegates who are residents of different countries, in the context of an international conference or meeting.
>
> (Hale, 2007: 30)

> Public service interpreting and translation are, as the name implies, interpreting and translation carried out in the context of the public services, where service users do not speak the majority language of the country. The term "public service" refers mainly to those services that are provided for the public by central or local government. *They include legal, health and the range of social services, such as housing, education welfare and environmental health*.
>
> (Corsellis, 2008: 4–5)

According to Hale (2011: 2–3), the different terms actually refer to the same professional activity with each term trying to capture a different characteristic of the activity. While Gentile, Ozolins and Vasilakakos (1996) highlight the settings and the consecutive mode of interpreting – though the whispered simultaneous mode is also used in these settings – Mason (1999) focuses on the dialogic format and face-to-face interaction; Hale (2007) highlights participants of the interaction being within the same community rather than in international conferences; and Corsellis (2008) summarises the types of public services that use this activity.

In terms of training, where relevant training is offered at the higher education level, dialogue or liaison interpreting is only offered as a traditional gateway tool towards the provision of conference interpreting training at the preliminary/preparatory stage. While the training of dialogue or liaison interpreting skills provides a well-proven gateway to more advanced interpreting skills and modes, such preliminary training is far from sufficient in providing professional preparation for would-be public service interpreters. It must be clarified from the beginning that PSI requires specialised competences, skills and role profiles that are different from those in conference interpreting, which will be discussed systematically in Sections 13.2 and 13.3.

With regard to previous literature, in spite of the fact that a great amount of literature has been published on other aspects of public service or community interpreting since the mid-1990s (e.g. Carr et al., 1997; Roberts et al., 2000; Brunette et al., 2003; Wadensjö et al., 2007; Hale et al., 2009; Schäffner et al., 2013), focused studies on curriculum and pedagogical design of a formal PSI programme in higher education are still scanty. Among the few relevant previous studies, de Pedro Ricoy (2010) points out that PSI training is a very complex endeavour that must balance pedagogical considerations and market requirements. In her paper, she discusses the interrelationship between academic programmes, qualifications, curriculum design and standards in PSI in connection with the perceived professional status and the desirability of regulated monitoring practices. The paper provides a comprehensive discussion about the context of PSI training though it only presents a brief introduction to a module in PSI offered as part of an MSc interpreting course. D'Hayer (2012) proposes communities of practice within a virtual learning environment as a useful way for PSI training. D'Hayer (2013) gives another useful discussion about building a virtual community of learners and professionals as a useful way to realise PSI training.

At the University of Leeds, we have been delivering the first MA/PGDip Business and Public Service Interpreting (MA/PGDip BPSI) programme in the UK since 2018. In this chapter, the particularities of PSI as being different from conference interpreting will be discussed. Accordingly, a framework of PSI competences will be proposed by drawing upon relevant research literature, textbooks and professional documents. Then the pedagogical and practical considerations in designing and delivering such a postgraduate-level BPSI programme will be discussed, and the structure and content of the programme and its core module on PSI will be presented. Based on the Framework of PSI Competences, a mini-survey was conducted among graduates of the programme to gauge the importance of PSI competences as perceived by practitioners and the adequacy of coverage of the competences in the training programme. The result will also be reported here.

13.2 Public service interpreting: What is special?

13.2.1 Typical settings using PSI

Different from conference interpreting, PSI happens in the settings of public services, which means it is conducted within the society rather than on international occasions. Typical settings where PSI is used include the following (ISO 13611:2014: 1): public institutions (governmental services, community centres, etc.), healthcare institutions (hospitals, nursing homes, etc.), legal settings (police stations, courts, prisons, etc.) that facilitate equal access to justice, human and social services (refugee boards, self-help centres, etc.), emergency situations (natural disasters, epidemics, etc.) and faith-based organisations (rituals, ceremonies, etc.).

13.2.2 PSI: A triangular model of communication and mediation

PSI is also different from conference interpreting in that PSI is done in a dialogic or two-way mode rather than monologic or one-way mode. As shown in Figure 13.1 (Wang, 2019), in PSI the interlocution between the two parties of monolingual interlocutors that is mediated by the interpreter can be represented by the three-cornered dialogic format, which is also the typical setting-up of seating positions of the participants in PSI settings such as police interviews and healthcare consultations. Such a triangular model means that the public service interpreter plays a more visible role in communication and mediation, including: (1) mediation of discourses from the interlocutors (Wadensjö, 1998; Roy, 2000; etc.); (2) mediation of communicative interaction; (3) mediation of cultural differences and (4) mediation of power relations between the interlocutors.

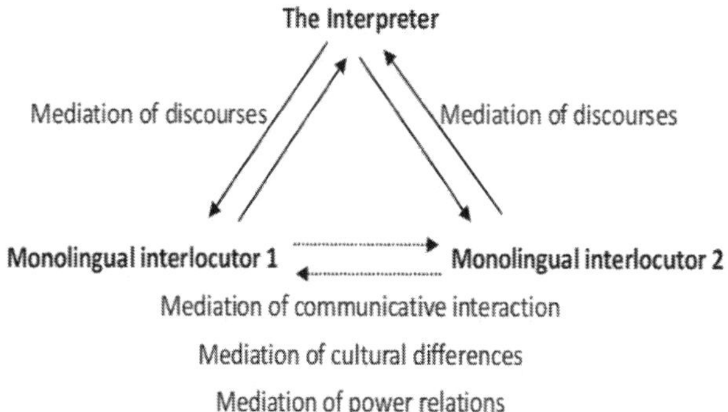

Figure 13.1 The triangular model of communication and mediation in public service interpreting.

13.3 A framework of PSI competences

According to the above discussion about the differences between PSI conference interpreting and the particularities of PSI, it is not feasible to apply indiscriminately general models of (conference) interpreting competence to the training of PSI. It is necessary to construct a framework of PSI competences. Previous research literature, textbooks and professional documents (e.g. Hale, 2007; Corsellis, 2008) have discussed the competences or skills required in PSI to varying degrees. Drawn from them, a Framework of PSI Competences is proposed here integrating representative constructs from previous research literature, textbooks and professional documents.

As shown in Table 13.1, the six competence sets in the framework, which are outlined in consideration of the typical settings and features of communication and mediation in PSI as analysed in Section 13.2, form an organic whole of the all-round competences required of a public service interpreter. While the competence sets of "interpreting techniques", "bilingual competence" and "extralinguistic knowledge and research skills" might be considered as similar to what are required of conference interpreters, the other competence sets including "interpersonal communication competence", "intercultural competence" and "profession-related awareness and qualities" are more salient in PSI, which is obvious from the list of their components.

13.4 PSI training: Programme structure and syllabus outline

13.4.1 MA/PGDip BPSI: Programme structure

The lack of provision of formal training of PSI in higher education means not only the lack of uniformity of entry requirements to the PSI profession but also a disparity in levels of competence and performance of public service interpreters, which have "obvious negative repercussions" on professional status, remuneration levels and professional identity (Hale, 2011: 5).

The provision of the postgraduate-level PSI programme has several major benefits as follows: (1) through the formal training programme, motivated and suitable trainees with appropriate aptitudes can be recruited; (2) through the formal programme, specialised training in PSI can be designed and provided systematically; and (3) through the formal programme, a standardised qualification framework can be put in place for PSI, with impartial and transparent assessment criteria and internal and external assessment review.

In 2017 the MA/PGDip BPSI programme was proposed and then approved for provision in the University of Leeds in 2018 after internal review by the Student Education Committee and the Quality Assurance Committee as well as external review by experts from outside the university. The rationale for designing such a programme can be summarised as follows (University of Leeds, Programme Catalogues).

Table 13.1 A framework of public service interpreting (PSI) competences and their components

PSI competence sets	*Components*
Interpreting techniques	Consecutive interpreting techniques Simultaneous interpreting techniques Whispering/*chuchotage* techniques Sight interpreting techniques
Bilingual competence	Listening comprehension ability after singular delivery from the speaker Oral expression ability in singular delivery Ability of immediate transfer from one working language to the other (Wang, 2021) Ability to comprehend language varieties in the working languages (e.g. dialects, regional varieties) Good command of a range of language registers Ability to use context- and register-appropriate language (ISO 13611-2014: 7)
Extralinguistic knowledge and research skills	Broad encyclopedic knowledge and intellectual curiosity Fundamental subject knowledge (e.g. about healthcare and legal settings and public institutions) (Wang, 2021) Ability to efficiently acquire terminological and specialised knowledge Capability in using task preparation and research tools (e.g. computer and software, internet, ICT, etc.) Ability to develop suitable strategies for the efficient use of the information sources available (e.g. terminology databases, parallel texts and corpus) (ISO 13611-2014: 7)
Interpersonal communication competence	Ability to relate well to people Exhibiting strong communication skills Managing and keeping up the flow of communication (e.g. turn-taking) Anticipating when to intervene during the interaction Using effective interjection skills when appropriate Effective intervention skills (ISO 13611-2014: 8) Being able to cope with communication breakdown Being able to cope with emotivity and tension between the interlocutors (Rudvin & Tomassini, 2011: 88)
Intercultural competence	Awareness and knowledge about cultural differences Awareness about culture-specific norms Ability to understand and render culture-specific elements Awareness and knowledge about intercultural pragmatics (e.g. politeness) Ability to use socio-culturally appropriate language (without violating social and cultural taboos) Intercultural intelligence in intercultural mediation (Wang, 2021)
Profession-related awareness and qualities	Awareness about professional roles and ethics (e.g. confidentiality) in PSI Awareness about interpreting client services and relationships (Wang, 2021) Exhibiting self-control and impartial behaviour in all situations (ISO 13611-2014: 8)

In the age of globalisation, both business and societies are increasingly multilingual. The rising need for interpreting and translation is marked by a rising acknowledgement from business and governments that using interpreting and translation services is an essential step towards ensuring good communication and fair public services. The MA/PGDip BPSI programme provides linguists, from the UK and abroad, who meet the entry requirements of the programme, with the opportunity to develop the skills of professional business and PSI and translation and consolidate these skills by acquiring familiarity with a range of issues in the fields of business, law, medicine and public services. It also provides specialised translation training and a module in methods and approaches to translation studies. The MA/PGDip BPSI programme is designed for those with an interest and aptitude for business and PSI who work bidirectionally within two languages and to enable graduates to apply the skills gained at a professional level in domestic and international courts and in medical settings as well as in business and international trade.

The entry requirements of the MA/PGDip BPSI programme are as follows (University of Leeds, Programme Catalogues):

1 Candidates must have a good undergraduate degree (normally a 2:1 Honours or above, or the equivalent).
2 They must have an excellent command of English and one or more foreign languages (International English Language Testing System (IELTS): 7.0 overall, with at least 7.5 in Listening and Speaking, and 6.5 in Reading and Writing).
3 Applicants seeking to enrol for Specialised Translation modules must pass a "Specialised Translation" entry test for each language combination they wish to study (up to two languages in addition to English).
4 Applicants must undertake and pass the aptitude interview to assess their suitability for interpreting training.

The programme structure of MA/PGDip BPSI is presented in Table 13.2.

As shown in Table 13.2, in terms of practical skills students in the MA/PGDip BPSI programme are required to study and pass six interpreting modules and the module of Specialised Translation. They also need to study and pass one optional module from the list of modules that are relevant to interpreting and translation. For those who want to get the MA degree, they are also required to study and pass the module of Methods and Approaches in Translation Studies (for two semesters) and finish the Summer Project (either Extended Translation with Commentary or Dissertation).

Among the six interpreting modules, the module "Interpreting Skills: Consecutive and Simultaneous" is provided for two semesters, in which consecutive and simultaneous interpreting skills are systematically introduced and trained progressively with one "component skill" (Moser-Mercer, 1997) for every 1 or 2 weeks. The core modules of "Public Service Interpreting" and "Business Interpreting" are practical interpreting modules

Table 13.2 Programme structure of MA/PGDip Business and Public Service Interpreting (BPSI)

Modules	*Credits*
Core modules	
Interpreting Skills: Consecutive and Simultaneous (Semesters 1 and 2)	15
Public Service Interpreting (Semester 1, two sessions/week)	15
Retour Interpreting: Consecutive (Semester 1)	15
Business Interpreting (Semester 2)	15
Simultaneous Interpreting (Semester 2)	15
Advanced Retour Interpreting: Simultaneous (Semester 2)	15
Methods and Approaches in Translation Studies (Semesters 1 and 2)	30
Specialised Translation (Semester 1 or 2)	15
Summer Project (Semester 3)	30
Optional modules	1×15
Introduction to screen translation; Genres in translation; Computers and the translator; Corpus linguistics for translators; Principles and applications of machine translation; Rhetoric and public speaking; Specialised translation; etc.	

targeting specialised competences, skills and topics in PSI and business interpreting respectively. As business and public service interpreters need to work bidirectionally, the two modules of "Retour Interpreting: Consecutive" and "Advanced Retour Interpreting: Simultaneous" are offered to train and consolidate skills and competences in interpreting into B language. The practical module of "Simultaneous Interpreting" is also provided to students of this programme, and is intended to lay a good foundation for their career development to an advanced level.

13.4.2 The core module of PSI: Teaching objectives, learning outcomes and syllabus outline

The main objectives (University of Leeds, Module Catalogues) of the core module of PSI in the MA/PGDip BPSI programme are to build upon the students' liaison and consecutive interpreting skills while introducing simultaneous interpreting skills and the technical and contextual knowledge required of public service interpreters. The focus will be on the development of specific techniques that support adequate source-language comprehension and target-language reconstruction in the various modes of interpreting used in the public service sector: consecutive, liaison and *chuchotage*/whispered simultaneous interpreting. These techniques include effective preparation and rapid assimilation of technical knowledge about the topic of the assignment, deverbalisation, note-taking and code- and register-switching to meet the needs of a specific audience or client. In addition to these skills, the module develops basic awareness and understanding of concepts in healthcare and legal interpreting and the institutional structures in which it is used.

In terms of learning outcomes, upon completion of this module, students should be able to (University of Leeds, Module Catalogues):

1 demonstrate an awareness of the professional and terminological requirements of public service interpreters
2 effectively research and prepare for assignments of a specialised and technical nature
3 proficiently take notes to support liaison and consecutive interpreting
4 interpret effectively in the liaison and consecutive modes
5 interpret effectively in the *chuchotage*/whispered simultaneous mode.

Accordingly, the core module of PSI has three strands on which it focuses: (1) PSI skills and their progression; (2) a strong activity focus featured by multiple modes employed in PSI and (3) professional literacy and ethics in PSI.

An indicative syllabus outline for the core module of PSI is presented in Table 13.3. The table outlines the training focus, teaching and learning content and modes and activities of interpreting for each week of the module. The class contact hours are 4 hours per week. Weeks 1–4 focus on healthcare interpreting with its content proceeding from simple liaison tasks to short and long consecutive tasks and then to sight interpreting of technical and specialised tasks. Weeks 5–8 focus on legal interpreting with progression in the technicality of content and in interpreting skills from rapid liaison interpreting in an interrogative context as well as long consecutive and sight interpreting to *chuchotage* and simultaneous interpreting. Weeks 9–10 focus on other settings in public services with knowledge and discussion on ethical and cross-cultural issues and professional issues in PSI while the interpreting activities are conducted in multiple mode and in the formats of video-conferencing and telephone interpreting.

The assessment of the PSI module takes the form of oral presentation, which includes interpreting tasks in which the student is required to interpret bilaterally in both the liaison and *chuchotage*/whispered simultaneous interpreting modes. The assessment lasts about 30 minutes in total (University of Leeds, Module Catalogues).

13.5 PSI training: Teaching activities and exercises

13.5.1 Teaching methods and organisation of the activities and exercises

As a practical, hands-on module, the training methods of the PSI module can be summarised as follows (University of Leeds, Module Catalogues): students are introduced to authentic materials from a range of recorded, live and written sources and engage in practical activities in which they acquire specialised knowledge about various settings in PSI and develop PSI skills introduced by the tutor. Regular, targeted and specific feedback is provided by the tutor in class for the students to further develop in their private study. Exercises take

Table 13.3 Public service interpreting (PSI): An indicative syllabus outline

Week	*Training focus*	*Content*	*Mode(s) and activities*
1	Healthcare interpreting: preparation and simple liaison tasks	Research basic healthcare terminology and learn how to prepare for assignments in general practitioners' consultations	Liaison interpreting and sight interpreting exercises
2	Healthcare interpreting: simple liaison tasks	Reinforce familiarity with basic healthcare terminology and a range of contexts in the healthcare interpreting field	Liaison interpreting and sight interpreting exercises
3	Healthcare interpreting: short and long consecutive	Familiarise themselves with the context of simple mental health assignments, such as the use of interpreting in cognitive behavioural therapy, evaluations and other forms of "talking therapy"	Liaison interpreting and sight interpreting but will also include short and long consecutive interpreting
4	Healthcare interpreting: technical and specialised tasks	More technical and specialised medicine, e.g. surgical consultations, coronavirus consultations, oncology consultations, etc.	Liaison interpreting and sight interpreting but will also include short and long consecutive interpreting
5	Legal interpreting: simple legal and paralegal contexts	Simple legal and paralegal contexts including attending police station assignments for witness statements, etc.; assignments with solicitors and legal advisors and assignments with adult and child services. The ethical concerns of working with children will be discussed as well as the lexical ramifications for public service interpreters	Rapid liaison interpreting in an interrogative context as well as long consecutive and sight interpreting
6	Reading week		
7	Legal interpreting: specialised contexts	Key differences in strategies and lexical choices between legal interpreting, healthcare interpreting and various forms of conference interpreting. The idea of translation by omission, paraphrasing, etc. and the consequences these strategies have for PSI	*Chuchotage*

(*continued*)

Table 13.3 Cont.

Week	*Training focus*	*Content*	*Mode(s) and activities*
8	Legal interpreting: specialised contexts	Contexts of court interpreting, prison interpreting, tribunal hearings, etc.	Simultaneous
9	Other public services: dealing with ethical and cross-cultural issues in PSI	Ethical and cross-cultural challenges of various aspects of legal and healthcare interpreting, such as how to deal with offensive language; how to work with vulnerable interlocutors; how to control the interpreting environment and ethical and professional strategies in that regard	Multiple-mode
10	Other public services: professional issues in PSI	Agencies, self-marketing, self-employment and tax as well as other relevant, non-interpreting aspects of the PSI profession	Video-conferencing in courts and probations offices; telephone interpreting
11	Final assessment		

a variety of forms of summaries, presentations, role-plays, liaison and sight interpreting as well as other skill-relevant exercises.

The teaching activities and exercises in each session are normally composed of the following four parts:

Part 1: Briefing and discussion on background knowledge and key skills
1 Briefing on topics of the week and skills of the week.
2 Discussion on background knowledge and key skills.

Part 2: Liaison interpreting exercises and feedback
1 Liaison interpreting and feedback on Scenario 1.
2 Liaison interpreting and feedback on Scenario 2.

Part 3: Sight interpreting exercises and feedback
1 Preparation on the text.
2 Sight interpreting exercises.
3 Feedback.

Part 4: Discussion, reflection and summary

13.5.2 An example of teaching activities and exercises

A session in Week 4 is used as an example here to demonstrate the teaching activities and exercises that are typical in PSI training.

13.5.2.1 Part 1: Briefing and discussion on background knowledge and key skills

- Topics of the week: healthcare interpreting – technical and specialised tasks.
- Skills of the week: understanding the role of public service interpreters in the healthcare setting; building rapport; managing boundaries; sight interpreting.
- Modes and activities: liaison interpreting and sight interpreting.

Prior to the class, students have been asked to do task-based preparation on the topics of the week and have been requested to watch a video entitled "Understanding the interpreter's role" (Interpreting in Health Care: Educational Resources) as an introduction to the skills of the week. They have also received the links to some online healthcare resources for interpreters to acquaint themselves with the topics of the week. Students are supposed to share what they have prepared with their peers via their WhatsApp study group, including glossary and any written or multimedia resources they have found on the topics given.

At the beginning of the class, the tutor shares with the students a summary of the topics of the week, i.e. knowledge relevant to the healthcare interpreting tasks in this session, including the symptoms of some common diseases and the most frequently seen scenarios in healthcare interpreting, with a focus on coronavirus-related information and the differences between coronavirus and allergies which are related to the scenario in the interpreting task. Then there is brainstorming on the glossary and a discussion about the video which is related to the skills of the week. Students are expected to talk about their understanding of the roles of interpreters in the healthcare setting and what they can do to build a rapport with clients and manage boundaries. The tutor would also stimulate the students in identifying the expectations of service users.

13.5.2.2 Part 2: Liaison interpreting exercises and feedback

In this part, there are usually two scenarios under the topics of the week, in which student interpreters are expected to do liaison interpreting for an English-speaking interlocutor and a Chinese-speaking interlocutor in the context of public healthcare services in England. Due to the page limit of the paper, only one of the two scenarios is displayed below.

13.5.2.2.1 SCENARIO OF THE PSI TASK

A language other than English (LOTE) speaker (Interlocutor B) sees a general practitioner (GP) (Interlocutor B) through an online appointment about concern over COVID-19 and allergies.

13.5.2.2.2 STUDENT INTERPRETER'S PROMPT NOTES

You are asked to interpret for the healthcare setting, and you should follow the professional standard of PSI. You will do liaison interpreting for the dialogue in liaison mode.

13.5.2.2.3 INTERLOCUTOR A'S PROMPT NOTES

You are a GP in the UK. You have received many inquiries about the possibility of contracting COVID-19, and you have just finished dealing with an online appointment before meeting Ms Linqi Zhao. You will ask questions regarding symptoms and medical history and move on to give advice to the patient on obtaining a COVID-19 test.

- What are your symptoms?
- Do you have any medical history? Explain the differences between symptoms of common allergic reaction and symptoms of COVID-19.
- Is there anyone else in your household? If yes, who are they?
- Has anyone in your household had any symptoms, like a high temperature, a new, continuous cough or a loss or change to their sense of smell or taste? If yes, have they done a COVID-19 test?

- Advise the patient to get a COVID-19 test and tell her that she can make an appointment for an allergy test if her COVID-19 test result is negative.

13.5.2.2.4 INTERLOCUTOR B'S PROMPT NOTES

You are Ms Linqi Zhao, a 41-year-old woman from Chengdu, China, and you have been in the UK for 2 years, accompanying your husband who is working as an engineer in the UK. You have a daughter, Anna Yao, who is a Year-8 student in a secondary school in the UK. Your English is not fluent enough for daily interaction, so you need an interpreter on formal occasions such as visiting your GP. With the COVID-19 pandemic, you have booked an online appointment with your GP and have required an interpreter to be present at the appointment as you are not sure whether you had allergies or COVID-19.

You have had a sore throat and have been coughing for 3 days, with a high fever of 39°Celsius. You have shortness of breath sometimes. There is no loss or change to your sense of smell or taste. You have taken some traditional Chinese medicine, but it did not work.

- You have had seasonal allergy but never coughed during these instances. That is why you thought your symptoms were caused by the virus instead of an allergy.
- You live with your husband and daughter in the UK.
- Your husband has been healthy. However, before you developed the symptoms, your daughter Anna had had a high fever and had been coughing for 5 days and recovered after taking some traditional Chinese medicine. You believe your daughter might have caught COVID-19 from other students at her school before the national lockdown and subsequently passed it on to you, but there was no proof of it as your daughter has never been for a COVID-19 test.

You want to know whether your symptoms were caused by coronavirus or allergy.

13.5.2.2.5 ROLES AND ORGANISATION OF THE ACTIVITY

INTERLOCUTOR A: The English-speaking GP
INTERLOCUTOR B: The Chinese-speaking patient

In terms of different roles in the teaching activity, the interlocutors are language assistants/volunteers who play the roles in class and who have received the prompt notes and detailed guidance from the tutor on how the conversation evolves. The student interpreters have received the topics and skills of the week in advance and have been informed of the scenarios and been prepared in background knowledge and glossary. The tutor listens to the student interpreters and takes notes before giving feedback about their performances.

Thanks to the small class size and the help of the language assistants, the tutor can watch the performances of all six interpreters who practise liaison interpreting in the two scenarios and give feedback to all of them. The tutor and language assistants listen to the interpreters in the two scenarios, each listening to one interpreter at a time and giving feedback to them later.

In the face-to-face class, two interpreters stay on site to do liaison interpreting for Scenario 1 while the other students do liaison interpreting for the same scenario, each in a simultaneous interpreting booth on site. Then another two interpreters work on Scenario 2, while the other students work in the booths.

In the online class during the lockdown caused by COVID-19, the tutor assigns the students to different interpreting channels on Zoom while listening to students' performances with different channels. Just like in the physical simultaneous interpreting booths, two of them can choose to do liaison interpreting while others are doing simultaneous interpreting. The tutor and language assistants can choose to tune in different language channels either to monitor their performances or to use the interpreting as customers. As the language assistants are two interlocutors who do not understand each other's language, they rely on the interpreters to keep the interlocution going. All the performances are recorded so that they can be played back and used for revision after class.

13.5.2.2.6 FEEDBACK TO THE INTERPRETERS

The tutor and language assistants will give feedback to the interpreters based on accuracy, delivery and use of language with a special focus on the interpreters' use of the skills of the week. It will be followed by a discussion among the tutor and student interpreters about how the skills of the week could have facilitated the interpreting process.

13.5.2.3 Part 3: Sight interpreting and feedback

A document about the differences between symptoms of allergies and that of COVID-19 is provided to students in the class. They normally have 5 minutes to prepare and then to record their sight interpreting performance on an online interpreting training platform, which can video-record their interpreting performances. The tutor can watch the live performances of Students 5 and 6 before giving feedback to the interpreters.

13.5.2.4 Part 4: Discussion, reflection and summary

Before the end of the session, the students are prompted to reflect on their learning activities in three aspects:

1. What have you done well in your performance today?
2. What haven't you done well in your performance today?
3. What will you need to do to improve your performance after the class?

Through the discussion, the tutor encourages students to sum up what they have learnt in terms of skills and knowledge.

13.6 A mini-survey on PSI competences: Relative importance and adequacy in training

13.6.1 The questionnaire and the survey

Based on the framework of PSI competences developed in Section 13.3, a questionnaire was designed to survey the relative importance of the PSI competences in delivering PSI training and the coverage of their components in the PSI programme at postgraduate level.

The "Questionnaire on public service interpreting competences: Relative importance and adequacy in training" comprises 38 questions covering two parts. The first part of the questionnaire contains six questions that survey about the relative importance of the six interpreter competence sets, in which respondents are asked to choose a value along the scales of "not important, slightly important, important, very important". The second part of the questionnaire contains 32 questions that survey about how adequately all the components of the six PSI competence sets have been covered in the current programme from which respondents graduated, in which they are asked to choose a value along the scales of "none, inadequate, adequate, extensive".

The survey was conducted among alumni of the postgraduate PSI programme who are working as practising interpreters. Though it would be better to conduct the survey among a bigger group of respondents, as the postgraduate PSI programme adopts strict admission criteria and is delivered in small class sizes, we have only managed to get six responses from alumni who have graduated from the programme and are working as interpreters.

13.6.2 Survey results

The survey results are analysed from two aspects: (1) relative importance of the six PSI competence sets, (2) coverage of the components of PSI competences in the current PSI curriculum.

13.6.2.1 Relative importance of the six PSI competence sets

As indicated by the survey results shown in Table 13.4, all the PSI competence sets, including interpreting techniques, bilingual competence, extra-linguistic knowledge and research skills, interpersonal communication

Table 13.4 Relative importance of the six public service interpreting (PSI) competence sets

PSI competence sets	*n*	*Min*	*Max*	*Mean*	*sd*
Competence set 1: Interpreting techniques	6	2.000	4.000	3.400	0.894
Competence set 2: Bilingual competence	6	3.000	4.000	3.800	0.447
Competence set 3: Extralinguistic knowledge and research skills	6	3.000	4.000	3.800	0.447
Competence set 4: Interpersonal communication competence	6	3.000	4.000	3.400	0.548
Competence set 5: Intercultural competence	6	2.000	4.000	3.600	0.894
Competence set 6: Profession-related awareness and qualities	6	3.000	4.000	3.400	0.548

competence, intercultural competence, profession-related awareness and qualities, are considered important by those alumni who are working as practising interpreters. The mean scores for the six PSI competence sets are all above 3.4, with bilingual competence, extralinguistic knowledge and research skills, interpersonal and intercultural competence scoring higher than 3.5, which means they are considered very important.

13.6.2.2 Coverage of the components of PSI competences in the current PSI curriculum

As shown by the survey results in Table 13.5, of all the 32 components of PSI competences that were surveyed, the respondents among the alumni of the MA/BPSI programme think that 29 components have been covered adequately in the current programme, while three components of the PSI competences are perceived as not being covered adequately, including "Sight interpreting techniques", "Being able to cope with communication breakdown" and "Being able to cope with emotivity and tension between the interlocutors". This suggests that training about interpersonal communication competence in PSI will need to be consolidated.

13.7 Conclusion

As traditional liaison or dialogue interpreting is no longer the sole context in which PSI is employed, PSI professionals must be equipped with the necessary competences, skills and role profiles required by the field and the market. The MA/PGDip BPSI programme at the University of Leeds has been designed and delivered to meet such needs. As domain-specific norms, expectations and demands are placed upon PSI professionals, such a programme providing specialised training in PSI will prepare students to meet those demands and expectations.

Table 13.5 Coverage of the components of public service interpreting (PSI) competences in the current PSI curriculum

Components of PSI competences	*n*	*Min*	*Max*	*Mean*	*sd*
Consecutive interpreting techniques	6	3.000	4.000	3.600	0.548
Simultaneous interpreting techniques	6	3.000	4.000	3.200	0.447
Whispering/*chuchotage* techniques	6	3.000	4.000	3.400	0.548
Sight interpreting techniques	6	2.000	3.000	2.600	0.548
Listening comprehension ability after singular delivery from the speaker	6	2.000	4.000	3.600	0.894
Oral expression ability in singular delivery	6	3.000	4.000	3.400	0.548
Ability of immediate transfer from one working language to the other	6	2.000	4.000	3.400	0.894
Ability to comprehend language varieties in the working languages (e.g. dialects, regional varieties)	6	2.000	4.000	3.600	0.894
Good command of a range of language registers	6	3.000	4.000	3.200	0.447
Ability to use context- and register-appropriate language	6	3.000	4.000	3.400	0.548
Broad encyclopedic knowledge and intellectual curiosity	6	3.000	3.000	3.000	0.000
Fundamental subject knowledge (e.g. about healthcare and legal settings and public institutions)	6	3.000	4.000	3.400	0.548
Ability to efficiently acquire the terminological and specialised knowledge	6	3.000	4.000	3.400	0.548
Capability in using task preparation and research tools (e.g. computer and software, internet, ICT, etc.)	6	3.000	4.000	3.600	0.548
Ability to use efficiently the information sources available (e.g. terminology databases, parallel texts and corpus)	6	2.000	4.000	3.000	0.707
Being able to relate well to people	6	3.000	4.000	3.400	0.548
Exhibiting strong communication skills	6	3.000	4.000	3.400	0.548
Managing and keeping up the flow of communication (e.g. turn-taking)	6	3.000	4.000	3.400	0.548
Anticipating when to intervene during the interaction	6	3.000	4.000	3.400	0.548
Using effective interjection skills when appropriate	6	3.000	4.000	3.400	0.548
Effective intervention skills	6	3.000	4.000	3.400	0.548
Being able to cope with communication breakdown	6	2.000	4.000	2.800	0.837
Being able to cope with emotivity and tension between the interlocutors	6	2.000	4.000	2.800	0.837
Awareness and knowledge about cultural differences	6	3.000	4.000	3.200	0.447
Awareness about culture-specific norms	6	3.000	4.000	3.200	0.447
Ability to understand and render culture-specific elements	6	3.000	4.000	3.200	0.447

(*continued*)

Table 13.5 Cont.

Components of PSI competences	*n*	*Min*	*Max*	*Mean*	*sd*
Awareness and knowledge about intercultural pragmatics (e.g. politeness)	6	3.000	4.000	3.200	0.447
Ability to use socio-culturally appropriate language (without violating social and cultural taboos)	6	3.000	4.000	3.200	0.447
Intercultural intelligence in intercultural mediation	6	3.000	4.000	3.400	0.548
Awareness about professional roles and ethics (e.g. confidentiality) in PSI	6	4.000	4.000	4.000	0.000
Awareness about interpreting client services and relationship	6	3.000	4.000	3.400	0.548
Exhibiting self-control and impartial behaviour in all situations	6	3.000	4.000	3.800	0.447

This chapter highlights the particularities of PSI as being different from conference interpreting. It proposes a framework of PSI competences by drawing on relevant research literature, textbooks and professional documents. Then it discusses the pedagogical and practical considerations in designing and delivering such a formal postgraduate-level BPSI programme. It also presents the structure and content of the programme and its core module on PSI as well as typical teaching activities. Based on the Framework of PSI Competences, a mini-survey is conducted among graduates of the programme to gauge the importance of PSI competences as perceived by practitioners and the adequacy of coverage of the competences in the training programme. The survey results show that all the PSI competence sets as outlined by the Framework of PSI Competences are considered important by the alumni who are working as practising interpreters while training about interpersonal communication competence in PSI training will need to be consolidated.

Acknowledgement

The main content of the paper was presented by Binhua Wang as a keynote in the Symposium on Public Service Interpreting: Practice and Training (Xi'an International Studies University, 18 December 2020). We would like to express thanks to the organisers of the symposium.

References

Brunette, L., Bastin, G., Hemlin, I., & Clarke, H. (eds.) (2003) *The Critical Link 3: Interpreters in the Community. Selected Papers from the Third International Conference on Interpreting in Legal, Health and Social Service Settings.* Amsterdam: John Benjamins.

Carr, S., Roberts, R., Dufour, A., & Steyn, D. (eds.) (1997) *The Critical Link: Interpreters in the Community. Papers from the First International Conference on Interpreting in Legal, Health, and Social Service Settings*. Amsterdam: John Benjamins.

Corsellis, A. (2008) *Public Service Interpreting: The First Steps*. Basingstoke: Palgrave Macmillan.

D'Hayer, D. (2012) Public service interpreting and translation: Moving towards a (virtual) community of practice. *Meta: Translators' Journal*, 57(1): 235–247.

D'Hayer, D. (2013) Public service interpreter education. A multidimensional approach aiming at building a community of learners and professionals. In Schäffner, C., Kredens, K., & Fowler, Y. (eds.) *Interpreting in a Changing Landscape: Selected Papers from Critical Link 6*. Amsterdam: John Benjamins, 321–337.

de Pedro Ricoy, R. (2010) Training public service interpreters in the UK: A fine balancing act. *Journal of Specialised Translation*, 14: 100–120.

Gentile, A., Ozolins, U., & Vasilakakos, M. (1996) *Liaison Interpreting*. Melbourne: Melbourne University Press.

Hale, S. (2007) *Community Interpreting*. Basingstoke: Palgrave Macmillan.

Hale, S. (2011) Public service interpreting. In Malmkjær, K. & Windle, K. (eds.) *The Oxford Handbook of Translation Studies*. Oxford: Oxford University Press, 1–9.

Hale, S., Ozolins, U. & Stern, L. (eds.) (2009) *The Critical Link 5: Quality in Interpreting – A Shared Responsibility*. Amsterdam: John Benjamins.

Interpreting in Health Care: Educational Resources. www.gla.ac.uk/research/az/gramnet/research/trainingmodel/resources/ (accessed on 20 February, 2021).

ISO 13611:2014. (2014) *Interpreting – Guidelines for Community Interpreting*. Geneva: ISO copyright office.

Mason, I. (ed.) (1999) Special issue on dialogue interpreting. *The Translator*, 5(2).

Moser-Mercer, B. (1997) Skill components in simultaneous interpreting. In Gambier, Y., Gile, D., & Taylor, C. (eds.) *Conference Interpreting: Current Trends in Research. Proceedings of the International Conference on Interpreting: What do we Know and How?* Amsterdam: John Benjamins, 133–148.

Roberts, R., Carr, S., Abraham, D. & Dufour, A. (eds.) (2000) *The Critical Link 2: Interpreters in the Community*. Amsterdam: John Benjamins.

Roy, C. (2000) *Interpreting as a Discourse Process*. New York: Oxford University Press.

Rudvin, M., & Tomassini, E. (2011) *Interpreting in the Community and Workplace: A Practical Teaching Guide*. Basingstoke: Palgrave Macmillan.

Schäffner, C., Kredens, K. & Fowler, Y. (eds.) (2013) *Interpreting in a Changing Landscape: Selected Papers from Critical Link 6*. Amsterdam: John Benjamins.

University of Leeds. Module Catalogues. http://webprod3.leeds.ac.uk/catalogue/dynmodules.asp?Y=202021&F=P&M=MODL-5048M (accessed on 7th February 2021).

University of Leeds. Programme Catalogues. http://webprod3.leeds.ac.uk/catalogue/dynprogrammes.asp?Y=202021&P=MA-BPSI%26TS (accessed on 7th February 2021).

Wadensjö, C. (1998) *Interpreting as Interaction*. London: Addison Wesley Longman.

Wadensjö, C., Dimitrova, B. & Nilsson, A. (eds.) (2007) *The Critical Link 4: Professionalisation of Interpreting in the Community. Selected Papers from the 4th International Conference on Interpreting in Legal, Health and Social Service Settings*. Amsterdam: John Benjamins.

Wang, B. H. (2021). What are (ir)replaceable by the machine in interpreting? Designing a framework of interpreter competence as the conceptual foundation for interpreting pedagogy in the AI era (in review).

Wang, B. H. (王斌华) (2019) Interpreting as communicative mediation. Is interpreting only a skill of cognitive processing? (口译的交际协调论——兼论"口译只是认知处理技能吗？.") *Journal of Foreign Language Education* (外语教学), 40(1): 78–83.

14 A proposal for the integration of social-haptic communication in the training of (tactile) Italian Sign Language interpreters

Laura Volpato and Lara Mantovan

14.1 Introduction

Sign languages are natural languages expressed in the visual modality through hand movements, facial expressions, and body positions. They constitute the primary way of communication of many deaf people, allowing them to access contents, participate in society, and interact without communication barriers. Providing access to information in all settings of their daily lives through sign language is of vital importance to promote their full inclusion in society.

The current situation in Italy shows that much has to be done in the field of accessibility: in particular, public service interpreting for Italian Sign Language (LIS) users is still an under-developed service. To illustrate, a few examples are provided. According to Giura (2017), it is not uncommon for court offices to put hearing signers without qualifications in charge of interpreting; also, LIS interpreters are not guaranteed in prison, forcing deaf prisoners into an extreme form of isolation. Hospitals and health-care facilities do not have sign language interpreters on site, although some hospitals have recently started providing remote interpreting in collaboration with Veasyt, a spin-off company of Ca' Foscari University of Venice.[1] At school, support teachers usually do not know sign language or have very basic skills preventing them from enabling full accessibility to mainstreamed deaf pupils. The presence of LIS interpreters on public television is scarce: this service used to be limited to 5-minute news bulletins and the end-of-year speech given by the President of the Republic (Fontana, Corazza, Boyes Braem & Volterra, 2017). The current pandemic crisis has recently led to a slight increase in sign language interpretation on TV (mainly TV news, government press conferences, parliamentary sessions; cf. Gulli & Volterra, 2020). One of the reasons for the limited accessibility in sign language is that LIS has been only recently officially recognised by the Italian Parliament (May 19, 2021).

There is another minority group who is even more neglected and often faces more severe challenges in accessing information and communication: the deafblind community. The definition of deafblindness approved by the

DOI: 10.4324/9781003197027-18

Deafblind Nordic Cooperation Committee is the following: "Deafblindness is a combined vision and hearing impairment of such severity that it is hard for the impaired senses to compensate for each other. Thus, deafblindness is a distinct disability".[2] The term deafblind, therefore, not only refers to persons who are completely deaf and blind, but can be applied to persons with varying degrees of hearing and vision. The World Federation of the Deafblind (WFDB), in an initial report presented in 2018,[3] states that individuals with deafblindness represent between 0.2% and 2% of the world population (WFDB, 2018). In Italy, individuals having a dual sensory loss (vision and hearing) were estimated at 189,000 (0.3% of Italian population) in the year 2013 (Solipaca & Ricci, 2016).

Deafblind individuals have special communication needs, most of which rely on touch as their preferred communication channel. Depending on the aetiology and the time of onset of the dual sensory deprivation, deafblind people can use different communication modes. One of these is tactile sign language, which is mainly used by those individuals who first experienced deafness and acquired a sign language in the visual mode, and secondly (partially or totally) lost their vision and had to adjust their sign language competence into a tactile modality. Many deafblind individuals who first experience deafness and then suffer from gradual vision loss are affected by Usher syndrome. As the vision loss progresses, the deafblind person can rely less on the visual cues of the sign language, which are gradually substituted by new elements, more related to a touch dimension. A tactile sign language is therefore the linguistic variant mostly used by deafblind signers who are competent in a sign language and can no longer rely on the grammatical system of the visual language as it is (Checchetto et al., 2018).

The European Parliament, in the Declaration on the rights of deafblind people (2004),[4] states that deafblind people have the right to receive one-to-one support where appropriate from communicator-guides, deafblind interpreters, and/or intervenors. On the basis of this European declaration, Italy recognised deafblindness as a unique and distinct disability in 2010 (Law No. 107 of 24 June 2010).[5] Despite the European and Italian regulations, deafblind people in Italy still face severe limitations in everyday life activities. The lack of services is reflected in the lack of proper training in deafblind interpreting, which requires specific skills such as interpreting of speech, environmental description, and guiding. Given the necessity of adjusting to the European and Italian regulations, deafblind interpreting training should become part of all LIS interpreting programmes. In addition, we propose that the deafblind interpreting programme should include a broad range of skills, including competence in social-haptic communication (SHC). This communication system is useful when guiding, when describing the environment and the emotional feedback of interlocutors, and therefore it is a major contribution to the quality of the service for the deafblind person.

The chapter is structured as follows. Section 14.2 provides a general overview of training courses in sign language interpreting in Italy. In Section 14.3, the focus shifts to tactile Italian Sign Language (LISt) and the training opportunities currently available for interpreters working with deafblind individuals. Then, in Section 14.4, we describe how SHC functions and why it can be useful for LISt users. Finally, Section 14.5 presents a proposal for the integration of SHC in the training of LISt interpreters.

14.2 Training in sign language interpreting in Italy

The present section is intended to present the state of the art of sign language interpreters' training in Italy. First, we offer a brief overview of the historical evolution of courses in sign language interpreting, from the launch of the first courses to the current situation (Section 14.2.1). Second, we propose a critical review of the available training opportunities, highlighting similarities and differences (Section 14.2.2).

14.2.1 Historical evolution of LIS training courses

Franchi and Maragna (2013) discuss the main stages of the evolution of the role of LIS interpreters. Before the 1980s, sign language interpreters in Italy were not acting as professionals, but as helpers, willing to assist deaf people on a voluntary basis. They were mainly family members, friends, teachers, priests, and nuns, i.e., people living in close contact with deaf individuals. It was not infrequent that they interfered with the communicative exchanges, making choices *in lieu* of deaf people. During voice to sign interpreting, an Italian-based manual sign system was used (i.e., Signed Italian) because LIS was not considered a prestige language, not even by deaf people. No formative training and no guidelines were available at that time.

The flourishing of academic research on American Sign Language (ASL) and Deaf culture in the United States triggered a new awareness in Italian interpreters and deaf people. On the one hand, interpreters began to follow self-imposed rules and pay attention to pre-assignment preparation as well as other organisational aspects. On the other hand, deaf people assumed a more proactive behaviour, actively participating in the activities of associations and indicating their needs as end users of LIS interpreting services (Fontana, Corazza, Boyes Braem & Volterra, 2017).

It is in this context that LIS interpreting gradually became a profession. The first training course for interpreters was organised in Rome in the years 1982–1984 by the Region of Lazio in collaboration with *Consiglio Nazionale delle Ricerche* (CNR: National Research Council). Despite the lack of a clear methodology, this pioneering experience set the basis for the LIS interpreting courses of the following years (Bove & Volterra, 1984). One year later, two experienced ASL interpreters, Sharon Newman Solow and Marina McIntire, were invited to Rome to hold an intensive course for three LIS interpreters who were about to work in an international congress. The first courses in LIS interpreting were mainly organised by ENS (*Ente Nazionale Sordi*, the Italian

National Association of the Deaf), included sign language classes (no entry level was required), and were aimed at training "technicians" and "operators" specialised in LIS.

Then, more exchanges of views among interpreters, colleagues from abroad, and deaf people led to a greater attention being paid to deontological issues. The increasing professionalisation of LIS interpreters culminated in the founding of the two national category associations in 1987: ANIOS (*Associazione interpreti di lingua dei segni italiana*, Association of Italian Sign Language Interpreters) and ANIMU (*Associazione nazionale interpreti di lingua dei segni*, National Association of Italian Sign Language Interpreters). Both associations established an admission exam and have been offering many formative courses to their members over the years (on admission exams and refresher courses within ANIMU, see Mazzoni, 2000).

After the beginning of the 1990s, training opportunities in LIS interpreting increasingly blossomed, especially within public entities such as regions and provinces (e.g., a 2-year course organised in collaboration with the Province of Bologna and the Region of Emilia Romagna in 1996–1997). In 2003, for the first time, language classes aimed at teaching LIS were excluded from an interpreting course. Since then, an entry exam has been regularly introduced to verify whether candidates have an advanced level of linguistic competence in LIS. Also, special attention was paid to Deaf culture, intercultural communication,[6] as well as ethical issues such as professional distance and neutrality (Buonomo & Celo, 2010).

An important turning point came in 1997, when the Ministerial decree of June 23 determined the inclusion of LIS among the disciplines clustered into the L09A (now L-LIN/01) scientific area. This decision opened up the possibility of teaching LIS at the university: indeed, the University of Trieste organised the first LIS course in the academic year 1998–1999, and Ca' Foscari University of Venice did the same the following year. In the academic year 2001–2002, LIS was offered at Ca' Foscari as a language of specialisation in BA and MA programmes. These pioneering academic experiences brought a new dignity to the language and paved the way for the organisation of LIS courses in other Italian universities (a.o., Bologna-Forlì, Milano-Bicocca, Roma La Sapienza, Catania-Ragusa). In 2005, the University of Naples "Suor Orsola Benincasa" organised a 1st Level Master degree specialised in LIS educational interpreting with the purpose of training interpreters for the school setting (Buonomo & Celo, 2010). After the implementation of LIS courses into BA and MA programmes, in the academic year 2006–2007 Ca' Foscari University proposed an advanced training course in Italian/LIS interpreting techniques (Mazzoni & Cardinaletti, 2007). Two years later, a specific training in translation into LIS was implemented into the programme. In 2012, this course became a 1-year 1st Level Master degree (*Teoria e tecniche di traduzione e interpretazione italiano/lingua dei segni italiana*, Italian/LIS translation and interpreting theory and techniques), unique of its kind in Italy. A recent step forward in the academic training of

LIS interpreters is the addition of a dedicated LIS curriculum into an MA course in interpreting and translation studies at Ca' Foscari (*Interpretariato e traduzione editoriale, settoriale*, Interpreting and translation for publishing and for special purposes). This is an important achievement because the academic training of LIS interpreters has finally aligned with the training standards of spoken-language interpreters in Italy and also with those of sign language interpreters in other countries. Indeed, the European Commission requires that interpreters obtain a postgraduate degree in translation and conference interpreting (Cardinaletti, 2018).

14.2.2 Available programmes in interpreting training

To provide an overview of what a prototypical training course in sign language interpreting offers in terms of contents and methods, we compare three programmes currently available: the MA course in interpreting and translation studies at Ca' Foscari University,[7] the course in LIS interpreting at ENS,[8] and the course in LIS interpreting at SILIS (sign language study and information group in Rome).[9]

To enrol in these courses, candidates must meet specific requirements. The MA course at Ca' Foscari requires the following: a BA degree (preferably in foreign languages) with a minimum grade of 90/110, at least 3 years of LIS study and 24 European Credit Transfer System (ECTS) credits in LIS, 36 ECTS in the other language of specialisation (either English or Spanish), and at least a B2 level in English. Moreover, candidates must pass an admission exam aimed at testing linguistic competence in Italian, LIS, and the other language of specialisation. As for the non-academic courses, ENS requires a high school diploma, at least 3 years of LIS study, good linguistic competence in Italian, and passing an admission exam, while SILIS requires 4 years of LIS study. Ca' Foscari and ENS limit their courses to a maximum number of students: 8 and 24, respectively.

The overall duration of these courses is 2 years. Class attendance is organised in different ways: from Monday to Friday according to the schedule of the courses (Ca' Foscari), every other weekend (ENS), two or three weekly classes and two Saturdays every month (SILIS). Attendance at the MA programme is free, while at ENS and SILIS students are required to attend at least 80% of the scheduled classes.

As for the structure of courses, the situation is very heterogeneous. The MA course at Ca' Foscari, like any other MA course in Italy, features a workload of 120 credits. Since one credit equals 25 hours of study work, the whole course consists of about 3000 study hours. Note that it focuses not only on LIS, but also on another language of specialisation, to be chosen by the student. In the second and last year, students are required to complete a 150-hour internship. The course organised by ENS includes frontal lectures (720 hours), group and individual practice, and an internship of 100 hours (50 hours of observation in real working environments and 50 hours of active interpreting in protected environments under the supervision of a tutor). The course organised by SILIS includes frontal lectures (750 hours) and an internship of 150 hours (in the first year, 50 hours of passive training/observation and 20 hours of active training/interpreting; in the second year, 30 hours of passive training and 50 hours of active training).

In all courses, there are both deaf and hearing instructors, including experts in LIS L2 teaching, theoretical disciplines, as well as professional interpreters. Contentwise, the three programmes differ significantly. As previously mentioned, the MA course at Ca' Foscari aims to train professional interpreters and translators in two languages of specialisation (i.e., LIS and English, or LIS and Spanish), like any MA course in interpreter training in Italy. This curriculum allows "mixed educational paths", combining pre-established courses with electives. It includes: (1) core educational activities (advanced LIS and discourse analysis, Italian/LIS translation, Italian/LIS simultaneous interpreting, advanced English or Spanish, Italian/English or Spanish translation, Italian/English or Spanish simultaneous interpreting, contrastive Italian-LIS linguistics, linguistics, computer science for consecutive interpreting and translation); (2) interdisciplinary activities (English/Spanish culture, translation theory and technique); and (3) elective courses (free choice credits). The non-academic courses, on the other hand, focus on LIS only. The programme offered by ENS includes: advanced LIS and advanced Italian, Italian/LIS (consecutive and simultaneous) interpretation, Italian/LIS translation, theories of translation and interpretation, professional ethics, sectoral languages, cultural mediation, professional practice, stress management, elocution, and legal and regulatory aspects. The programme offered by SILIS includes the following courses: advanced LIS, interpreting techniques, consecutive and simultaneous interpreting, liaison interpreting, history of professional associations of interpreters, comparative linguistics, linguistic registers in Italian/LIS, elocution, professional ethics, psychological issues, and self-evaluation.

The three courses also differ in terms of student assessment and final qualification. In the MA programme at Ca' Foscari, in order to gain credits, students must pass the written or oral exam of each course. The final exam consists in a dissertation on a research project developed by the student. Once the programme has been completed, students earn a graduate degree, that is, an academic title. The ENS course includes intermediate exams and a final examination. In case of positive evaluation, students earn a certificate of qualification, which is claimed to be equivalent to Level C2 of the Common European Framework of Reference for Languages (CEFR). In case of negative evaluation or poor attendance, students are given a certificate of attendance. In the SILIS course, admission to the second year is subject to passing an intermediate exam at the end of the first year. In case of negative evaluation, students are given a certificate of attendance. At the end of the second year, students are required to pass a final exam to obtain the qualification of LIS interpreter.

Overall, in all three courses an advanced linguistic competence in LIS is taken for granted, and the focus is mainly on the acquisition of professional knowledge and practical skills. They significantly differ in terms of prerequisites for admission, programme, and final qualification.

14.3 Tactile sign language training in Italy

The present section aims at presenting the state of the art regarding tactile sign language interpreter training in Italy. In Section 14.3.1, we provide a brief description of LISt and its main features, and in Section 14.3.2 we present the training opportunities for (public-service) interpreters working with deafblind individuals currently available in Italy.

14.3.1 Tactile Italian Sign Language

LISt is the tactile variant of visual LIS. It is performed by placing one or both hands on top or beneath the hand/s of the interlocutor, depending on whether one is receiving or producing a message, respectively (for LISt, see Checchetto, 2011; Checchetto et al., 2012; Checchetto et al., 2018; for hand position, see Mesch, 2001, 2011, 2013).

Tactile sign languages are no natural languages in the ordinary sense. They virtually have no native signers, although some deafblind individuals use tactile sign language as their primary mode of communication. As already mentioned, tactile sign languages are often used by deafblind individuals who already had a visual sign language before losing sight (Checchetto et al., 2018).

Like other visual sign languages, LIS makes great use of non-manuals. This term includes facial expressions and head and body movements (Branchini & Mantovan, 2020). In the transition from the visual to tactile modality, LISt users lose access to the information conveyed by non-manuals and "make up for this loss by modifying some pre-existing manual items, or by introducing novel manual signs (or by combining some of these options)" (Checchetto et al., 2018, p. 2). Not only do tactile signers seem to encode linguistic information in a different way (tactile vs. visual), but deafblind signers seem to reinscribe or access relevant interactional information that participants normally perceive through sight or hearing in a different way. The information can regard, for instance, who is in the room, what is the expression on the interlocutor's face, who wants to intervene in the discussion. The way in which such information is conveyed to a deafblind signer is somehow similar to what we call "non-verbal communication" for spoken languages (Willoughby et al., 2020) but, still, it has to be transmitted through touch in order to be perceivable.

In addition to the purely linguistic features that distinguish a tactile sign language from a visual sign language, a deafblind cultural perspective must be taken into account as well. Edwards (2012, 2014a, 2014b, 2015, 2017, 2018) provides an account of the integration of such a perspective into the language used by the deafblind community. The world is perceived through touch, and this moulds the way concepts are expressed and the way touch itself is considered from a different "angle".

14.3.2 Training opportunities for tactile sign language interpreting in Italy

As stated by the World Association of Sign Language Interpreters in the *WASLI Deafblind Interpreter Education Guidelines* (2013),[10] the availability of deafblind interpreter education can vary widely from country to country. In some countries, deafblind training is included in their sign language interpreting programmes, while in many others it is not. The reasons for this are various and complex. In part, the reasons might be linked to countries' access to resources (financial, human, technological, knowledge), as well as the level of political awareness and involvement on the part of deafblind communities.

In Italy, there is currently no official specific training in deafblind interpreting. The few opportunities available mainly concern LISt and its linguistic properties, as well as background information on deafblindness. We describe some concrete examples below.

Since 2011, Ca' Foscari University (Department of Linguistics and Comparative Cultural Studies) in cooperation with Lega del Filo d'Oro (i.e., an Italian association that assists and rehabilitates deafblind people) has been delivering a course on LISt (30 hours, 6 ECTS credits).[11] The course aims at training students who already have a basic knowledge of visual LIS in the use of its tactile variant. Students of LISt also learn background information about the deafblind population and their special communication needs. This course can be chosen as free choice credits by students enrolled in the MA course in interpreting and translation studies (see Section 14.2.2), thus enriching their professional profile.

The one-year 1st Level Master degree on LIS interpreting, since its first edition at Ca' Foscari University in 2012, has always included a laboratory session (approximately 10 hours of lectures) on deafblind interpreting.

In other training programmes for LIS interpreters, LISt is usually not included.

In 2019 and 2020, Ca' Foscari School for International Education (SIE) organised a programme open to everyone dedicated to sign languages which includes intensive LISt courses (10 hours). In summer 2021, the intensive course of LISt was organised by the Department of Linguistics and Comparative Cultural Studies.[12]

Training in LISt can also be found in the programmes organised by ENS for students and teachers of LIS, but these courses are not specifically meant for interpreters (cf. interpreting training course offered by ENS in Section 14.2.2).

ANIOS periodically organises refresher courses on LISt and deafblind interpretation strategies. These training opportunities are mainly reserved to the member associates of ANIOS.

The lack of specific training in this field can be better comprehended if we consider that: (1) the profession of LIS interpreters is relatively young in Italy (see Section 14.2.1); (2) training opportunities for such interpreters are scarce; and (3) attempts to bring interpreters' training to academic level are even scarcer.

14.4 Social-haptic communication

In this section, we describe SHC and its important role in enhancing touch-based accessibility. Specifically, we provide a description of this system (Section 14.4.1), we describe the state of the art in SHC at the international level (Section 14.4.2), and we present the current situation of SHC in Italy (Section 14.4.3).

14.4.1 Social-haptic communication as an additional source of information

SHC consists of brief tactile messages performed on the body of the deafblind person, in order to convey information regarding the environment and the emotional feedback of the interlocutor. Usual places of articulation for SHC are: the back, the upper arm, the hand, the leg/knee, and the foot (Bjørge et al., 2015). In Figure 14.1, we provide an example of how a social-haptic message can be performed on the back of a deafblind person.

SHC can help people with deafblindness to understand better what is happening around them and therefore master the situation more autonomously. It is a useful resource for different situations, for example when the

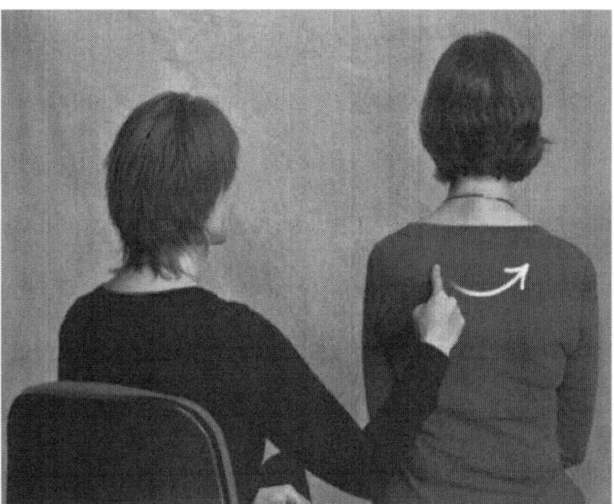

Figure 14.1 Example of social-haptic communication. Haptice for "smiling" (Hesse & Nielsen 2018, p. 126).

hands of the deafblind person are busy (touching something or communicating with someone through tactile sign language); or when the environment is too noisy for the deafblind person to use her/his residual hearing (Hesse & Nielsen, 2018). SHC should not be intended as a substitution of the deafblind person's first or preferred communication system, such as, for instance, tactile sign language. It rather represents an additional source of information.

14.4.2 Social-haptic communication: State of the art

Despite touch signals having been used for a much longer time, the earliest research about SHC started in the 1990s. The development of SHC in many different countries benefited from the contribution by Riitta Lahtinen and Russ Palmer (Lahtinen, 1999, 2003, 2008; Lahtinen & Palmer, 1996, 1997, 2000, 2005; Palmer & Lahtinen, 1994, 2005, 2013; Lahtinen, Lahtinen & Palmer, 2010; Lahtinen, Palmer & Ojala, 2012; Lahtinen, Palmer & Tuomaala, 2016; Lahtinen, Groth & Palmer, 2018). Riitta Lahtinen is a Finnish researcher and interpreter who investigated haptices. She mainly works in cooperation with her husband Russ Palmer, a deafblind international music therapist and vibroacustic therapy practitioner. In their "grammar of touch", they call *haptemes* those minimal touch variables that can be combined into more complex and complete messages, what they call *haptices* (Lahtinen, 2008).

In Norway, Trine Naess, a young deafblind woman, contributed to the collection and standardisation of haptices. In 2010, Berit Øie, another Norwegian deafblind woman, introduced SHC to the Helen Keller National Center for Deaf-Blind Youths and Adults (HKNC) in New York. In doing so, she paved the way for further cooperation between the United States and Norway, which resulted in the book *Haptic Communication: The American Edition of the Original Title Haptisk Kommunikasjon* (Bjørge et al., 2015).

The National Association of Deafblind people in Denmark has been working on the collection, standardisation, and sharing of their social-haptic variant (see Hesse & Nielsen, 2018).

In Sweden, a collection of the most important haptices used in the country is available on the website of the Swedish Nationellt kunskapscenter för dövblindfrågor (National Knowledge Center for Deafblind Issues).[13]

Recently a country-wide project started collecting, developing, and standardising haptices in the Netherlands.[14]

14.4.3 Social-haptic communication in Italy

In contrast to what happens in Northern Europe, SHC is mostly unknown in Italy. Deafblind individuals tend to use home-made haptices, but there is no actual collection and standardisation of such messages.

The Erasmus+ project Social Haptic Signs for Deaf and Blind in Education[15] aims to collect haptices used in four European countries (Estonia,

Italy, Portugal, and Sweden) and make them available online through video-recordings, pictures, and simple descriptions. Ca' Foscari University coordinates the Italian team and collaborates with Lega del Filo d'Oro in the project, which started in September 2019 and will end in August 2022. As a result, an open-source online dictionary for SHC will be created. Once the dictionary is available, it will be possible to organise SHC courses in which, with the support of deafblind trainers, SHC will be taught to deafblind people, interpreters, intervenors, family members, and caregivers.

14.5 A proposal

The WFDB defines deafblind interpreting as "a requirement in order for people with deafblindness to achieve full participation, equality, independence and self-determination in every area of society".[16] It consists in the provision of visual and/or auditory information via an intermediary, which is realised through three, fully integrated elements: the interpreting of spoken or signed language, the environmental description, and the physical guiding. Each of these elements requires specific studying and training. LISt competence represents just a part of one of the three elements, that is, the interpreting of spoken and signed language, and therefore, alone, it is not sufficient for the preparation of qualified deafblind interpreters.

Part of deafblind interpreting can be incorporated into any regular LIS interpreter training curriculum,[17] and specific dedicated programmes should be provided as well. Based on what has been discussed so far regarding deafblind interpreting skills and SHC, and following the guidelines provided by WASLI (2013), a proposal for the topics to be included in a deafblind interpreting programme in Italy is provided below and commented on further. The integration of specific training on SHC is highlighted in italics.

1 Communication methods and interpreting:
   - a LISt: tactile signing
   - b visual frame signing, restricted space signing, and close vision signing
   - c tactile manual alphabet
   - d tracking
   - e pro-tactile
   - f Malossi
   - g *SHC: history and fundamentals*
2 Environmental description:
   - a physical surroundings
   - b people
   - c happenings
   - d social exchanges
   - e *SHC: environmental description*
   - f *SHC: emotional feedback*

3 Guiding techniques:
   a orientation and mobility
   b *SHC: guiding and orientation*
4 Ethics:
   a assessing communication match
   b determining preferences
   c issues of power
5 Roles:
   a interpreter
   b support service provider
   c guide interpreter
   d intervener
6 Environmental conditions:
   a lighting
   b attire
   c background
   d scents
   e seating arrangements
   f *SHC applied to environmental conditions*
7 Community issues:
   a deafblind culture and perspectives
   b organisations and resources
   c technology
   d *SHC applied to technology and devices*

SHC can be considered as a very versatile tool, which can become pervasive of many aspects of a deafblind interpreting educational programme. Interpreters who use SHC will need to know its origins and its fundamentals, in order to fully comprehend its use and application. SHC represents a precious resource for environmental description (in its physical, atmospheric, and social declinations), and it can be used to support guiding and orientation (in both physical and technological environments). In this perspective, the collection and standardisation of SHC in Italy through the Erasmus+ project Social Haptic Signs for Deaf and Blind in Education can help in the process of inclusion of SHC into deafblind interpreting education.

In addition to the design of a specific, comprehensive, and rigorous training programme in deafblind interpreting, having qualified teachers is fundamental. Current interpreting instructors are therefore encouraged to support deafblind people in their efforts to contribute to deafblind training. Members of the deafblind community can be invited to share with students their expertise and perspectives in a variety of ways: as guest lecturers, language mentors, language models, staff for interpreting lab, office staff, and more. The subsequent step would be to identify qualified instructors who are deafblind and who can play an integral role in developing and implementing appropriate interpreter training.

14.6 Conclusion

The deafblind community in Italy faces severe limitations in terms of mobility, access to information, and communication. Despite international and national regulations, public service interpreting for this specific population is not guaranteed. This is also due to the unavailability of dedicated training programmes focusing on specific deafblind interpreting skills.

In this paper, we outlined a deafblind interpreting programme covering the main issues that an interpreter working with deafblind people should be aware of. We propose that SHC should be integrated within the training, as an important source of additional information. SHC could find application in each macro domain (i.e., communication, environmental description, orientation, etc.), significantly contributing to the transmission of a wider range of information. In the collection, systematisation, and teaching of haptic signals, the deafblind community should play a prominent role.

Notes

1 Veasyt has developed a professional video remote interpreting service in LIS, allowing deaf people to interact with public institutions directly in LIS (for more details, see www.veasyt.com).
2 Retrieved from: www.fsdb.org/Filer/DBNSK%20English.pdf [accessed on 10 April 2021].
3 Report available at www.internationaldisabilityalliance.org/sites/default/files/wfdb_complete_initial_global_report_september_2018.pdf [accessed on 10 April 2021].
4 Available at www.europarl.europa.eu/sides/getDoc.do?pubRef=-//EP//TEXT+TA+P5-TA-2004-0277+0+DOC+XML+V0//EN [accessed on 10 April 2021].
5 Full text available at www.gazzettaufficiale.it/eli/id/2010/07/13/010G0128/sg [accessed on 10 April 2021].
6 Cultural awareness was probably due to the influence of the Bi-lingual-Bi-cultural Model (Bi-Bi Model) from the United States. According to this interpreting model, it is important for interpreters to master both languages and, at the same time, have a deep knowledge of both cultures (Cokely 2003).
7 Information on the programme offered by Ca' Foscari is retrieved from www.unive.it/pag/25172/ [accessed on 10 April 2021].
8 Information on the programme offered by ENS is retrieved from: https://formazione.ens.it/images/immagini/2016/POF_2016/1._POF_2016-Introduzione_valido_per_i_progetti_presentati_fino_al_22_Settembre_2017.pdf.pdf [accessed on 10 April 2021].
9 Information on the programme offered by SILIS is retrieved from: www.grupposilis.it/corso-lis/interprete-lis [accessed on 10 April 2021].
10 Full text available at http://wasli.org/wp-content/uploads/2013/06/279_wasli-db-interpreter-education-guidelines-1.pdf [accessed on 10 April 2021].
11 Information about LISt university course (academic year 2020–2021) is available at www.unive.it/data/insegnamento/310851 [accessed on 10 April 2021].

12 For more details about LISt programme (summer 2021), see www.unive.it/pag/16981/ [accessed on 10 April 2021].
13 See https://socialhaptisk.nkcdb.se [accessed on 10 April 2021].
14 See https://dbconnect.info/2018/07/social-haptic-communication-cursus/ and www.kentalisshop.nl/nl/op-het-lijf-geschreven-basiscursus-over-social-haptic-communication [accessed on 10 April 2021].
15 General information about the project is available at https://ec.europa.eu/programmes/erasmus-plus/projects/eplus-project-details/#project/2019-1-SE01-KA201-060404 [accessed on 10 April 2021].
16 See www.wfdb.eu/interpretation/ [accessed on 10 April 2021].
17 In particular, see WASLI (2013) at *5.3 Program content – General courses* (http://wasli.org/wp-content/uploads/2013/06/279_wasli-db-interpreter-education-guidelines-1.pdf).

References

Bjørge, H. K., Rehder, K. G., Øverås, M., Keller, H. National Center. (2015). *Haptic Communication: The American Edition of the Original Title Haptisk Kommunikasjon* [Kindle DX version]. Retrieved from Amazon.com.

Bove, M. G. & Volterra, V. (1984). *La Lingua Italiana dei Segni. Insegnamento e Interpretariato*. Rome: Centro Regionale di Formazione Professionale.

Branchini, C. & Mantovan, L. (2020). *A Grammar of Italian Sign Language (LIS)*. Venice: Edizioni Ca' Foscari.

Buonomo, V. & Celo, P. (2010). *L'interprete di lingua dei segni italiana. Problemi linguistici, aspetti emotivi, formazione professionale*. Milan: Hoepli.

Cardinaletti, A. (2018). La lingua dei segni italiana a Ca' Foscari. Didattica, ricerca e progetti sull'accessibilità. In A. Cardinaletti, L. Cerasi & P. Rigobon (eds.), *Le lingue occidentali nei 150 anni di storia di Ca' Foscari*, 341–353. Venice: Edizioni Ca' Foscari.

Checchetto, A. (2011). Interpretare in LIS a favore di persone sordocieche. In C. Vallini, A. De Meo & V. Caruso (eds.), *Traduttori e traduzioni*, 341–356. Naples: Liguori Editore.

Checchetto, A., Cecchetto, C., Geraci, C, Guasti, M. T. & Zucchi, A. (2012). Una varietà molto speciale: La LISt (lingua dei segni italiana tattile). In A. Cardinaletti, C. Cecchetto & C. Donati (eds.), *Grammatica, lessico e dimensioni di variazione nella LIS*, 207–218. Milan: Franco Angeli.

Checchetto, A., Geraci, C., Cecchetto, C. & Zucchi, A. (2018). The language instinct in extreme circumstances: The transition to tactile Italian Sign Language (LISt) by deafblind signers. *Glossa: A Journal of General Linguistics*, 3(1), 66.

Cokely, D. (2003). *Il processo di interpretazione. Un modello sociolinguistico*. Rome: Kappa.

Edwards, T. (2012). Sensing the rhythms of everyday life: Temporal integration and tactile translation in the Seattle deaf-blind community. *Language in Society*, 41(1), 29–71.

Edwards, T. (2014a). From compensation to integration: Effects of the pro-tactile movement on the sublexical structure of Tactile American Sign Language. *Journal of Pragmatics,* 69, 22–41.

Edwards, T. (2014b). *Language Emergence in the Seattle DeafBlind Community*. PhD dissertation, University of California, Berkeley.

Edwards, T. (2015). Bridging the gap between DeafBlind minds: interactional and social foundations of intention attribution in the Seattle DeafBlind community. *Frontiers in Psychology,* 6, 1497.

Edwards, T. (2017). Sign-creation in the Seattle DeafBlind community: A triumphant story about the regeneration of obviousness. *Gesture*, 16(2), 305–328.

Edwards, T. (2018). Re-channeling language: The mutual restructuring of language and infrastructure among DeafBlind people at Gallaudet University. *Journal of Linguistic Anthropology*, 28(3), 273–292.

Fontana, S., Corazza, S., Boyes Braem, P. & Volterra, V. (2017). Language research and language community change: Italian Sign Language, 1981–2013. *Sign Language Studies*, 17(3): 363–398.

Franchi, M. L. & Maragna, S. (2013). *Manuale dell'interprete della lingua dei segni italiana*. Milan: Franco Angeli.

Giura, V. (2017). L'accessibilità per la persona sorda. Talk presented at the conference "La lingua dei segni: diritto alla comunicazione. Diritto Universale", Rome, February 8. Available at www.radioradicale.it/scheda/499502/la-lingua-dei-segni-diritto-alla-comunicazione-diritto-universale [accessed on 10 April, 2021].

Gulli, T. & Volterra, V. (2020). La comunità sorda segnante italiana all'epoca del coronavirus: Lingua dei segni e accessibilità. *MicroMega*. Available at: www.istc.cnr.it/sites/default/files/micromegagullivolterra.pdf [accessed on 10 April, 2021].

Hesse, P. & Nielsen, G. (eds.). (2018). *Haptic Signals – 139 New and Known Signals*. The Danish Association of the Deafblind. Retrieved from Fddb.dk website: www.fddb.dk/media/141088/haptic-signals-139-new-and-known-signals-english.pdf [accessed on 10 April, 2021].

Lahtinen, R. (1999). Holistic and interactive communication methods. In B. Peckford & L. Hawcroft (eds.), *Proceedings of an International Symposium in Interpreting for Deafblind People*, 64–65. Durham: Prontaprint.

Lahtinen, R. (2003). *Development of the Holistic Social-Haptic Confirmation System. A Case Study of the Yes & No – Feedback Signals and How They Become More Commonly and Frequently Used in a Family with an Acquired Deafblind Person*. Licenciate thesis, Department of Teacher Education, University of Helsinki.

Lahtinen, R. (2008). *Haptices and Haptemes: A Case Study of Developmental Process in Social-Haptic Communication of Acquired Deafblind People.* Doctoral dissertation. Frinton-on-Sea: A1 Management UK.

Lahtinen, R., Groth, C. & Palmer, R. (2018). Sound descriptions of haptic experiences of art work by deafblind cochlear implant users. *Multimodal Technologies and Interaction,* 2(2), 24.

Lahtinen, R., Lahtinen, M. & Palmer, R. (2010). *Environmental Description for Visually and Dual Sensory Impaired People*. Helsinki: Art-Print.

Lahtinen, R. & Palmer, R. (1996). Holistic family communication: Spoken language by touch is more than just words. *The 4th European Deafblind Conference*, Espoo, June.

Lahtinen, R. & Palmer, R. (1997). Theoretical basis of holistic communication for dual-sensory impaired people & family members. *EUSSG & 4th IAEDB (DbI) European Conference Proceedings*, Madrid.

Lahtinen, R. & Palmer, R. (2000). *Holistic & Interactive Communication Methods with Acquired Deafblind People & Families – A Practical Approach. Joint Training Initiative, Distance Learning Course* (incl. video). Manchester: Manchester University.

Lahtinen, R. & Palmer, R. (2005). *The Body Story: Creating Musical Images Through Touch (CMIT)*. Tampere: City-Offset.

Lahtinen, R., Palmer, R. & Ojala, S. (2012). Visual art experiences through touch using haptices. *Procedia – Social and Behavioral Sciences*, 45, 268–276.

Lahtinen, R., Palmer, R. & Tuomaala, S. (2016). Using haptices in health care settings. *DbI Review*, 56, 18–19.

Mazzoni, L. (2000). Formazione e aggiornamento degli interpreti LIS. In L. Gran & C. Kellett Bidoli (eds.), *L'Interpretazione nelle lingue dei segni: Aspetti teorici e pratici della formazione*, 69–70. Trieste: EUT Edizioni Università di Trieste.

Mazzoni, L. & Cardinaletti, A. (2007). Proposta di standardizzazione dei contenuti per i corsi di interpretazione italiano-LIS. In *Dall'invisibile al visibile: 3. Convegno nazionale sulla lingua dei segni*, Verona 9–11 March 2007. Rome: Ente Nazionale Sordi Onlus.

Mesch, J. (2001). *Tactile Sign Language: Turn Taking and Questions in Signed Conversations of Deaf-Blind People*. Hamburg: Signum.

Mesch, J. (2011). Variations in tactile signing – The case of one-handed signing. Eesti ja soome-ugri keeleteaduse ajakiri. *Journal of Estonian and Finno-Ugric Linguistics*, 2(1), 273–282.

Mesch, J. (2013). Tactile signing with one-handed perception. *Sign Language Studies*, 13(2), 238–263.

Palmer, R. & Lahtinen, R. (1994). Communication with Usher people. *Deafblind Education*, July–December, 7–9.

Palmer, R. & Lahtinen, R. (2005). Social-haptic communication for acquired deafblind people and family: Incorporating touch and environmental information through holistic communication. *DbI Review*, January–June, 6–8.

Palmer, R. & Lahtinen, R. (2013). History of social-haptic communication. *DbI Review*, 50, 68–71.

Solipaca, A. & Ricci, C. (eds.). (2016). *Studio sulla popolazione di persone sordocieche, con disabilità sensoriali e plurime in condizioni di gravità*, 44–48. Trento: Erickson.

Willoughby, L., Manns, H., Iwasaki, S. & Bartlett, M. (2020). From seeing to feeling: How do deafblind people adapt visual sign languages? In K. Allan (ed.), *Dynamics of Language Changes,* 235–252. Singapore: Springer.

World Association of Sign Language Interpreters (WASLI) (2013). Deafblind Guidelines for Interpreter Education. Montreal: WASLI. Retrieved from: wasli.org/wp-content/uploads/2013/06/279_wasli-db-interpreter-education-guidelines-1.pdf (accessed 27 July 2021).

World Federation of the Deafblind (WFDB) (2018). At Risk of Exclusion from CRPD and SDGs Implementation: Inequality and Persons with Deafblindness. Initial Global Report 2018. Oslo: World Federation of the Deafblind. Retrieved from: www.wfdb.eu/wp-content/uploads/2019/04/WFDB-global-report-2018.pdf (accessed 27 July 2021).

Index